RELIGIOUS EDUCATION

Religious
Education

THE FOUNDATIONS
AND PRACTICE OF NURTURE

J. Donald Butler

HARPER & ROW, PUBLISHERS
NEW YORK AND EVANSTON

To *L. M. B.*

Contents

Preface

*T*his book is broadly sectarian in approach, an admission which needs to be made and justified for the reader before his serious study of it begins. While it is assumed, not without some reason, that the sectarianism represented in this volume is not narrow, it is nevertheless sectarianism. This, in the judgment of the author, is unavoidable; yet he wishes to share the most inclusive fellowship with those who do not believe as he does, as well as with those who have no religious faith at all.

Sectarianism is unavoidable in a book such as this because religious belief is not an abstraction. Instead it is both an observable phenomenon and an experience of concrete communities of faith which have a history. More specifically, therefore, religious education or nurture in and by a faith is also of necessity an aspect of the life of concrete communities of faith. It cannot be abstracted and separated from such communities for purposes of study without sacrificing both precision and vitality. Because of this, it would be superficial, and for this author insincere, to conceive and to write a book such as this except from within his own community of faith. The student and reader will therefore turn very few pages before he recognizes that the man who writes is a Protestant Christian, and the reader may even perceive quite accurately the particular brand, among the many varieties of Protestant Christianity, to which the author is committed.

It is believed however that the broadly sectarian character of this book does not prevent its being useful as a reference and guide for study for those whose faith is divergent from that expressed here. In addition to Protestants to whom this book will be generally congenial, although many of them will not agree with its general approach and certainly not with every position taken in it, particular adaptations and omissions may make the volume also useful to both Roman Catholic and Jewish readers.

For the Roman Catholic student, it is believed that Chapter

ix

1 on the nature of the Church will have both relevance and value. Certain modifications and additions will of course be desired, but what is made explicit in the chapter will not be strange and unwelcome. The historical portion of the book, Chapters 2 through 8, should be both useful and helpful, with two possible exceptions. Chapter 2 on the Protestant Reformation and Chapter 6 on the thought of Horace Bushnell, being peculiarly related to the Protestant tradition, will lack revelance to the historical perspective in which religious education stands within the Roman Catholic Church. Chapters 9 and 10, on the functions in nurture of theology and the Bible respectively, will no doubt prove to be the most controversial parts of the book for Roman Catholics. Their value consequently may be chiefly in the raising of some vital issues on which Roman Catholics and many Protestants honestly disagree. Chapter 11 on the secular community and Chapter 12 on parish educational agencies should prove of virtually as much worth as in the Protestant frame of reference, except that some of the parish agencies are not as common in the Roman Catholic Church. The two chapters on psychology, 13 and 14, may be quite helpful to the Roman Catholic student, as long as due allowance is made for the fact that they do not proceed from Thomistic presuppositions and are more empirical than Thomist psychology. Chapter 15 on methods of teaching will be quite as adaptable to Roman Catholic education as to Protestant, except for the presupposition, especially regarding discussion method, that no intellectual formulas are final. Chapter 16 on curriculum deals only with the curriculum literature used in a number of Protestant denominations and will therefore be largely informative to the Roman Catholic reader. Because of marked differences in polity between the Roman Catholic Church and most Protestant communions, Chapter 17 on administration will require considerable adaptation and correction to be made applicable to the Roman Catholic parish. And the final chapter, on the ministry of the Church, is so markedly Protestant in conception that the Roman Catholic reader will doubtless find it a matter of conscience to oppose its central thesis that both clergy and laity are one in the common ministry of the Church.

Jewish readers will have reservations at those points in the book at which christology becomes most explicit and determinative. While all of these cannot be itemized, the major ones can be indicated and the values of the book which may stand even though there is such a decisive difference regarding christology can be suggested. The nature of the Church as presented in Chapter 1 is so completely centered in christology that the only common element for the Jewish student is the communal context of nurture in Israel as the people of God, comparable to the communal context of nurture in the Church as a living body, understood by the Christian as the body of Christ. The historical chapters will be uneven in their relevance, but by no means as decisively controversial as the first chapter. The origin of the Sunday School (Chapter 4) because of the adoption of this movement by the Jewish community, the psychological movement in education (Chapter 5) because of its warm humaneness and its familiar secular sources, and Horace Bushnell (Chapter 6) because of his revival of the Jewish emphasis on the family in religious nurture, will all three be of interest and may win a good degree of acceptance. The same may be true in large part for the chapter on John Dewey and progressive education (7) and the chapter on the religious education movement (8), because Jewish religious educators were influenced as much by and participated as much in these movements as Protestant religious educators. Chapter 9 on the function of theology in education and Chapter 10 on the Bible in nurture may not present as difficult issues to the Jewish reader as to the Roman Catholic, because the Jewish mind, like the newer Protestant theology, is more inclined toward empiricism and less toward rationalism. Therefore a theology which is not assumed to be a deposit of doctrinal formulas is neither foreign nor unwelcome. This may be an obverse way of pointing out that the newer theology of Protestantism holds more closely to the ancient biblical way of thinking than earlier theologies have done; herein at least is one motif in common with Judaism. Chapters 11 through 17 do not appear to raise fundamental problems for the Jewish reader. The analysis of the secular community (Chapter 11) is familiar ground to many Jewish students and a welcome concern. The majority of the parish agencies discussed (Chapter 12) are quite common in Judaism, although there may be variants in their names. Psychology (Chapters 13 and 14) and methodology (Chapter 15) as discussed here are quite as familiar and congenial to the Jewish student as to the Protestant. But with curriculum (Chapter 16), as in relation to Roman Catholicism, the discussion may not do more than inform and provide a basis of comparison, since it deals predominantly with Protestant curriculums. The discussion of administration (Chapter 17) does not present such a problem however, as a number of the patterns of organization and relationship proposed are quite as possible to Judaism as to Protestantism. Finally, since the last chapter (18), on the ministry, reflects Protestantism so distinctly and uniquely, it will probably not be embraced readily by the Jewish student; however it may not be as forbidding to him as to the Roman Catholic.

It is of course impossible for a person to acknowledge, or even consciously to ferret out, all of the resources upon which he has been dependent in writing a book. He can strive for the appropriate humility, however, out of which sincere thankfulness is born. Among the many acknowledgments which could be made, it is imperative that three be written down here for all to read. To the patient and inspiring students, now quite a company, who struggled together with me over the contents of this book, goes my appreciation and continued good wishes. A good number of them were in courses with me at Princeton Theological Seminary; a small group at Garrett Biblical Institute during a summer session there; and another large body of them in Austin Presbyterian Theological Seminary. To two faithful secretaries, successively Mrs. John Hammons and Mrs. Philip Samuelson, I owe profound gratitude for their patience, hard work, and careful proficiency in "writing" this book for me, as it were, in all the several stages through which it grew before reaching the presses. To Austin Presbyterian Theological Seminary and particularly its President, David L. Stitt, my deep appreciation is expressed for making available to me such full and competent secretarial help that I could write this book while carrying full academic responsibilities during my three years there. I offer a final note of gratitude to Macalester College, its President, Harvey M. Rice, the Board of Trustees, and Mr. DeWitt Wallace because of the gracious terms of the James Wallace Professorship of Religion which gave me time for research and writing.

J. DONALD BUTLER

Macalester College, St. Paul, Minnesota
January, 1962

xii

RELIGIOUS EDUCATION

CHAPTER 1

The Church and Nurture

THE ACTUALITY OF THE CHURCH

*B*efore taking up an understanding of the Church, we should recognize that it is significant that the Church is a present fact in the world. It exists now and has existed in every generation since its inception. And by its very existence the Church is a spokesman in the world.

It is by virtue of this actuality of the Church that the opportunity for faith is opened to men in every generation; it is by virtue of this that the demands of faith are made upon us. Although it may be argued that men are converted by the Bible, and in a few rare instances this may happen apparently quite apart from the Church, yet much more universally it is because men are touched by the Church that they are brought to faith. It is usually because the Bible is taught or preached by the Church that men come to faith. It may be argued that on occasion great ideas or doctrines of the Christian religion burn themselves into the minds or consciences of men, and it is because of their inescapable impact that men come to believe. But it is rare when these occasions are not immediately connected with the Church at work in preaching, teaching, or writing—to say nothing of occasions when the Church is a more remote influence.

The actuality of the Church is the point at which revelation confronts each individual and each generation. For children of Christian homes, it is by virtue of the Church in their homes, or at least the influence of the Church in their homes, and because of the vital relation of the home to the Church that the child and the Christian faith become related. For those who are born in homes where there is no belief, when and if they are brought to a vital faith, they are so brought because of the fact of the Church which somehow or at some point touches their lives and evokes their response. And for those who reject the faith and do not believe, the actuality of the Church is likely in some way to be involved in their act of rejection.

This existential aspect of the Church is noted in order to call attention to the point of departure of the life of faith for most men. We do not in this generation reach back by some transcendence of history to the original events of revelation, and there begin our life of faith. Rather, we begin with the Church as it is now; or else the Church begins by touching us and moving us. Through the thought and life of the Church and through Scripture, the events of God's revelation are brought to bear upon us. Truly, in historical sequence the Incarnation preceded the New Testament and the Church, and all three preceded the centuries of the history of the Church between now and then. But the sequence of history is not the sequence of faith or of nurture; that is another sequence which begins with the present-day Church as it touches a man in this generation, or any other man in any other generation, and draws him into a present meeting with God which is revealing and redeeming. In this sense it can be said that there is a kind of transcendence of history, and by means of the Church a man is taken back to the original events from which the faith began.

But this existential aspect of the Church is only one aspect; it is the "thatness" of the Church. As such it is significant, but what we want to know even more, when we have been arrested by the fact of the Church, is what it is in its inner essence. And it is to this that the discussion now turns.

THE NATURE OF THE CHURCH

The Church is not, of course, its buildings, this scarcely need be said. While it will affect the way in which it arranges its activities, a congregation can suffer loss of the building in which it meets without affecting its life in a lasting way. By deliberate intent an old church building is demolished in order to make way for a new

2

one standing on the same site without serious effect. There may be temporary inconvenience while the transition is being made, but the new building when completed will be not only the symbol of a larger and fuller life for the congregation, but also the physical provision for it.

Institutional Forms

To say, therefore, that the church building is not an essential part of the Church is easy. But what may be more significant is to go on to say that the institutional forms which the Church has in any denomination or generation are similar to the building; i.e., they are scarcely more a part of the essence of the Church than its buildings. But this may need some explanation.

What do we mean by the institutional forms of the Church? Well, there are the denominations, of which we have more than enough, and there are organizations by which many denominations are interrelated. Within each denomination or sect there is also organization by which the day-by-day business of each particular religious body is done. There are offices and bureaus in the Church just as there are in government and in commerce, whether we like it or not. They have become an expedient, at the least, in order to keep the affairs of the churches in hand.

Explicitness at the congregational level requires first of all that we scan some of the usual structural elements in the congregation. Usually there is a minister, ordained or set apart in some way as the "spiritually" qualified and therefore officially appointed or installed leader of the congregation. He may be the only paid staff-member in smaller congregations, and these are far more numerous than those in which the minister has paid assistance. In somewhat larger churches there is a single paid secretary and an office in the church building, open for business through most of the regular business hours of the week. In congregations of varying larger memberships, the secretarial, janitorial, and professional staff is proportionately larger; and in accordance with the larger membership and larger staff, the "temporal" and business affairs of the congregation are more complex.

Among the members of the congregation, in addition to paid staff, there are organizations and designations of responsibility. The congregation usually sits at regular intervals as a voting body, prob-

3

ably no less than once a year, making decisions concerning the affairs of the church. There is at least one official body within the congregation, commonly elected by the members and given a mandate to administer, as an executive board, the affairs of the congregation. The number of these official bodies and the peculiar character of their duties will vary among denominations and also among congregations of the same denomination. In addition to such executive organizations within the congregation, there is a variety of "program" organizations—the Sunday Church School, the youth fellowships, men's and women's organizations, and choirs, to mention only some of the more common ones. Now our argument, in relation to this sketch of congregational organization, is that this institutional structure in the congregation has little more to do with the essential nature of the Church than does the building in which the congregation is housed.

A similar judgment can be made concerning the institutional structure of a denomination to the effect that this too is no more a part of the essence of the Church, which may be in the denomination's life, than the various buildings in which denominational headquarters are housed. There of course is variety in denominational organization; this is one of the reasons why we have denominations. There are differences in doctrine among denominations, but there is also a difference in "discipline," in the way in which the Church is organized and in the value judgments as to which particular form of organization is best. Generally speaking, there are three kinds of discipline: congregational, episcopal, and presbyterian. It will be noted that the names for these types have not been capitalized. Commonly they are names of denominations, but they are also names of types of organization.

Congregational organization is an attempt at approximating pure democracy in church organization. The presupposition of congregational organization is that the people who comprise the membership of the local congregation should have full say as to what transpires in the life of the Church. It is based on the argument that the congregation should be completely autonomous and should not be governed by any higher authority. To use figures from civil government, it is local autonomy or states' rights without any controlling centralized or federal government. The Congregational, Baptist, and Christian Churches are examples of denominations which follow the congregational system.

The direct antithesis of this type of church discipline is episcopal organization. Its presupposition is that the Church should be governed primarily by bishops. In the Roman Catholic Church there is an earthly head, namely, the Pope, and from his centralized authority and control stems the appointment of bishops of different rank, thence reaching down to the local parish level at which the minister or priest receives his appointment to the congregation by a higher authority. According to the analogy of civil government, this discipline in theory is centralized government more than local autonomy. Two other denominations, in addition to Roman Catholicism, which follow generally this type of organization are the Episcopal and Methodist Churches. For them, however, there is not a single head of the Church, as in Roman Catholicism,[1] and the authority of the bishops is also less autonomous, being derived as it is from governing bodies in the Church.

Between these two antithetical forms of Church organization is the presbyterian system. It may seem to be a compromise, but possibly it is better understood as a synthesis combining local autonomy and centralized authority. The Church is governed, in the presbyterian system, by presbyteries and therefore the name. The presbyterian idea in discipline is that the bishops of the Church should be corporate entities and not single persons; these corporate entities are all considered to be courts of the Church, and they have an ascending order moving from the congregation upward. The local congregation, in which all members have a part, is a court of the Church. The chief governing body of the local Church, elected by the people, is the next highest court. In the various Reformed Churches this court is called the consistory; in the Presbyterian Churches it is called the session. The next highest court, usually governing a number of congregations in a manageable geographical area, is called the presbytery by the Presbyterian Churches, and the classis by the Reformed Churches. Higher above this, and governing a larger region, is the Synod, of which there are commonly several in a given denomination. And highest of all the

[1] Except in England where the Monarch is the titular head of the Anglican Church.

courts, the body from which the entire denomination is controlled, is the general assembly or the general synod.

Whereas different denominations hold quite consistently to one of these systems in principle, there are various adaptations in practice which blur the lines of distinction, so that in actual practice such a neat classification as is attempted here does not apply literally. One way in which this can clearly be seen is that all denominations must have centralized offices; the larger and more extensive the affairs of the denomination, the larger these offices will be and the more people they will have to employ in order to handle the business of the church. Now even congregational churches, which in principle do not hold to centralized control, have to yield because of complexity to this much centralization.

But the point of all of this discussion of denominational organizations and the necessary bureaucratic structure which they have is to argue again that none of this is a part of the essence of the Church which truly may be in these denominations. This may very well be necessary human organization which the Church cannot avoid having, but it is not the Church.

There is yet another form of organization common to the churches, structures by which denominations are related to each other. This is seen most simply at the local level. In small communities in which there may be only a few churches, there may be a simple and possibly very informal organization of ministers. In larger communities and cities, it is very common for there to be a council of churches with at least one full-time, paid staff member. At higher levels there are state councils of churches, with a staff and an organization of varying complexity depending largely on size. In most of the nations of the world there are national councils of churches. And, as is commonly known, for somewhat more than a decade now there has been the World Council of Churches.[2] So there are structures for interdenominational or ecumenical relations and concerns at the different levels of the life of the Church, ranging from the local to the global. And in addition there are some organizations by which the denominations are related, as it were, as families. For example, the various Reformed denominations and the various Lutheran denominations of the world have respective organizations in which their representatives meet to deal

[2] Formed in Amsterdam in 1948.

6

with matters of common interest and concern. But having said this by way of description, we now return to our argument for which we have been contending throughout. This is that all of these various interdenominational organizations are scarcely any more closely allied to the essence of the Church than are the buildings in which the headquarters of the various organizations are housed.

What then is the Church, if its essence is not to be found in these institutional forms? This is the central and rather difficult question which we want to answer. The answer proposed here cannot of course be complete; this is a major theological problem and many books have been devoted to it. However, if we are to make an authentic approach to the understanding of nurture in the Church, we have an obligation to be aware of the nature of that which is the context for nurture. This understanding must be derived in great part from the work of theologians who have devoted major attention to defining the nature of the Church, but it must somehow bypass the trap of second-hand knowledge to have its own ring of truth and its own theological integrity.

How the Church Came to Be

Possibly we may come near to the being and essence of the Church if we ask how it came to be. Of what events or causes is it the consequence? What substratum of reality does the Church have, which insures that, in every generation and in almost every culture, there will be a Church, whatever institutional form it may have?

The Christian Church had its antecedents, if not its beginnings, in the Apostles whom Jesus chose as his intimates and followers and also in a small remnant of faithful and devoted men and women who persisted in following him, constant in their faith in contrast to the acclaiming multitudes who occasionally gathered around him when they sensed a flare of popular appeal. But Apostles and faithful followers alike were not equal to the tragic element which Jesus embraced as a part of his life and mission, without enthusiasm, but, nevertheless, with determined tenacity. They would not hear him when he talked about his death in prospect, and they could not see anything but unrelieved despair when he was actually crucified. When his life and mission became an open public issue on which people had to take sides, they did not have the courage to stand by him and be recognized as his friends. And when his death came, it was the tragic and disappointing end of what they had hoped would be a new and messianic era. This is the rather unpromising antecedent out of which the Church came as a sequel.

But unpromising as the antecedent may have been, there was a sequel. Despairing and scattered though they were, those followers of Jesus nevertheless came back together and became the Church. And there were two convictions about events which brought them back together and welded them into a community. They were convinced that Jesus had risen from the dead and had revealed himself to them, to some individually before they had come together again as a group, and to the group itself after they had come back together. They were also convinced that the Spirit of God, which he had promised, had come among them, uniting them as one and giving them power to stand for what they believed to be true about Jesus, against an unfriendly world which regarded their belief as foolishness.

In its origins at least, it is clear that the Church was centered in Jesus. It was he who brought the Apostles and followers together by that peculiar attraction which was his; enough reference to their squabbles and quarrels is on record to indicate that they had little else in common. It was his return to them, and not pious dedication to any of his teachings, which brought them together again after his death had nearly destroyed them. It was the Spirit which he had promised that gave them their new manifestations of power and unity. At least in terms of the origin of the Church, therefore, if it is not also confirmed by the later experience of the Church, to understand the Church is to see it necessarily as intimately tied to the person of Jesus Christ.

The Church of course may be described as a phenomenon of human events having institutional forms which make it appear externally very similar to any other human institution. But if this apparent Church has any substratum of reality which is more fundamental than the phenomenal and institutional Church, this substratum consists of Jesus Christ, the second person of the Trinity, and of the Holy Spirit he promised, both of whom came from God the Father—with whom and of whom they are, yet together all three are one. It may be that the being of the Church is

8

resident in the tragedy of the death of Christ, more than in any other possible base of existence. If God so loved the world that he wanted to share with or somehow give to man eternal life similar to his own, how could this be done except, that God not only come among men, but that God should die, laying open and laying down his eternal life and his abiding existence so that man could take it up and acquire a new existence, an eternal life? And if this is so, then the Church in essence is that company of people who have partaken of this life which has been laid down, this existence which has been opened up to man in the tragic death of the Son, and who are one body, one unified community, because they all partake of him and have their existence in him. If the Church has a substratum of reality, this is it. If the Church is a unified body, if it is in any sense a corporate entity, it is because of this foundation of its being that it is.

The Body of Christ

There are a number of concepts and metaphors, used in the first instances in the New Testament, but perennial in the thought of the Church, which symbolize or characterize the Church. Some of these are nearly total in their scope, and some are more partial, referring only to some aspect of the Church. All of them derive their meaning from the convictions of the original, first-generation Church concerning Christ. And accordingly they can only validly communicate the nature of the Church as they symbolize the ontological foundation of the Church in the death of Christ and the work of the Holy Spirit in the Church. We will discuss these concepts and try to suggest how they refer symbolically to the substratum of reality underlying the phenomenal and institutional forms of the Church whenever these forms become instrumentalities of the life of the true Church.

One of the more common of these metaphors is that the Church is the body of Christ. This symbol was used by Saint Paul, especially in his later letters. Apparently the major occasion for first using this figure was to correct dissension in the churches. In answer to the contention that some gift is superior to another, for example, that preaching is superior to healing, he argued that all people serving in the Church, regardless of the nature of their particular service, are like the parts of the human body. Each has its peculiar

9

function to perform without which the health of the body would be impaired. And no one part of the body can be declared to be superior to another. Christians are all "members" of the one body. Interpreting the metaphor to the Church in Corinth, Saint Paul said, "Now you are the body of Christ and individually members of it." In some uses of the figure there is mention of the "head" of the body, i.e. the directing and controlling head or authority of the Church. This language is tied to the sacrament of the communion in the famous words of institution which the liturgy of many denominations has incorporated verbatim from Saint Paul's statement in I Corinthians, chapter 11. In the sacrament the members of the Church partake of bread as the body of Christ and wine as the blood of Christ. And this classical statement of Saint Paul's concerning the communion has its antecedent of course in a symbolic act in which Jesus engaged with his disciples just before his death, according to the record in the Gospels. In this act he gave them the bread to eat saying, "This is my body," and giving them the wine to drink he said, "This is my blood."[3]

The tying of the figure of the body of Christ to the sacrament of the communion is significant because it suggests that the validity of the symbol is in the underlying substructure which Christ is to the Church. It is only as the members of the Church partake of Christ who was broken for them that they are members of the Church. It is only because of this that they are a part of a corporate entity which transcends the solitariness of their individuality. It is only because of this that the particular ministry of each individual Christian has a dignity and worth which is equivalent to the particular ministry of any other member. It is only because of this, it may even be said, that the metaphor may be made to say Christ is the head of the Church. He is the head not as some arbitrary authority who controls and governs because he is in the position of power which gives him this prerogative. He is the head because he is the one who, by giving of himself in brokenness, has given the Church its existence. In a way beyond that apparently intended by

---

[3] See especially I Corinthians 12:4–31 and 11:23–26; also Romans 12:4–8; I Corinthians 10:16–17; Ephesians 1:23; 4:12; 5:30; Colossians 1:18, 24; 2:19; 3:15. For the account of the first communion in the Gospels see Matthew 25:20–29; Mark 14:17–25; Luke 22:14–23.

the hymn ascribed to Bernard of Clairvaux, he is the "sacred head now wounded"—not just the physical head of the incarnate Jesus torn by a crown of thorns, but the sacred head who is the head of the Church, the underlying being of the Church, because his whole being was wounded for the Church and for mankind.

The Fellowship of the Spirit

A second and also very common concept referring to the Church is that it is the fellowship of the Spirit. The concept easily loses its meaning in translation and in the bending and slanting to which it is subjected by different cultures. The ambiguity is in the word "fellowship." The New Testament word *koinonia*, which is often translated as "fellowship," implies a bond of relationship which is more intimate, more communal, and more genuinely serious than our word "fellowship" suggests. To mention the more concrete first, the word in some contexts is quite correctly made to mean "a contribution."[4] Members of the early churches were asked on occasion to make a gift to help those of other churches which were in need, and this collection of money to be sent to their fellow Christians in another church was sometimes called a *koinonia*. In another set of instances, the word is made to mean "a sharing," or in the verb form, "to share." In one instance Christians were admonished "to share what you have,"[5] referring to material goods. In another instance, referring to the less tangible, the reference was to sharing the sufferings of Christ[6] and in still a third to "the sharing of your faith."[7] "Participation" is the meaning given the word *koinonia* in two other instances. In one of these instances Saint Paul spoke of "participation in the Spirit"[8] and in the other he asked the rhetorical question, "The cup of blessing which we bless [referring to the sacrament of communion], is it not a participation in the blood of Christ?"[9] In addition, one other word is used as an English equivalent; this is the instance in which *koinonia* is made to mean "*partnership* in the Gospel."[10]

4 II Corinthians 9:5; 9:13, and Romans 15:26.
5 Hebrews 13:16.
6 Philippians 3:10.
7 Philemon 4.
8 Philippians 2:1.
9 I Corinthians 10:16, my italics.
10 Philippians 1:5, my italics.

Now what nuance of meaning can we draw from uses of this word which may be rather strange to us, the same word which refers to the fellowship of the Spirit which is the Church? It is something so intimate and so much a part of one's own being that it is like a gift that a person makes to relieve the sufferings of someone for whom he has compassion. It is allied to the act of sharing, of letting someone else have a part of what I myself have, be it materials, faith, or sufferings; and conversely it is the act of having a part of whatever someone else is willing for me to have in common with him. It is the act of participating in something which is shared in common, and particularly in the Spirit and in the blood of Christ in the communion sacrament. It is a partnership, a common joning together like members in a business enterprise.

These are the different facets of meaning the word has, which more commonly in the New Testament and by derivation in the life of the Church, become a part of the phrase, "fellowship of the Spirit," which the Church is supposed to be. This is what the members of the first Church perceived as coming into being on the day of Pentecost when the Holy Spirit came among them—a new emergence which they could only describe as like an earthquake and as though flames of a common fire had come among them and had touched each one of them. It was as though, by some flight of speech or transcendence of language, they had been given powers of expression so that anyone hearing them could understand, no matter what his native tongue was. To them it was so much to be made one in a common sharing that they could not see how they had any right to call any possession their own.[11]

It is impossible and beyond our scope here to go into the problem of relationship between Christ and the Spirit as the common basis of their unity. They were one by the common foundation of existence which Christ had opened to them by his crucifixion; they were one by the common bond of the Spirit which came among them. There is some distinction between these two sources of their commonality, but there is no duality or conflict in the distinction.

The Hope of the Church

There are three other common concepts besides the two that have been discussed which indicate in some measure the nature of

[11] Acts 2.

the Church. These ideas are common, but they are less central than the body-of-Christ figure and the Fellowship-of-the-Spirit concept. They are (1) the hope of the Church for the Kingdom of God, (2) the Church as the people of God, and (3) the Church as being in the world. And this last more than either of the first concepts may return our thought to an earlier subject, namely, the institutional form of the Church.

We will take up first of all then the hope of the Church. In theological language, this is the eschatological aspect of the Church, its hope for the Kingdom of God. This conception has to do with the future toward which the Church looks, and it depicts the dynamic and moving character of the Church. That is that the Church is not in the past and the present alone, but it looks forward to the consummation of that which has been initiated and promised in the Church, namely, the coming of the Kingdom of God.

Incidental to this understanding of the Church there is involved, of course, the conception of the Kingdom of God. While this subject cannot now be taken up for primary consideration, two things should be said.

1. In our particular generation we have exaggerated somewhat the conception of the Kingdom of God as the rule of God. There are many references which could be made to the Bible as the basis for the view of the Kingdom of God as an order in which God's rule is effective and all members of the order live in harmony with this rule and in obedience to God. The question can at least be raised, however, as to whether this conception may overwork the monarchical element in the metaphor. The word "Kingdom" is a monarchical figure; more precisely it refers in human terms to a form of government in which there is a monarch who rules, whose decisions, judgments, and will are final. Up until recent centuries when symbolizing the social order it was understandably normal to take the word "Kingdom" to represent political order, if not social order. It was a figure which would communicate far better previously than it does now because political order was virtually synonymous with monarchical organization. Jesus used this figure, and possibly with deliberate intent, but there is reason to assume that he used the figure, as he may very well have used many other words and figures, because they would communicate with the

people of his time. This is the language he had to speak in order to be understood. It may at least be inferred from this that the monarchical element is not primary in the figure, but instead that it refers to the order of God—a new order which transcends and supplants the human order which very commonly is as much disorder as it is order. To single this monarchical element out and define the Kingdom as the rule of God is to distort the figure at least in some measure. Another way of understanding the Kingdom of God, and one preferred by this author, is that it is the new society of God which is founded upon the Son who gives it existence and which is bound together as one by the Spirit. In this new order there is truly enough the rule of God, but the rule of God is present by means of internal bonds which tie the members together in unity. The orderliness of the society comes from the internal compulsion of love rather than from the external rule of force. Inadequate as this digression is, it may possibly be enough for the present purpose so that we can return to the conception of the Church which specifies the hope of the Church for the Kingdom of God. Our primary concern at this point is that the Church lives in the hope of this coming order of God. In fact, there is some sense in which the Church now participates in this coming Kingdom.

Two symbols in the New Testament portraying this hope of the Church for the Kingdom are the earnest or guarantee and the Christian's true citizenship. Let us take these up in order. There is a word[12] in II Corinthians 1:22 and 5:5 which is translated "earnest," or in the Revised Standard Version, "guarantee," and which is used in relation to this hope of the Church. The implication of this word is that we already have in the Church something very close to what is hoped for in the Kingdom, but not the full realization of it. It is as though in the Church we already have a sample of the Kingdom—as it were, a down payment or a first installment. Now a down payment or a first installment is the very same kind of money that is used to make the final payment on a purchase. A home owner in building a house will pay the builder a percentage on what the cost of the construction will be, and this is commonly termed earnest money. Wherever the rest of the

[12] αρραβῶνα.

14

money comes from to complete the deal when the house is finished, it's all money, it's all currency, it's all the same stuff as the down payment. Now this word translated "earnest" or "guarantee" has the possible meaning that the Church already has something of what this ultimate Kingdom will be; at the least it has the guarantee that the Kingdom will come.

2. The other figure relating to this hope is borrowed from government. It comes from a reminder by Saint Paul, in Ephesians 1:14, that the Christian has his abiding citizenship in heaven. While he is and should be a participant in human affairs and even a citizen, of course, in one of the nations of men, he is also a citizen in an order which is above things human. Put another way, the Church may be considered a colony of heaven that is located on earth and among men of earth, but having the Kingdom of God as its mother country. This last is certainly an exaggeration; we understandably shrink back from the suggestion that human society is only a colony of heaven. But nevertheless Saint Paul's statement that the true citizenship of the Christian is in heaven vividly symbolizes the eschatological hope of the Church.

The People of God

The second of these three less central conceptions of the Church is the reference to the Church as the people of God. This is based largely on the word *ekklesia*, used in the New Testament not only for the Church, but also for the public assembly of people. This word, rather frequently used in the New Testament, on many occasions does not refer to the Church. For example it is used in the Book of Acts, chapter 19, to refer to an assembly of people which came together as an excited mob in the city of Ephesus.[13] This is the incident in which Demetrius the silversmith created a commotion among the people of Ephesus because of his worry that the preaching of Paul would bring an end to the lucrative business of making silver shrines of Artemis, the goddess of a great temple in Ephesus. The word here refers not to the Church, but to the crowd of people who came together in a theatre to hear Demetrius. There are those who are convinced that the usage of this word is not helpful in attempting to understand the Church. The Swiss

13 Acts 19:23–41.

theologian, Emil Brunner, for example, argues this in his book, *The Misunderstanding of the Church*.[14]

There may be some significance in the word, however, when used to refer to the Church. By implication the word may say that the members of the Church are called by God to be his people; not uncommonly the word has been interpreted in this way. It may also imply that as the Church, these people who are called out constitute a separate and distinct people, as compared to other men who are not men of faith in Christ. These may be two valid implications in the word; however it is primarily a descriptive word. By descriptive we mean that the word merely tries to denote or describe and that is all. It refers to the Church externally in its public or institutional aspects; it does not refer to the Church essentially, nor does it predicate anything concerning the inner nature of the Church. It refers rather to the observable assembly of people which any Church is when it is gathered together. Without too great distortion, it may be said that this is a phenomenological word, that is, it deals only with the phenomenology of the Church. It deals with the Church externally as a phenomenon in human events. It refers to the "thatness" of the Church, as we have already tried to do earlier,[15] the evident Church as a fact in human events. In addition to this actuality it does not tell us much about the Church. It does not help us in understanding the essence, the inner nature of the Church, nor does it tell us much about the ontological ground of the Church's being.

The Church in the World

We now turn to the third of these common but less central concepts—the Church in the world. While the concept may be less central as compared to the body of Christ and the fellowship of the Spirit, it is of no mean importance. It would be helpful if we had in English a word which means "Church-in-the-World." For from the standpoint of the necessary relation of the Church and the world, we are not denoting the Church truly unless we refer to the Church-in-the-world, all telescoped together as one word. This concept is, among other things, a correction of romantic tendencies

[14] Trans. by Harold Knight, Philadelphia: Westminster, 1953.
[15] See pp. 1–2.

to make the Church a purely mystical retreat in which man can escape from the stern realities of human life and have the assurance of heaven without getting under the burden of human responsibility. The famous and much quoted invitation of Jesus to the disciples, after they had come back from some arduous travels, "Come ye apart in to a desert place and rest a while,"[16] has been more generally applied than is warranted. The Church is not primarily a place to which we retreat for rest. An earnest believer may rest for a while, but he is going to get burdens, compulsions, imperatives, urgencies, and responsibilities if he stays very long, and if the Church is truly the Church. The Church is not a mystical retreat which can feed a romantic heart, and the conception of the Church-in-the-world very properly corrects this mistaken understanding. However else the Church is to be understood, it can never be separated from the world of man's affairs—corrupt though these affairs may be—and still be the Church. The locus of the Church is in intimate relation to the life of man and not in the aloofness of separation. There is abundant reference to this in the New Testament, and while the Church historically has not always recognized this responsibility as it should, relation to the world has been stressed repeatedly by the Church throughout its history.

The common distinction made in this connection is that the Church is in the world, but is not of the world. This, apparently, is a valid distinction. Jesus' prayer for the infant Church, just before his crucifixion, makes this very distinction.[17] When he prays for the disciples, he does not pray for them to be taken out of the world; he prays that the Father will "keep them and make them one" as the Trinity is one.[18] And in making this prayer, he confirms that their true place and the true place of the Church is in the world, as he himself was in the world up to the time of his death. In passing, it should be remarked, however, that this is not to imply that the Church is an extension of the Incarnation.

Further exploration of the in-the-world aspect of the Church necessarily involves the servant figure, one of the more common figures of the Bible. It is used in the Old Testament[19] most fre-

[16] Mark 6:31.
[17] John 17:15.
[18] John 17:22.
[19] Especially *Isaiah* 41–49.

17

quently to refer to Israel, sometimes to refer to the anticipated Messiah, and occasionally to refer to a person who has no apparent connection with the people of God. In one instance which is an example of this last, Cyrus is called the servant of God[20] apparently because the events with which he was connected were in harmony with the purpose of God for his people at that particular time.

Jesus adopted the servant figure very openly and decisively. He adopted it in his teaching, admonishing us—in relation for example to our problem of status—that he who would be the greatest, let him be the servant.[21] He also adopted the figure in his symbolic acts, for example, in the foot-washing incident.[22] Because of their great concern for status, none of his disciples was going to sacrifice his dignity and stoop to washing the feet of his brethren. No doubt this very meaningful account is familiar to you—Jesus girded himself with a towel and proceeded to go around the group washing the disciples' feet. While this act certainly must have had a decisive meaning in the human struggle for status which it resolved, it was also a symbolic act in which Jesus fully embraced the servant form for what it would say apart from any words.

The servant figure is also urged upon Christians in a passage which is attributed to Saint Paul, but which may have been taken from an early liturgy in the Church.[23] It lays upon Christians as their appropriate posture the servant motif. If it was a kind of poem or hymn in the early liturgy, it sings about one who existed on an equality with God, but one who counted not this equality a thing to be grasped, one who humbled himself to become a servant, one who became a servant to become a man, one who became a man to die the death that man has to die, and even more than this, to die a death that no man has to die. All figures can be overworked of course; nevertheless the servant figure has a great depth of meaning, and it speaks to some of our most difficult current human problems. To the extent that we are beset today with the struggle for power—and it appears that we are so beset more than ever before—the servant figure is most relevant.

We have been dealing with the servant figure incidental to our effort to understand more fully one aspect of the Church, namely

[20] Isaiah 45:1–4.
[21] Matthew 20:27.
[22] John 13:1–20.
[23] Philippians 2:5–11.

its relation to and involvement in human affairs. This aspect of the Church necessarily draws upon the servant figure, because this figure when applied to the Church, by derivation from Christ's application of the figure to himself, says that the Church is in the world *as a servant.* In other words we can say more than the simple assertion that the Church is in the world; we can go on to specify in part how and in what way the Church is in the world. And this more particular statement is that the Church is in the world as a servant, that in some sense the Church is the Church in essence by virtue of being a servant in the world. Claude Welch, in his book, *The Reality of the Church,*[24] points to the human nature of Christ as not being something at which we should be surprised; rather we need to recognize, he says, that his Sonship is revealed by means of these very human elements, and not in spite of them. Now there is a parallel to this in the Church, namely that the Church is the Church, not in spite of its being in the world or in spite of its being a servant, but the Church is the Church because it is in the world and because it is a servant.

Possibly it might be helpful to summarize here before moving on to a new major topic. On the nature of the Church it has been contended that we do not find the essence of the Church in its human institutional forms. Secondly, we approached an understanding of the Church by trying to see how it came to be, before considering conceptions of it. Here it was contended that the Church came as a kind of miracle out of complete despair and desolation; there was and is a Church because Christ came back to his scattered followers, so the argument ran, and therefore any understanding of the Church necessarily has to be rooted in Christ who is the foundation of the Church. From this point our study turned to metaphors or concepts in the New Testament for the Church: (1) the Church as the body of Christ, (2) the Church as the *koinonia* or the fellowship of the Spirit, (3) the eschatological hope of the Church for the Kingdom, (4) the Church as the people of God, and (5) the Church in the world.

Now the point of all this, if it has any relevance in this book apart from a theological interest, is that it may throw some light on nurture. If it is correct to argue that nurture is integral to the

[24] New York: Scribner's 1958, pp. 74-146.

Church, that we cannot understand nurture without understanding the Church, and that any definition of nurture must at least in context be derived from the nature of the Church, then the validity of the foregoing discussion is contained in the question: "What does this say about nurture?" And that is the subject of the next and last section of this chapter. What understanding of nurture can be derived from the understanding of the Church?

NURTURE AS DERIVED FROM THE CHURCH

In trying now to define nurture by deriving its meaning from this understanding of the Church, it may still prove necessary to speak in metaphor rather than in direct and explicit statements. Unless this is done, nuances may be lost which are essential to a vital and authentic understanding of nurture. Simple and direct statements will at least have the illusion of clarity, but they may also fail to convey or participate in essence.

Since the Church is an intimate and communal matrix, it would seem valid to infer that nurture has this same intimate and communal character. It is an action of the Church performed upon its members and upon those who may become members which is similar to a body extending itself by adding new parts. It is also similar to a body doing something to its members which makes them more completely members than they were before. This is, of course, to carry over the figure of the body and to see what it implies for an individual function of the Church, in addition to what it says about the nature of the Church in all of its functions. While it now breaks down as a metaphor, it yet says something about nurture which would seem to be valid.

The human body can only be monstrously imagined as adding new members, such as a finger or an eye. But were such biological generation a possibility and an appropriate metaphor, it would imply that the new member would be added not as a mere increase in mass, but by means of being made qualitatively and functionally an integral part of the body. The human body may exercise in its entirety as a single unit, or it may exercise particular parts to keep the body healthy, to make a part a better part, or possibly to correct the effects of disease or injury. But the kind of action which nurture is, is not just an exercising, a going through one's paces. It is more qualitative than this, involving changes in quality and essence; it is neither just a maintenance of what is nor a correction of deficiency. Nurture in the Church is an action upon individuals so involving internal relationships that by it members are not just quantitatively or statistically added or quantitatively maintained in external relationship; they are made to have the kind of being that Christ has made possible to them and to become qualitatively more and more a part of his body.

Turning now for a moment from the body metaphor to the fellowship concept, it may be said that nurture is the act of sharing the Church with the individuals who are members of it and also with those who are brought within such proximity to the Church as makes sharing possible. It is an act of offering a gift. It is an overture or invitation to come in and participate in a partnership or community, and to enjoy it more fully.

Nurture, as it is implicit in both of these conceptions, is an action by which men are brought to share the kind of being the Church has by virtue of its *foundation of being* in Christ and because of the one Spirit who is the common corporate possession of the Church, shared individually by its members. It is to bring individuals into the stream of history which the Church is in its temporal dimension and to cause them to have part in it more fully. It is also to make of individuals fingers of the Church, which reach out into the society of man.

Although this attempt at deriving the meaning of nurture from the nature of the Church may appear allegorical and mystical, it may yet say something significant and be neither mysticism nor allegory. At the least it says that nurture is not all an affair of words. Though words may frequently, and even most commonly, be used either in "telling" or in the reciprocity of "conversation," we should not be misled by this. Words do not equal nurture, although they may be a common vehicle of it. The communication or "communion," by which the Christian community brings to birth in a new existence its own children or those whom it "calls" from the world, is a giving of itself, a reaching "out" and "down" to embrace, a living with, a bringing unto itself. And in such a movement words are the means and not the essence.

Admittedly this does not constitute a definition of nurture that fully explicates or includes all, or even most, of the predicates

21

which may be stated with some degree of validity. There has been no attempt here to approach nurture in terms of the forms it has taken in the history of the Church. Neither has an attempt been made to state the place and degree of importance that the Scriptures or doctrine has in nurture. Beyond this no implications have been drawn for nurture from an authentic theological doctrine of man or from a psychological description of man's need. Conceivably all of these will have some place in an explicitly formulated definition. Several of the chapters which follow in this book will be addressed respectively to these other aspects of nurture and what they imply for a definition of it. Nevertheless, what has been stated here, largely in metaphor, is prior to any and all of these formulations. Since the Church and each of its succeeding generations, from which we depart in all excursions of faith, are existential facts in history, it is important to understand both the essence of the Church and what this essence implies for its teaching function. This has been the sole focus of the effort made in this chapter. From this beginning, profitable efforts may be made in formulation. Without it such efforts may be without foundation and lacking in authenticity.

CHAPTER 2

Nurture in the Early Church

We next turn to consideration of the forms nurture has taken in the history of the Church. As there are other approaches to nurture or its dimensions with which this book will wrestle, it is not possible for the history of the forms of nurture to be in any sense full and complete. We have had to choose those backgrounds in history which relate more especially to teaching in the parish church, rather than in the educational institutions of the church. In part this is why the historical portion of this book will omit reference to the medieval period.

We begin in this chapter by viewing nurture as it was in the primitive church, and in the following chapter we will move directly to nurture as it was conceived in the Protestant Reformation. The subjects of subsequent chapters relate only to relevant developments in modern times.[1] This historical overview, sketchy as it may prove to be, will we believe, give essential perspective for dealing with the plight of Christian education in the parish of today. This is one of the major concerns to which we will try to speak in later chapters, with reference to both theory and practice.

---

[1] Some knowledge may be gained of Christian education in the medieval period by consulting Lewis Joseph Sherrill, *The Rise of Christian Education*, New York: Macmillan, 1944, which is a history of Christian education up to the Reformation. Except for Chapter 2, the historical section in this book will supplement Dr. Sherrill's history, which does not deal with the Protestant Reformation nor with modern times.

BACKGROUND FOR NURTURE IN THE EARLY CHURCH

It may be helpful first of all to consider the kind of community that the early Church was. A very simple community as compared to the Church today, it was based on belief in the validity of the Apostles' experience of Christ and the conviction that the Holy Spirit was in the Church, empowering it and unifying it. It was scattered in cells or congregations in many parts of the Mediterranean world; commonly these small units had their meeting places in homes, and often they were subject to the hazard of persecution.

The background of the members offers some clue as to what the task of teaching was in this primitive Church. As far as cultural practices and intellectual understandings were concerned, this infant Church had to cope with both the heritage of Judaism and the contemporary cultures surrounding it. We may take up each of these; it is usual to look first at the roots of the early Church in Judaism.

Although the Old Testament history, law, and prophecy had great relevance to the experience of the Church and to the Christian gospel, this legitimate background was also a hazard. It was all too easy, when trying to fill in the intellectual understandings which were to accompany the new way represented by Christianity, to fall back into the old ways of Judaistic culture and teaching.

In the time of Saint Paul one of the most vital issues was whether Christianity was just a sect of Judaism or whether it was a distinctly new way. Were these early Christians to conform to all the Judaistic practices, or did they constitute a new emergence in history, distinct and different from all antecedents? They faced this problem in particular ways in their teaching. They were under the necessity of preserving the valid heritage and antecedent which their Hebrew background constituted, but at the same time they had to stand against it. Accepting Jesus as the Christ, they had to stand against all things in their heritage which by implication would make Christianity a segment of Judaism and thereby, something less than a universal faith. As we go further and look into such documents as the *Didache*, we will find that they were not altogether successful in this.

In addition to the Hebrew background there were many mystery cults and, most especially pervasive, the culture of Ancient Greece with its many human achievements of an unusually high order. The Greek culture constituted a background which was comparable in magnitude and influence to the Hebrew heritage. There was such congeniality toward Greek thought—as later exemplified by Saint Augustine in the fourth and fifth centuries—that another line of least resistance, comparable to falling into Judaistic thought and practice, was to embrace Greek thought, fusing it with Christian belief and borrowing from it patterns for Christian thought. This is still a problem today. The Christian Church has largely moved beyond the Judaistic problem; in fact Christians have set up separations between themselves and the Jews many of which are neither desirable nor valid. But if we are to believe many of our contemporary speakers or writers who deal with Christian thought, we have not moved beyond the Greek problem. In part this is so because Augustine was so dependent upon things Greek and was so influential for centuries; in part also it is so because in the thirteenth century Saint Thomas, drawing heavily from Aristotle, fused Greek and Christian thought in the *Summa Theologica*, a *magnum opus* which is still without parallel in Roman Catholic thought. The reformers changed this somewhat; in their concern to reach back to sources, they bypassed Saint Thomas and Augustine and returned to the Scriptures in the original languages. But even so the problem is still with us: what in our thought is Greek in its origin and what is Christian? It may very well be that our generation is riding this distinction too hard; often it appears that everything, which in our judgment is not Hebraic or Christian, is Greek, the assumption being that no union or fusion is possible. However that may be, the early Church had to find its way against the pervasive influence of Greek culture and was not entirely successful in doing so. As it sought to teach converts, making them ready first of all for baptism and then preparing them to live as baptized and confessing Christians in the world, it had to cope with Greek culture as well as a Hebrew heritage.

NEW TESTAMENT WORDS

Some significance may be drawn from three words that are used in the New Testament to refer to teaching or to some aspect of it. These three words may tell us something about forms of nurture which were initiated in the early Church. The first of these words is *paideia*. This word is translated variously as "education," "training up," "nurture," "instruction," "discipline," "correction," or "chastisement." There is a very famous passage for example which is commonly quoted, "Fathers do not provoke your children to anger but bring them up in the nurture and admonition of the Lord."[2] The Revised Standard Version translates this ". . . bring them up in the discipline and instruction of the Lord." In the use of the word "discipline," a somewhat rigid and precise meaning is given to *paideia*, a meaning narrower and more specialized than our word "nurture."

A second word that was used is the word *didache*. This word has been translated "instruction," "the giving of instruction," "the content of teaching," and "the act of teaching." It has been translated as "doctrine"; in certain contexts it is also made to refer to the modes of teaching and in others to the kind of doctrine taught.[3]

The last of these three words is *catecheo*, to use its verb form. As can be easily observed, this word contains the stem of our noun "catechism" and our adjective "catechetical." It also has in it the root for the adjective "catechumenal." This word has been translated as "to sound in the ears," "to make the ears ring," "to instruct orally," "to instruct," "to inform," "to be taught," "to be instructed," "to be made acquainted," "to receive information," "to hear a report." Each of these words and their various meanings may provide some background for the forms which nurture actually took in the early Church. There is no attempt made here to redefine our words "nurture" and "education," making them convey the meanings of these three words. It would appear rather that the word "nurture," used in the context of the Church, may have valid meanings beyond those contained in any or all of these three words.

CATECHUMENAL INSTRUCTION

To go directly now to actual teaching endeavors in the primitive Church, the earliest form they assumed was preparation for bap-

[2] Ephesians 6:4.
[3] Matthew 16:12; John 7:16, 17; Matthew 7:28; Mark 1:27.

tism, known as catechumenal instruction. In fact what we today, in some of our communions, call catechetical instruction was in the early Church catechumenal instruction. Catechetical instruction was used to refer to another form with which we will deal later. Our confirmation classes and communicants classes, we might say, are direct descendants or modern equivalents of this first form of nuture, preparation for baptism.

The importance of this early form can be recognized in its context if we think somewhat imaginatively of the significance of profession of faith and baptism in the primitive Church. To profess faith in Christ and to receive baptism was an awesome step compared to what it is today. This may be a rather proper reflection of the lack of seriousness and decisiveness in our present practice. When a person became a Christian in the first or second century, it was like taking sides in warfare, and accepting the discipline of military life. It was also in many cases to give up one's livelihood and source of income until some new employment could be found. And this may have been one of the contributing reasons that the early Church had a kind of communism of goods reflected in the Book of Acts.[4] We are told that they held all things in common. One of the reasons for this, in addition to their belief that they were part of their brothers and that they should share all things, was that many times they had to take on the support of a new member until he could get re-established economically. There were two stages in becoming a member of the church. The probationers, when they were going through instruction and before they were baptized, were not admitted to all of the worship. They were excused at a certain point in the service, and the remainder of the service was restricted to those who had already confessed their faith.

The content of profession of faith in the New Testament Church and early thereafter was especially confession of the faith that Christ is Lord. It was commitment to him as a Person and not commitment to a set of doctrines, a simple and central confession of faith. Gradually, however, commitment to certain propositions entered as a part of the profession. These came in as a protection of the Gospel, a protection against teachings which in some part embraced Christianity, but added to it ideas which were foreign to

[4] Acts 4:32–37; 5:1–11.

27

it. The different forms of Gnosticism are excellent examples of this. Also this more specific confession was protection against documents circulated among Christians which were not authentic, either historically or in their expressions of the faith.

One of the early documents used in the teaching which prepared people for baptism was the *Didache*.[5] It throws some light on nurture in the early Church because of what it reveals regarding prebaptismal teaching. It may be that the *Didache* was a manual of instruction; it may also have been an outline or syllabus of instruction based on other writings only summarized in the *Didache*. A very short writing of pamphlet length, it first came to light in modern times in the latter half of the nineteenth century and was published in 1883. It is believed, however, to have been written late in the first century or early in the second century. Some parallels may be drawn between the *Didache* and the manual of discipline of the Qumran Community, one of the more familiar documents which came to light among the Dead Sea Scrolls. The *Didache* opens with the announcement that there are two ways, the way of life and the way of death. The way of life is to love the God who made us and to love one's neighbor as one's self: "whatsoever thou wouldst not have done to thy self, do not thou to another." This section on the way of life is interlarded with quotations from the New Testament, introduced apparently at random. The way of life, as the teaching moves on, involves such ethical matters as alms-giving, the duty of the catechumen to the Church, and the avoidance of hypocrisy, to mention a very few specifics. After the middle of the document, the way of death is taken up very briefly, and this is followed in the latter paragraphs by discussion of some religious practices. There is a paragraph for example on baptism, one on fasting, one on prayers, and one on the eucharist. There is also reference to traveling teachers, introducing a note of precaution as to how long they are supposed to stay when they come to a church. There is a short paragraph on Sunday worship, a section on bishops and deacons, and at the very end a warning that the last days are near at hand. This is a most random sketch, but it may convey the temper of the *Didache*; it is apparent

[5] See, for example, *The Apostolic Fathers*, trans. by Kersopp Lake, vol. I, Cambridge, Mass.: Harvard University Press, 1952.

that it is the earliest manual we know for the confirmation or communicants class.

CATECHETICAL EDUCATION

The second form of nurture in the early Church was a kind of advanced education for Christians who had been baptized and fully received by the Church; this was called catechetical instruction. In a sense this is an antecedent for the Christian higher education of today and for the parochial school, because the intention of this teaching was not to make the person a Christian or to get him ready for making his profession of faith. Rather its intent was to take the fully convinced Christian and help him to know how to think as well as to act as a Christian, though living in the midst of a clearly non-Christian culture. Geraldine Hodgson in her book, *Primitive Christian Education*,[6] concludes that in the early Church there was no disdain for education; on the contrary it was regarded highly. There was concern to condemn false learning, but there was no reluctance concerning education as such.

One of the examples of this kind of education is to be found in the writings of Clement of Alexandria, particularly in his book, *The Instructor*.[7] The reason for the title, as is made clear in the beginning, is the presupposition that Christ is the ultimate teacher of all Christians. It would be interesting to speculate as to what the book would have been if Clement had proceeded on this theme throughout. Instead of doing this, the book gives major attention to details of living and focuses on a pattern of life, apparently seeking to guarantee that all aspects of the life of a Christian shall reflect Christian character. A random selection of subjects indicate the range covered by the book. There are sections on the following topics: laughter, filthy speaking, clothes, embellishment of the body, and behavior in the baths. If we remember the characteristics of the civilization at the time, we can understand that this last had peculiar relevance to their living. With whom were they to associate? What were the exercises in

[6] Edinburgh: T. & T. Clark, 1906, pp. 37–38.
[7] See Ante-Nicene Christian Library, vol. IV, ed. by Alexander Roberts and James Donaldson, Edinburgh: T. & T. Clark, 1867.

order to a good life? It would seem to be quite clear that this book is largely ethical and deals primarily with pattern of life rather than with theology. Another writing of Clement is the *Stromata*,[8] which indicates a further range of this form of teaching intended for the more mature Christian. There is a section against the Sophists and another which asserts that the human arts as well as divine knowledge proceed from God. The following titles of other selected portions will further suggest the character of the book: "Philosophy, the Handmaid of Theology," "Human Knowledge Necessary for the Understanding of the Scriptures," "What Is the Philosophy Which the Apostle Bids Us Shun," "All Sects of Philosophy Contain a Germ of Truth," "In What Respect Philosophy Contributes to the Comprehension of Divine Truth," "The Jewish Institutions and Laws of Far Higher Antiquity than the Philosophy of the Greeks," and "Plato an Imitator of Moses in Framing Laws."

We may conclude from this sketch that there were two main forms of nurture in the early church. The first was strictly within the life and fellowship of the Church, preparing people for baptism and for full membership in the Christian fellowship. The second, a liberal or general education following baptism and entrance into full membership, sought to enable Christians more adequately to cope with the world's culture, and thereby it prepared a new generation of leaders for the Church. Monasticism, following in later centuries, constituted a third form, weighted in the direction of withdrawal from the culture of man. But the concern of the second form to cope with the culture suggests yet another form which is to be found especially in Martin Luther many centuries later. As a reformer and a new spokesman for the Church, he stood over against the secular culture and urged upon it what he conceived to be its responsibility in education. It will be to this fourth form and some other matters relative to it that we will turn as we take up consideration of the Reformation and nurture in the next chapter.

[8] *Ibid.*

CHAPTER 3

The Reformation and Nurture in the Church

MARTIN LUTHER (1483–1546)

*M*artin Luther is singular among the Reformers in his concern for education. None of the Reformers had the concern for education Martin Luther did, and none was as vocal about it, with the exception of John Amos Comenius, who will be studied later and who may not have been a Reformer in the strict sense. Luther was a man of great vigor; being a German and living close to his own people he could speak to them with a directness and almost a brutality which is surprisingly refreshing. In him is theological vigor and at the same time a great concern for nurture and education. While Luther's interest in education is expressed in many different places in his work, it is most clearly found by referring to two documents which have become famous as Luther's manifestoes on education. The first is "The Letter to Mayors and Aldermen of All the Cities of Germany in Behalf of Christian Schools," and the second is his "Sermon on the Duty of Sending Children to School."[1]

There may be some disadvantage in our heavy dependence on these two documents for Luther's ideas on education. One interesting and possibly significant implication we may be able to draw from other writings is that Luther may well have been more interested in the *volkschule*, the German popular elementary school for all the people, than in the *gymnasium*, the oldest classical secondary

---

[1] See Robert Ulich, Editor, *Three Thousand Years of Educational Wisdom*, Cambridge, Mass.: Harvard University Press, 1947, pp. 218–249. From *Luther on Education*, translated by F. V. N. Painter, St. Louis, Concordia, 1928, by permission of Concordia Publishing House.

school.[2] However, if we are limited to Luther's writings translated into English, the two documents on which we focus in this discussion are still the fullest and the most convenient sources to which to turn for his thoughts on education.

There is a variety of minor themes in Luther's educational thought to which attention is given in passing. One of these was a sense of urgency that both Greek and Hebrew should be taught in the schools. His reason for this was his conviction that he had been delivered from what he considered the twilight of Roman Catholicism by his command of these tongues, which enabled him to study the Bible in the original languages. In fact, one of his most significant achievements was the translation of both Old and New Testaments into German. He was firmly convinced that the preservation of true religion depended on the preservation of the means by which men could go to the original sources of the Scripture. In one place he goes to such extremes as to say that he was sure the Devil was more afraid of his command of Greek and Hebrew than of whatever measure of the Spirit he had. Another minor theme in which Luther both echoes and anticipates other writers on education is his argument that childhood is the time for learning. A third is his contention that schools are a better agency for learning than private tutoring; in making this argument, he takes a clear stand on one of the perennial issues in educational literature.

But we can do no more than sample these minor themes; we must reserve major attention for the three central educational themes in Luther. The first of these is the importance of education, the second is the responsibility of parents for the education of their children, and the third is the responsibility of government to educate children. These themes constitute a new stance taken by the Church on the broad conception of nurture—a new stance compared to the catechumenal and the catechetical forms of the early Church and Monasticism of the medieval Church. The two famous writings in which these themes are promulgated constitute a significant phenomenon in history: a spokesman of the Church urging upon society the responsibility it should bear for education.

To analyze this new stance of the Church, taking up its three

---

[2] Bokumin Tsuchiyama, *Martin Luther on Education*, Princeton Theological Seminary, Th.M. Thesis, 1957.

major components, what did Luther have to say, first of all, regarding the importance of schools? His first argument is that
schools are as important as public works. Modern times offer a
better analogy than the public works of Luther's day. Schools are
as important as the various public works we have to provide in
order for society to be able to live in decency and order. Water
supply, sewage disposal, roads, means of communication and
travel—Luther says that the schools are every bit as important as
these. Occasionally direct quotations will be included here because
of the vigor and directness with which Luther makes his points. On
the subject of importance, he says: "If we must annually expend
large sums on muskets, roads, bridges, dams, and the like, in order
that the city may have temporal peace and comfort, why should we
not apply as much to our poor, neglected youth, in order that we
may have a skilled school-master or two?"[3]

If this is rephrased in modern terms to refer to the money we
are spending for instruments of atomic war and for offensive and
defensive missiles, it becomes all the more powerful. Of course we
have the historic advantage of learning something from Luther and
others like him and are spending considerably on education; nevertheless the urgency is as great as ever, if not greater. Another one
of his arguments in relation to the importance of education is that
schools are the source of religious leaders. He says concerning this:
"We must have persons qualified to dispense the word of God and
the sacraments and to be pastors of the people. But where will we
obtain them, if schools are not established on a more Christian
basis, since those hitherto maintained, even if they do not go
down, can produce nothing but depraved and dangerous corruptors
of youth."[4]

He also argues that the liberal arts are the basis of the very order
of society. This is an interesting theme because it equates the
liberal arts and education, and it is a point on which the Reformers and their Roman Catholic forebears were together. Concerning
this Luther says:

> Without scholars it would not be long till business men in
> their perplexity would be ready to dig a learned man out of
> the ground ten yards deep with their fingers; for the mer-

[3] "Letter to the Mayors and Aldermen," in Ulich, op. cit., p. 221.
[4] Ibid., p. 234.

chant will not long remain a merchant, if preaching and the administration of justice cease . . . where theologians perish, there perish also the Word of God, and nothing but heathen and devils are left; when jurists perish, there perish also law and peace, and nothing remains but robbery, murder, outrage and force—the reign of wild beasts. But what the merchant gains when peace vanishes, I shall let his ledger tell him.[5]

The fourth argument on the importance of education is that schools are necessary on secular grounds alone, a most interesting argument for Luther, since he virtually says that were there no religion at all, we would still need schools for the maintenance of the society of man. Here are two quotations:

Though there were no soul, nor heaven, nor hell but only civil government, would not this require good schools and learned men more than do our spiritual interests?[6]

And again

Even if there were no soul . . . for the establishment of the best schools everywhere, both for boys and girls, this consideration is of itself sufficient, namely, that society, for the maintenance of civil order and the proper regulation of the household, needs accomplished and well-trained men and women.[7]

At first this kind of argument may not be expected from the pen of Luther, but it does harmonize with his conception of the two realms, the religious and the secular, a separation being rethought today by some German theologians. The need for this re-examination comes from the conviction that the Church did not resist National Socialism early enough. When the Church was abiding consistently by this separation of the sacred and the secular, the National Socialists could make great inroads and become a real threat before the threat was apparent. In their illusion, churchmen could say, "We don't have anything to do about this; this doesn't touch the religious realm." It was too late when they learned that they were encircled by the Nazis and were forced to take a stand.

Let us turn now to the second of these major themes, that parents are responsible for the education of their children. This is

[5] "Sermon on the Duty of Sending Children to School," Ulich, op. cit., p. 247.
[6] "Letter to the Mayors and Aldermen," op. cit., p. 231.
[7] Ibid., p. 232.

both an old theme and a current one, held at least as early as Luther and practiced today in such communions as the Christian Reformed Church and Missouri Synod Lutherans. It is the policy in the Netherlands, one of the nations through which this tradition has been transmitted, to the extent that the parents decide whether their children shall attend Roman Catholic, Reformed, or public (in the sense of secular) schools. True to the more specific character of this tradition, the Protestant communions establishing their own schools commonly call them parent-controlled schools rather than parochial schools. Their principle is that it is not the official body of the church which controls the school; it is an organization of parents who are members of the church that exercises control. This is a current form of the old theme of parental responsibility for education.

Luther argues for parental responsibility by saying first of all that it is God's command that parents should educate their children, for which he finds authority in the *Book of Deuteronomy* and the Seventy-eighth Psalm.[8] However Luther is very realistic in his expectation of parents, asserting that they do not fulfill this responsibility and implying that they will not. He asserts that it is a sin that parents neglect this responsibility and that it is also sinful that they have to be aroused to recognize that they have such a duty. Consequently, he lets go with some strong speech on this point. He says: "Children are daily born and grow up among us, and there are none, alas! who feel an interest in them; and instead of being trained, they are left to themselves."[9] And so he exhorts the parents:

> You must indeed be an insensible and ungrateful creature, fit to be ranked among the brutes, if you see that your son may become a man to help the emperor maintain his dominions, sword and crown—to help the prince govern his land, to counsel cities and states, to help protect every man his body, wife, child, property and honor—and yet will not do so much as to send him to school and prepare him for this work![10]

With human understanding, however, he goes on to recognize

---

[8] Especially Deuteronomy 32:7; Psalm 78:5–8.
[9] "Letter to the Mayors and Aldermen," *op. cit.*, p. 223.
[10] "Sermon on the Duty of Sending Children to School," *op. cit.*, pp. 240–241.

35

the reasons for parental neglect. And the first of these is that the parents do not have the desire to educate their children: "The real difficulty is found alone in the absence of an earnest desire to educate the young, and to aid and benefit mankind with accomplished citizens. The devil much prefers blockheads and drones, that men may have more abundant trials and sorrows in the world."[11] The second reason is that parents lack piety. "There are some," he says, "who are so lacking in piety and uprightness that they would not do it if they could, but like the ostrich, harden themselves against their own offspring and do nothing for them."[12] This apparently is the source of Horace Bushnell's reference to ostrich mentality in his book, *Christian Nurture.*

The third reason why parents do not educate their children is that they are not qualified to do it. He contends, "the great majority of parents are unqualified for it, and do not understand how children should be brought up and taught."[13] However he also excuses them on the basis that they do not have the time. "On account of other employments and household duties they have no time for it, so that necessity requires us to have teachers for public schools, unless each parent employ a private instructor."[14] We should be reminded that the word *public* as he uses it here does not necessarily mean public school in the sense of being government supported and controlled. It means a public institution of learning as opposed to private tutoring in the home.

Luther's judgment on parents as possible teachers causes him to turn to his third major theme, the responsibility of government to educate children. Two quotations will show the strength with which he makes this argument; remember if you will that this is a letter to the mayors and aldermen, the people who have the power to instigate what he proposes.

> How if parents neglect it: Who shall attend to it then? Shall we therefore let it alone, and suffer the children to be neglected? How will the mayors and council excuse themselves, and prove that such a duty does not belong to them?[15]
> But I maintain that the civil authorities are under obligation

[11] "Letter to the Mayors and Aldermen," *op. cit.,* p. 234.
[12] *Ibid.,* p. 223.
[13] *Ibid.,* pp. 223–224.
[14] *Ibid.,* 224.
[15] *Ibid.,* p. 223.

> to compel their people to send their children to school, especially such as are promising . . . For our rulers are certainly bound to maintain the spiritual and secular offices and callings so that there may always be preachers, jurists, pastors, scribes, physicians, schoolmasters, and the like; for these cannot be dispensed with. If the government can compel such citizens as are fit for military service to bear spear and rifle, to mount ramparts, and perform other martial duties in times of war; how much more has it a right to compel the people to send their children to school, because in this case we are warring with the devil, whose object it is secretly to exhaust our cities and principalities of their strong men, to destroy the kernel and leave a shell of ignorant and helpless people whom he can sport and juggle with at pleasure.[16]

This is something quite different from what we found in the early Church and its two forms of nurture; some clarification may therefore be needed. That the concern of Luther expressed here is not just for religious nurture within the Church can easily be seen. It is somehow mixed up with and possibly confused with the secular process of equipping the young to take responsibly their places in society. There is no separation here; what he asks for is considered somehow essential to religious nurture, and so the two are more or less fused and mixed together. Nevertheless, the Church cannot be unconcerned with this broader educational responsibility. The Church is concerned that this education exists; it is concerned that it be of a high level of quality. There are modern parallels here: e.g., many times when under pious cloaks of one kind or another we talk about our godless schools and the importance of getting some religion into them, we may have jumped a few intervening steps and may have forgotten to be concerned first of all that the schools be very good schools. It is a religious concern that schools be good schools, and the Church must express urgency about this. While the major responsibility for performance, taking Luther here at his word, belongs to the secular order, the Church must be influential in this obligation, it must be related to it, it must be involved in it, though it must not officially carry responsibility for management, control, and maintenance.

There is an evident connection, at least in principle, between Luther's two major contentions (parent responsibility and govern-

---

[16] "Sermon on the Duty of Sending Children to School," *op. cit.*, pp. 248–249.

ment responsibility) and the first educational acts of civil authority in the United States. There may also be direct historical sequence, as cause and effect, between Luther's statements and what happened in these first two education acts of the Massachusetts Bay Colony; at least the principles are the same, and the similarity is a very interesting one. The Act of 1642 of the Massachusetts Bay Colony reads in part as follows:

> The Court, taking into consideration the great neglect of many parents and masters in training up their children in learning, and labor and other employments which may be profitable to the commonwealth, do hereupon order and decree, that in every town the chosen men appointed for managing the prudential affairs of the same shall henceforth stand charged with the care of the redress of this evil, so as they shall be sufficiently punished by fines for the neglect thereof, upon presentment of the grand jury, or other information or complaint in any Court within this jurisdiction; and for this end they, or the greater number of them, shall have power to take account from time to time of all parents and masters, and of their children, concerning their calling and employment of their children, especially of their ability to read and understand the principles of religion and the capital laws of this country.[17]

As the text probably makes clear, this law provided that the selectmen—comparable to what we know now as county commissioners, members of a township committee, or city council—have the responsibility to see to it that parents educate their children, subjecting to fines those who neglect this parental responsibility. This is clearly the first principle of Luther.

Five years later, in 1647, another law was passed which contained the second principle of Luther; this law has been known as the Old Deluder Satan Act. Luther, who, as you may recall, had some ideas about what Satan liked to do, reputedly threw an inkwell at him on one occasion! So maybe there is some direct influence of Luther even in the figure to which reference is made in the law.

> It being one chief project of the old deluder, Satan, to keep men from the knowledge of the Scriptures, as in former times by keeping them in an unknown tongue, so in these latter times by persuading from the use of tongues, yet so at

[17] E. P. Cubberly, *Readings in The History of Education*, Boston: Houghton Mifflin, 1920, p. 298. Modernization of language mine.

least the true sense of meaning and the original might be clouded by false glosses of saint seeming deceivers, that learning might not be buried in the grave of our fathers in the church and commonwealth, the Lord assisting our endeavors. . . . It is therefore ordered, that every township in this jurisdiction after the Lord hath increased their number to 50 householders, shall then forthwith appoint one within their town to teach all such children as shall resort to him to write and read, whose wages shall be paid either by the parents or masters of such children, or by the inhabitants in general, by way of supply, as the major part of those that order the prudentials of the town shall appoint. . . .[18]

This law went beyond the law of 1642 by requiring under penalty of fine that every village make provision for teaching the children. At first the fines were not very much, and some of the villages chose to pay the fine rather than hire a schoolmaster. And some of the churches stooped to such subterfuge as adding a couple of words to the call of a minister to designate him as schoolmaster as well as minister. But eventually the law was made too strict. Step by step, the fines were increased so that eventually it became cheaper and more prudent to establish a school. And so here is the very beginning on the North American continent, indeed in English-speaking countries, of common education by legal enactment of the principle that government has the responsibility for education. This is one reason why we cannot separate a history of Christian education from a history of education generally. They are intertwined, because the Protestant Churches, and especially the Reformed family of Churches, were most influential in producing the kind of social ethic that made education the responsibility of the government.

We should remember, when we fret today about our problems of religion and public education, that the Protestant Reformation was a strong influence in bringing into existence this separate institution. This is not to say that we do not have our problems, but rather to observe that we are in no position to talk loosely about so-called godless schools. Indeed some of the schools may be godless, but nevertheless our own Reformation history had very direct connection with the rise of this institution as a government-supported and government-managed institution. The Church follow-

---

[18] Cubberly, op. cit., p. 299.

ing the Reformation had something to do with the emergence of this institution which may be correctly denoted as the fourth major form nurture took. Specifically this "form" of nurture is in society and not within the Church—as the result, however, of a religious compulsion coming from within the Church and causing society to give birth to a new secular institution. An important component of the compulsion was the concern that people be literate enough to read the Bible for themselves and to understand sermons. It is interesting that the English Dissenter Academies arose out of this same compulsion, but related to the other side of the pulpit.[19] Many if not most of the boys in these academies were being prepared eventually for the ministry. If they were going to preach, they had to know how to use the English language, just as in Luther's concern, if people were going to understand sermons and read the Bible, they had to be able to use the vernacular language. The motivation was the same, but the two routes were different; one was on one side of the pulpit, and the second on the other side of it.

JOHN CALVIN (1509–1564)

Under this larger caption, "The Reformation and Nurture," we next turn to John Calvin, with the intention of understanding something of his interest in education and the ideas he held concerning it. Although Calvin was not as explicit on these matters as Martin Luther, such documents as the proceedings of the Council of Geneva, at which Calvin was frequently present, may reveal to careful inquiry his ideas concerning education. There is of course significance in the fact that Calvin established the College of Geneva. He was concerned that there be a school and college of high quality in Geneva, and this concern also expressed his conviction about the importance of the liberal arts. This notion he shared with Luther, and both of them held it in common with their Roman Catholic antecedents. There apparently was no significant innovation in the College of Geneva which would make it stand out as a landmark in the history of educational thought or practice. In fact some of its practices were not at all commendable;

[19] See J. W. Ashley Smith, *The Birth of Modern Education*. London: Independent Press, 1954.

for example, it is reported that Saturday mornings were set aside for bringing to account students who had committed misdemeanors during the week and flogging them commensurately for their offenses.

One of Calvin's earlier writings was a little book called *Instruction in the Faith*. Although this is a title which today might imply some discussion of teaching religious faith, this little document is in fact a kind of manual of preparation for baptism and confession of faith. It is in the tradition of the *Didache* and of catechumenal instruction; it has the format common to many catechisms. The most, therefore, that can be said about Calvin on education and nurture must be based on inference from his theological writing—most especially from his *Institutes*, a *magnum opus* of theological writing by any standards. In the *Institutes*, one of the more evident subjects to which to turn for such inferences, though, not necessarily the most significant or determinative for Calvin, is to his doctrine of man. While he dealt fully with the doctrine of man and has become famous for his conception of human depravity, nevertheless his insistence upon the sovereignty of God may say more concerning education than this more famous doctrine. Since, however, the discussion here is necessarily short, and since inferences from his conception of man are more obvious, we will center this discussion of Calvin upon his doctrine of man. Our limited concern will be to ask what, in Calvin's view, was the nature of the human material with which education and nurture must work.

First of all, let us look at the knowledge of God which, according to Calvin, man possesses. This is to be found in book I, chapters 3 and 4 of the *Institutes*. Apparently, since Calvin held that the human mind is naturally imbued with the knowledge of God, there is some kind of general or original revelation available to man; there is something natural and in some sense innate in him which is a knowledge of God. This is not the usual position taken today in the newer theology, which commonly rejects the ideas of general or original revelation. Calvin himself qualifies the idea considerably; this original knowledge of God, he says, is very limited and imperfect, necessarily so because of the Fall of Man. It has been stifled or corrupted, ignorantly and maliciously, by the Fall— the verbs and adverbs used here are all Calvin's. It would follow therefore in education or in religious nurture, if we take Calvin seriously on this point, that we should not bank very heavily upon the native knowledge of God which on occasion it has been assumed children possess in their innocence. In fact such original knowledge as there may be is not very innocent knowledge. A child of three or four may display some evidence of this knowledge; for example he may tell his parents that before he was born, God told him what to tell them. In doing this he may appear to give evidence of original knowledge; however it may also be as much an evidence of the acculturation of a religious home. But whatever the knowledge is, original revelation or not, the child is perverting it to the end of bypassing parental authority.

Calvin speculates about man as he was before the Fall in book I, chapter 15, but for the most part he appears to approach this as an academic exercise. He was convinced that the only man we can actually know is man after the Fall; man as he was before the Fall is purely a speculation. For the sake of his discussion in this chapter of the *Institutes*, he honors the philosopher's convention of cataloguing man's various capacities, but evidences no strong conviction that any of these philosophical definitions of man have validity. First of all, he says that man consists of body and soul. It would be incorrect to say that a dualism of soul and body is intended, but little is said to clarify the ambiguity in much of the Christian tradition, according to which man is both a unity and a combination of body and soul. Secondly he says that man is created in the image of God and that this image is especially seen in the soul of man, which tends to weight the above dualism on the side of the soul. Traces of Platonic influence are suggested when he goes on to say that the soul consists of two parts, intellect and will. Becoming more explicit, he lists the faculties of man as the so-called five senses, imagination, reason, will, irascibility, and concupiscence (this last especially suggesting Aristotle). This all constitutes a rather ordinary definition of man, not far different nor in any way distinct from the kind of statement almost any student could have made in Calvin's day. It is in the academic tradition, and, not at all strangely, traces of Plato and Aristotle can be seen in it.

The third subject in Calvin pertaining to the nature of man is the consequence of the Fall of Man, discussed in book II, chapters 1 and 2 in the *Institutes*. The Fall is regarded as an event in history, and men, as a result of it, "without a single exception, are polluted as soon as they exist," to use Calvin's words. "Adam was not only the progenitor, but as it were the root of mankind, and therefore . . . all the race were necessarily vitiated in his corruption."[20] Therefore what was formally a good and pure nature is now depraved. Implicit in this is the idea of the inheritance of original sin, the impurity of parents being transmitted to their children. It may be that Calvin was striving to say something more than he made explicit here. Had the concept of racial inheritance been available to him, possibly he would not have conveyed his thought so much in terms of biological inheritance. By racial inheritance is meant a transmission by social means, rather than through the genes, so that when a new individual is born into the human race, he is not born into a neutral order. Instead he is born into a matrix which embraces him and very quickly does something to him before he knows anything has happened. And how can a helpless infant be on his guard? Of course there are different kinds of cultures, and one culture does one thing to an individual and another culture does another. But generically every culture does something to those who are born into it, and what it does, regardless of cultural differences, is to reproduce and perpetuate the Fall. More specifically the consequences of the Fall are that man is now deprived of freedom of the will and is miserably enslaved. "Man is not possessed of free will for good works, unless he be assisted by grace."[21] We would need to infer from what Calvin says about the consequence of the Fall that we are mistaken when we think of children as innocent or when we approach them in education and nurture as though they were natively and actually good.

JOHN AMOS COMENIUS (1592–1670)

John Amos Comenius is not as well known as Luther and Calvin, but he is nevertheless a significant figure in the history of educational thought and of Christian education. Because of the general unfamiliarity with Comenius, it may be well to look briefly at his

[20] John Calvin, *Institutes of the Christian Religion*, 7th American Ed., trans. by John Allen, Philadelphia: Presbyterian Board of Christian Education, Vol. I, 1936, p. 271.
[21] *Ibid.*, p. 286.

life and work. In spite of his late start in getting an education, at an early age he became a bishop in his particular branch of the Moravian communion; in fact he was ready for ordination as a minister at the age of twenty-two, but had to wait two years because of a minimum age regulation then in force in his church. Being a Moravian, he was in the particular Reformed tradition of John Huss (1369–1415) which antedated Luther and Calvin. This tradition was more pietistic and less theologically vigorous however than the later traditions. Comenius took his advanced education in the Netherlands where he also spent the closing fifteen years of his life. After World War II he was honored by the Netherlands, when they negotiated with Czechoslovakia to permit his remains (or what are assumed to be such) to be transferred to Holland and buried there in the village of Naarden. This was made possible by an overture on the part of the government of the Netherlands to deed the property on which the tomb of Comenius stands to Czechoslovakia.

Comenius spent a short period in England (1641–1642), pursuing his pansophic idea which will be discussed later. Some members of parliament had given Comenius hope that money would be made available by parliament for this idea, but this hope failed to materialize. Following this he spent six years in Sweden writing Latin textbooks for the schools of Sweden, although rather half-heartedly. Although he did not like this kind of writing, he achieved his greatest fame in this capacity, and not without good reason. He really made a breakthrough in the teaching of languages because of two rather revolutionary ideas. Because of some sad experiences in his own education, he queried: "Why not relate these Latin words to vernacular words? And why not also relate these words to sensory objects whenever possible?" These were two radically new ideas in his time, however tame they may be for us. Even so he didn't like the work and often went off making speeches here and there, when he should have been at home in Sweden with his textbooks. Accordingly he had some matters of conscience to work out with himself and problems of relationship to work out with the Swedish government. Eventually, however, he got the job done.

Two things for which Comenius no doubt wanted to be remembered are his major writing, *The Great Didactic,* and his pansophic idea. The latter was a scheme of universal wisdom, comprised of two aspects. He proposed that an encyclopedia of universal learning be compiled, in which all knowledge would be brought together in one place. The other aspect was his plan for a pansophic institute, in which all areas of knowledge would be represented by specialists in the respective areas, so that knowledge could be pursued in its universality and wholeness. This is the pansophic idea for which he would want to be remembered, although he was never able actually to do anything with it.

The *Great Didactic* is his other achievement of note, and this will receive our full attention in the remainder of our discussion of Comenius. This book was a *magnum opus* in which Comenius envisioned the kind of education he hoped his own Moravian people could have when they were once again restored to their homeland. They had been made a wandering and exiled people by the turmoil and persecution of the Thirty Years' War, and Comenius consequently lived in a period of twilight and gloom, hoping for the time when his people would be restored to their native soil. This was the pressure which caused him to write *The Great Didactic*. Often it has happened in the history of education that great advances were conceived in times of crisis and suffering. A notable example in our century is the Education Act of 1944 in Great Britain which was conceived when German bombers were making regular shuttle trips to England. In this instance the most significant act so far in the entire history of English education came out of the gloom and crisis of the Second World War. Great advances are not as commonly conceived when men are comfortable and prosperous; in such times we do not dream dreams; we do not yearn for the time when the lights will come on again all over the world. It may be that the threat of missile warfare and unresolved tension between East and West will try us to the extreme in our time, and possibly new and significant things may be conceived as a consequence.

In *The Great Didactic*, Comenius attempted a realistic approach both to the Bible and to natural science. He presumed that he could combine these two in one unified system. The realism spoken of here is a naïve philosophical realism greatly stressing knowledge gained by the senses. This book was first published in Latin in 1657, and this is the reason why we know this man by a Latin name, "Comenius" instead of "Komensky," a Czech name. It is very strange that, in view of its magnitude the book was not translated into English for two centuries. The ideas of Comenius were not well received by his own and immediately succeeding generations, a circumstance which puzzles the historians. One of the most commonly advanced reasons is that as a Moravian he was so radically democratic that he was not readily accepted, the ascendancy of aristocracy still being very strong. For example, the Moravian brethren would not admit a person of noble birth to their church, unless he first renounced his nobility. A strange contrast to Comenius' lack of acceptance in his own time is that today historians of education, of all stripes and loyalties, are rich in their praise of him; his contingent of enemies is probably the smallest of any figure in the history of education.

We turn now to *The Great Didactic* itself and take up a few of its central ideas. The first of these is Comenius' definition of man, a rather clear contrast to the conception of man held by John Calvin. Comenius makes his understanding of man the source of the objectives for education, deriving them from the nature of man. He says that the ultimate end of man is "eternal happiness with God."[22] The "subordinate" end of man (keeping to his terminology) can be drawn, Comenius held, from God's words, according to the accounts in Genesis, spoken at the time of man's creation:

> Let us make man in our image, after our likeness; and let them have dominion over the fish of the sea, and over the fowl of the air, and over the cattle, and over all the earth and over every creeping thing that creepeth upon the earth.[23]

Now Comenius does a rather remarkable thing with this passage from the creation story; he draws from it three functions of man. They are that man is a rational creature, that he is the lord of all creatures, and that he is a creature which is the image and joy of his Creator. From these three characterizations of man, Comenius makes a transposition into objectives to be achieved by man and therefore to be achieved by his education. From the characterization of man as a rational creature, he infers that one objective for man's life is erudition or knowledge. From the principle that man is the lord of all creatures, he infers that virtue is another objective.

[22] M. W. Keatinge, *Comenius*, New York: McGraw-Hill, 1931, p. 23.
[23] Genesis 1:26.

And from the conception that the image of the Creator is in man, he infers that piety is the third objective. No order of importance is implied here. Consequently, we have inherited from Comenius three famous objectives for education—knowledge, virtue, and piety.

Let us proceed now to see how the Fall of Man is dealt with in the thinking of Comenius. First of all we must observe that the Fall is far more incidental in Comenius than in either Calvin or Luther. There is a sense in which we could use the word *accidental* to refer to Comenius' doctrine of the Fall. That is that it was an event that happened and with which man has to cope. When he speaks of nature, he does not mean "the corruption which has laid hold of all men since the Fall"—on which account we are naturally called the children of wrath, unable of ourself to have any good thought—but rather he means to lay stress on "our first and original condition, to which as a starting point, we must be recalled."[24] It is clear that Comenius assumed that we can know man as he was before the Fall and indeed that the man with whom we deal within the Church is redeemed man who has been restored in some significant measure to his original state. The "voice of nature" he understood as the "universal Providence of God or the influence of Divine Goodness which never ceases to work in all things."[25] This of course gives evidence that Comenius had a much more hopeful approach to man—perhaps even a romantic one—than is to be found in Calvin or in Luther. He contends that we can say of man that "no matter how disorganized by his fall into sin, he can, through the grace of God and by certain methods, be restored again to harmony."[26] It is interesting to note that Comenius used the verb "can" in this statement and also surprisingly links "certain methods" with the grace of God as though they were somewhat comparable. This last betrays his romantic enthusiasm for the *method* of teaching and learning which he was convinced could be discovered.

The next theme to be discussed is individual man's need for human culture. Comenius was impressed by reports, which he had received and judged to be valid, that certain children had been left

[24] Keatinge, *op. cit.*, p. 25.
[25] *Ibid.*
[26] *Ibid.*, p. 32.

47

inadvertently as infants to grow up among animals and had thereby taken on animal behavior. There have of course been comparable reports in the nineteenth and twentieth centuries. As a result of his reflection on these reports he says, "Let none believe . . . that any can really be a man, unless he has learned to act like one, that is has been trained in those elements which constitute a man."[27]

It is in this very necessity that education becomes important. Education is the institution by which human culture takes hold of a biological man and makes of him a human being by giving him both the patterns and forms as well as the content of human life and its discourse. By biological inheritance nature supplies the potentiality, but the potentiality will not take on human form unless human culture supplies it and guides the individual into it. As a consequence, Comenius' most famous figure for the school is that it is "a true forging place of men."[28] Put at its worst, what he was saying in this figure is that a school is like a factory, for example, as in heavy industry, where there are certain moulds or dies by which molten metal is cast into particular forms and shapes. If you have ever been on a guided tour through an automobile plant, you have seen raw metal poured into a cast and shaped so that it becomes an engine block. This may seem to be a very crude and even offensive figure for what the school is: a forging place in which human raw material is cast into human form. Actually it does express certain very naïvely realistic assumptions. But Comenius didn't intend it quite as grossly as this exaggeration of the figure has made it appear. He meant to say that if human culture does not take hold of the infant, even though the infant has the biological and psychological potentiality which is human, he will not take on human ways but will become something other than human. The reverse of this is represented by experiments in which psychologists have taken apes of high mentality and adopted them into the home as though they were human infants. They have diapered them, fed them, and given them a nursery (with the addition of bars to the windows), loved them, and played with them—with the result that in the more successful experiments, if we can

[27] *Ibid.*, p. 34.
[28] M. W. Keatinge, *The Great Didactic of John Amos Comenius*, Part II, London: A. & C. Black, 1921, p. 228.

48

trust the reports, the infant animal, though an animal, has learned to speak a few words. The intent of these experiments has been to demonstrate the importance of the emotional matrix in learning. What is interesting to us at this point is that it exemplifies the obverse of what Comenius was contending. Both the argument of Comenius and these experiments point to the same thing: if man is to take on the culture of man, it is necessary for him to live in this culture and be formed by it. For Comenius it was this cultural formation which is the function of the school.

Comenius therefore argues, and this is the next major point, that there should be a school in every human community. He says that there should be "a school or a place of education" erected in "every well-ordered habitation of man" (whether a city, a town, or a village.)[29] This of course is the same thing that Luther argued a century earlier, and Comenius alludes to Luther's position, heartily concurring with it, but making the observation that there was little more than Luther's wish in existence after the passing of a century. History indeed admonishes us to be humble when we observe that there was still scarcely more than a wish for another century or century and a half after Comenius. The reasons Comenius uses to support his argument that there should be a school in every place of human habitation are very spotty ones, providing an example of his frequent lapse into romantic uses of the argument from analogy. These arguments range from the need for division of labor in society, which is not a bad argument, to others which are rather far fetched. For example, he argued that Nature produces things in quantity in one area; that is, it produces wood in the forest, grass in the fields, etc.: therefore, children should be educated in schools. In arguments and analogies such as this we see a man of a different century at work, somewhat romantic, rather a dilettante, and apparently a man who derived great personal enjoyment from his platform lectures before whatever the seventeenth century equivalent may have been of parent-teacher associations and other civic groups. Although The Great Didactic stands among the great writings in educational thought, it is still clear that Comenius did not penetrate very deeply.

Comenius tried to propose in this his major work that a principle

[29] Ibid., p. 214.

of order for teaching and learning existed just as much as a principle of order in Nature. In fact it appears that he believed that this principle of order is to be borrowed from Nature. This was his dream of finding the method of education. It was a will-o'-the-wisp; he never found the method, but he assumed that there was such a thing and that when it was discovered, it would be the real panacea, solving the whole problem of education. It is now clear that there is no method that can be referred to by the definite article, the, and accordingly whenever a presupposition such as Comenius' is adopted, the warning flag of suspicion should be raised. There are no methods and probably no systems of method which can be given this status; nevertheless Comenius believed that there was such a thing and the mission of his life was to find it.

In his attempt to bring this principle of order from Nature, we see quite clearly his attempt to tie religion and Nature together as one. He said, for example, "as soon as we have succeeded in finding a proper method it will be no harder to teach school-boys, in any number desired, than with the help of a printing-press to cover a thousand sheets daily with the neatest writing."[30]

Alluding to the parable of the sower and carrying his argument further, he says, "The savior here shows that it is God who operates in everything, and that nothing remains for man but to receive the seeds of instruction with a devout heart; the process of growth and ripening will then continue of themselves, unperceived by him."[31] So much for this belief in a principle of order and a simple union of Nature and religion.

We go on now to the chapter in The Great Didactic on the method of instilling piety, which narrows the focus from the general educational task to religious nurture specifically. "Piety," Comenius says, "is a gift of the Holy Spirit, but since the Holy Spirit usually employs natural agencies, that is parents, teachers, and ministers, it is right that these should appreciate the extent of their duties."[32] What is piety for Comenius? He evidently assumed that he had defined piety in his opening arguments about the nature of man and the objectives of education. Piety, as he understands it, is to seek God everywhere, and after we have found him

[30] Ibid., pp. 248–249.
[31] Ibid., p. 263.
[32] Keatinge, Comenius, p. 188.

to follow him, and when we have attained him, to enjoy him. Now the sources of this piety or exaltation he says are Holy Writ, i.e., the Word of God, the world as God's handiwork, and ourselves as inspired by God. Without telling us too much more, he moves on to the priority and superiority of the Bible as a subject of study in Christian schools. In this we can see implicit in Comenius at least two assumptions. The first is the identification of the culture of his day with the Christian faith. His assumption, that the people generally would be a people of one faith and thereby homogeneous, did not leave room for the more complex religious pluralism which we face today. Comenius also apparently assumed that something magical was going to happen when children studied the Bible; he does not tell us any more than that the Bible is prior and superior. "Whatever is taught to the young in addition to the scriptures [for example, science, arts, language, etc.] should be taught as purely subordinate subjects. In this way it will be made evident to the pupils that all that does not relate to God and to the future life is nothing but vanity."[33]

We will conclude by summarizing the thought of Comenius. First, he does not make a separation between education and nurture. The possible reason for this is the homogeneity among his people regarding the Christian faith to which we have just alluded. Secondly, he is greatly interested in education as a human endeavor and institution, much more interested than this last quotation from *The Great Didactic* would imply. Comenius tried to get the Bible and natural science together—with how much success is a question, but he assumed that he had gotten them together. In his own romantic way he really liked to play around with natural science and with human institutions. While he managed to put a religious gloss on this fondness, he was much more interested in education even as a secular thing than his statement about the priority and superiority of the Bible would suggest. Finally, regarding piety, he makes the Bible both prior and superior as a subject of study in the schools. He does not elaborate this with any fullness, and he does seem to assume that there is a perfect harmony between the Bible and human knowledge. Of course the conflict of science and religion is perennial. There have been periods in which it seemed that the conflict was irreconcilable; then other periods in which we

[33] *Ibid.*, p. 190.

have assumed that the problem is rather easily resolved. This history of the conflict would caution us not to be too facile in getting science and religion together, and it also advises us that a bit of tension here may be healthy. Comenius contributed at least in a small way to this history.

CHAPTER 4

The Rise of the Sunday School

*N*ow that we have looked at the primitive Church to learn what beginnings were made there in nurture, and then at the Protestant Reformation to sample its thought concerning education and nurture, we turn by way of transition to eighteenth-century England for another significant chapter in the history of nurture in the Church. Of course, this would not be the next point of focus in a closely knit sequence which would constitute a definitive history of nurture. But within our limits, making it necessary for us merely to sketch significant episodes, the next step that we must take is to look at the rise of the Sunday School.

The Sunday School was one among several educational efforts produced in eighteenth-century England by the benevolent and religious motives that were shared by scattered groups of people. In other words, the one educational agency of the local church which has persisted rightly or wrongly into the twentieth century as the single agency of nurture and is most frequently depended upon by the Church in the United States had its inception in connection with the charity school movement of eighteenth-century England. History requires us to make this observation regardless of the virtues, strengths, and weaknesses that we may attribute to the Sunday School today. Indeed it may be in a very poor state of repair, and possibly its survival should neither be hoped for nor encouraged; nevertheless it still remains the major agency of nurture on which the Protestant Church depends. And in this connection, being the next most significant focus for this brief history, we have in the

Sunday School the fifth form which nurture in the Church historically assumed. This is to consider the catechumenal education of the early Church as the first form; the catechetical school, equipping the Christian to live in the midst of his secular culture, the second form; monasticism the third form; the Reformation's address to the world, urging upon the secular order what it must do in the education of its young, as the fourth form; and the Sunday School the fifth form. To the extent that this sequential scheme is a valid one, we would have to say that the twentieth century Church is very largely committed by habit and circumstance to this fifth form and places its chief dependence upon it. Therefore some of the significance of the discussion of this chapter is to be seen in the contemporaneous prevalence of the Sunday School, as we go back to the eighteenth century to see how it came into existence.

THE CHARITY SCHOOL MOVEMENT IN ENGLAND

The eighteenth century, as well as the late seventeenth century, in England was a time in which dramatic social changes brought into focus the need of the masses of the people for some kind of education. Among the more benevolent leaders of the people, there were those who recognized the hazards involved in not making some attempt to meet this need, and even though it meant sacrifice, they helped to give birth to a new kind of educational institution in their endeavors.

Some of the circumstances which brought attention to this need for education should be mentioned. First of all, by this time the Industrial Revolution had already wrought significant changes. England was changing over from a rural and pastoral nation to a country with vigorous and growing industries. Factories were becoming more and more numerous, and certain normal centers of commerce were becoming centers of population. Large numbers of people were drifting from the simple life of the country and crowding together in complex and unhealthy industrial centers, where conditions prevailed for which they were ill-prepared. The social and moral aspects of this suddenly new kind of life, as would be expected, were not good. The change from simple bartering to an economy in which currency was a man's wage and also the measure of his livelihood left unprepared people in poverty. They did not know the value of their wage nor how far it had to reach if liveli-hood were to be maintained. The pubs and other commercial estab-lishments, offering the enticements of pleasure and indulgence, got hold of their money and their time before the real necessities of life had a chance to make their claims. This improvidence was itself an immorality, but in its turn, as can easily be imagined, it became the occasion for other and more gross social and moral ills.

This infant industry, in the same kind of improvidence, utilized child labor and demanded excessively long hours. Children from very early ages, sometimes as young as five or six years of age, were put to work around the clock on a two- or three-shift basis. Many of them seldom saw the light of the sun, being shut up in the fac-tory or having to sleep during the day.

Parallel to such blighting practices as this, but of an entirely dif-ferent character, the vernacular language was beginning to have a dignity it had not known before. The King James Bible had no small part in bringing this new regard for the language of the people and eventually even came to have significance for education. For ex-ample, the suspicion was starting to grow that it might be possible to get some kind of education without benefit of Greek and Latin. This had far-reaching social import, for as long as Greek and Latin were the currency of education, the masses of the people were very largely excluded from it. But as soon as the doors began to open to the possibility that the language of the people could become the language of education, new vistas promised to open for society. It was virtually a social revolution to widen the circle of privilege to include even some of the masses in the schools, or at least for this ambition to emerge as a public ideal, however visionary.

The variety of educational efforts evoked by these circumstances should be dealt with briefly as we move on to a particular and major focus upon the Sunday School, for there were several dif-ferent benevolent efforts to provide minimal education for the underprivileged. They were put forward, feeble as they were, as attempts to meet the needs of the common people so highlighted by the changed circumstances of the period. While these efforts were genuinely benevolent, it should not be assumed they were nothing but benevolent, for they were also mixed with fear, fear of what would happen to the so-called better people, and to English society as a whole, if these evils of a newly concentrated mass society were allowed to thrive and grow unchecked. This is one instance of a phenomenon which history reveals to be very common, namely, that few if any great social advances are achieved by pure motivation. Most moves which we accept as social advances have in them a drag, a backlash, and a twisted motivation which is by no means good but nevertheless is favorably related to the task at hand. Sometimes rather good things are done for rather bad reasons.

The Society for the Promotion of Christian Knowledge

Three of these philanthropic movements of eighteenth-century England will be discussed briefly before turning to the Sunday School. The first of these chronologically was constituted by the schools of the Society for the Promotion of Christian Knowledge. You may have heard of this Society when named only by its initials, the S. P. C. K. It is still in existence in fact, primarily now as a publication agency of the Church of England. It originated in 1699, or possibly a year earlier, and was designed to encourage the establishment of schools in the parishes of the Established Church of England. It secured some funds, but did not have the larger sums of money needed for the maintenance of these schools. As a result, the schools were established and maintained largely by local management and benevolence. Primarily the function of the Society was to provide study literature for the schools and to offer a degree of supervision so that there might be some fairly acceptable standards of performance in the teaching that went on in them. The schools of the S.P.C.K. were largely devoted to the teaching of the catechism and the Bible. And the Society constituted a national body—not an authority, because it was purely private and voluntary—which could give some broad guidance to these local schools, helping to lift them somewhat above the limitations of parochialism.

The Infant School

The second of these movements was the Infant School, originating in Scotland largely under the encouragement and vision of Robert Owen, otherwise famous as an industrialist who turned to socialism and eventually became a member of the experimental community established at New Harmony, Indiana. Owen, even

56

though a young and promising leader in the mercantile industry who stood to lose by it, became morally burdened by the child-labor practices of industry. It was in an attempt to give relief from these practices and do something for these children who were so neglected and exploited that he was instrumental in having the first Infant School established. This school had in it a little of the vision that childhood is not only a time for learning, a correction of the idea that it is a time for gainful employment, but also that it is peculiarly a time for play. He came to believe that children should have the right to play, that there should even be freedom and lilt in their learning, such as exemplified in dancing and free play. In this sense, these early Infant Schools of Robert Owen were certainly progressive for their time and anticipated some of the freer educational practices of the early twentieth century.

It so happens that Owen's effort was paralleled by a movement in France, known by the same name and initiated by Jean Frederic Oberlin. Oberlin as a young minister accepted appointment to a most deprived and isolated little parish down in the Vosges Mountains of Southern France. Among the social needs which he recognized in the deprived little world of this community, in addition to good agricultural methods and usable roads, was the great need for education. He therefore originated a school for small children, using the same name as Owen. This little school caught on in France; indeed so well was it eventually accepted that even at the present time the lowest class in the French national school system is called the infant class or the *classe enfantine*. Most communities of any size in France have an Infant School, roughly comparable to our kindergarten, and the idea, if not some of the practices of this segment of the French system, have their ancestry in the work of Jean Frederic Oberlin.

The Monitorial School

The third of these philanthropic institutions, in addition to the Sunday School, was the Monitorial School. This innovation was fathered independently by Andrew Bell, within the Church of England, and by Joseph Lancaster, a kind of free lance who worked independently with very little continuing sponsorship. Andrew Bell had had some missionary experiences in India which suggested to him the monitorial idea. Joseph Lancaster, a very different kind of person from Bell, was somewhat erratic and unstable, but he never-theless hit upon the same idea, shallow and eventually unimportant as it was, which helped to advance the cause of education for the people. The idea of the Monitorial School was that one good teacher could take the more mature students and teach them what was to be taught to the rest of the students; in turn they would teach the others, and in this way one good teacher could multiply his efforts by as many monitors as he could gather around him. Consequently, there may have been among these schools some which had as many as a thousand students, but strictly speaking only one teacher.

This, of course, was very poor education; in fact, it was scarcely education at all. But what it did was to make it possible for a youth to acquire at least the appearance of literacy and some kind of mastery of number combinations. It is difficult to see how it could have done more than this. But in spite of this, the historical value of the Monitorial School was greater than its educationad achieve-ments would imply. While it virtually had no inherent value as education, it did provide a cheap way of promoting a degree of literacy and thereby demonstrated that at least some education, however little, could be provided for the masses. In turn, this demonstration helped to sharpen the social conscience; it opened the way to a wider acceptance of the belief that some education was possible for the many and that with small means something could be done to dispel widespread ignorance.

THE SUNDAY SCHOOL

We have sketched briefly three of the institutions which consti-tuted the charity school movement in England, in the context of which the Sunday School arose. We must now focus attention on the Sunday School, the particular charity school institution which is our special concern. What is important to note at the outset is that the Sunday School, which could be characterized as half within the Church and half outside of it, arose out of the same conditions and the same concerns as these other charity school efforts. We greatly need this particular historical perspective in the Church today, disappointing as it may be; in fact, we cannot under-stand the plight and problem of the Sunday Church School as we have it today, unless we understand this setting out of which it came and the kind of relation or lack of relation, with the Church which has characterized its history. Of course, it is gratuitous to say that it is by no means a first century institution. The Sunday School is a very modern institution, in terms of age, and arose out of secular conditions and influences, as well as religious concern; it by no means arose completely within the Church. And it is important to understand this in order to deal with it responsibly and knowingly today.

Robert Raikes and Early Beginnings

It is not far from the truth to designate Robert Raikes (1735–1811) the father of the Sunday School, as has commonly been done. Truly enough, there were scattered instances of other Sunday Schools which arose outside of the Raikes influence and the movement which began under his leadership, e.g., the occasional schools of this sort inspired by Francis Asbury, the Methodist leader. But these were outside of what might be called the main stream of the Sunday School movement and by themselves would probably not have grown into a movement as the Raikes-inspired schools did.

It is interesting to note how Robert Raikes came to apply his benevolent endeavors to the Sunday School, for he was by no means a theologian and did not foster the institution out of deep conceptions concerning the Faith or the Church. Circumstantially he came to an interest in the Sunday School by way of prison reform, in which he had been interested for some years, partly at least as an accompaniment of his duties as a journalist. However, his acquaintance with the prisons and criminals disillusioned him as to the hope of reforming them. He had tried it in his many relations with prisoners in the gaols, where he was a very frequent visitor. He eventually came to the conclusion, as the result of his experiences, that rehabilitation was a losing battle. To try to reform a person after a career of crime has once been launched involved odds which he regarded as too great, because the tendency to repeat crime is too strong. Raikes therefore turned from the prisons to the Sunday School, strange as it may seem, and made this apparently far-fetched move because he was trying to find a way by which crime could be prevented and the terrible waste of trying to correct it avoided. It will be recognized that this is largely

59

moral and social motivation, and not intellectually profound, but we cannot quarrel with it as being benevolent and very well-intended. In the case of Raikes, it so happened, it was surprisingly successful.

He believed that there were two chief conditions in which the seeds of crime flourish and grow; this belief is the intellectual root from which the Sunday School idea grew in his mind. The two conditions favoring the tendency to criminal acts, he believed, are ignorance and idleness. So Raikes launched the Sunday School as an effort to supply knowledge to take the place of ignorance and constructive engagements in school to take the place of idleness. This is why he took some of the little "ragamuffins" of the city of Gloucester and tried to give them the seeds of "knowledge, virtue, and probity," to use his own words.[1] Some of these children did not work on Sunday, and because of their comparative freedom this one day of the week, they frequently got into trouble, occasionally as bad as vandalism and the like. Their pranks and so-called delinquency would no doubt be looked upon in a different light today because of our tendency to think that freedom and leisure are essential to a healthy life; of course, this was not the pattern of life in Raikes's time. He occasionally had to work on Sunday at his newspaper, and he was therefore aware of what was going on in the streets of Gloucester. Attributing this delinquency to idleness and ignorance, and not apparently to some evil inherent in man, he proposed that the Sabbath day could properly be devoted to edifying pursuits which could supply these children with knowledge in the place of their ignorance and wholesome study, if not pious pursuits, in the place of their weekly idleness.

By 1780 Raikes was ready for the first school to be launched. It opened in July of that year in the home of a Mrs. King on Saint Catherine Street in Gloucester. Mrs. King was employed to be the teacher of this first school. Mr. Raikes and his parish minister, Thomas Stock, were partners in sponsoring this first effort, although they did not actually teach. The curriculum was simply designed to teach the children to read and to nurture them in the Christian religion. The curriculum was comprised of reading, spelling, worship, Bible study, and study of the catechism. The weekly

---

[1] As quoted by Guy Kendal in *Robert Raikes, A Critical Study*, London: Nicholson and Watson, n.d., p. 89.

sessions, a good bit longer than ours today, lasted from 10:00 to 12:00 in the morning and from 1:00 to 5:30 in the afternoon; apparently Raikes was trying to schedude as much as possible of the free time these children had on Sunday. All the children attended church after the first lesson in the afternoon, and Raikes himself very commonly met many of them early in the morning before church began and enticed them into going to the service of worship with him. Not knowing anything about modern educational psychology, he carried sweetmeats in his pockets and a few coins. It would be a warranted surmise that Robert Raikes had quite a following of "ragamuffins" when he went to church Sunday mornings before the morning session of the Sunday School.

However Robert Raikes's function in relation to the Sunday School was largely that of publicity agent, and if the consequences for the Sunday School movement are a valid index, he was a very clever public relations man for it. He had the good sense not to make a big splash about it until he had something to report. And the first time that the Sunday School ever hit the pages of the *Gloucester Journal* was as an item of news. It was already a going thing, and this first news report did not occur until more than three years after the school on Saint Catherine Street had opened. It appeared in the issue of November 3, 1783, whereas that school was started in July of 1780. But what is even more significant was the way in which this news announcement was written. Raikes of course had very largely engineered the thing and had done the work behind the scenes, and he had managed to get his own minister involved with him in the effort, but you wouldn't gather that Raikes had anything to do with the Sunday School by the way the news item was written. It read as follows: "Some of the clergy in different parts of the country, bent upon attempting a reform among the children of the lower class, are establishing Sunday Schools for rendering the Lord's Day subservient to the ends of instruction which has hitherto been prostituted to bad purposes."[2]

This announcement was at the same time an understatement and an exaggeration. The understatement was that he omitted any reference to himself or any other laymen, although he himself was the guiding force in getting the Sunday School launched. The over-

[2] As quoted by Alfred Gregory in *Robert Raikes, Journalist and Philanthropist*, London: Hodder and Stoughton, 1880, pp. 67–68.

statement was the reference to the clergy as the sponsoring group; apparently, except for Thomas Stock, they had little to do with it. Even so, this announcement was an astute and clever piece of publicity.

Early Success and Rapid Growth

In response to the item and evidently to others which followed, inquiries came to Raikes from many parts of England and Wales requesting information about these schools. This was not unusual, except that it concerned a philanthropic cause and apparently reached considerable volume. Raikes had often printed advertisements in his *Journal* calling for a reply; e.g., some subscriber would want a barrel of choice wine and would advertise to this effect, and normally replies would come back to the *Journal*, advising him that the respondents could supply the quality of wine he wanted. In the same way, when Raikes announced the launching of these schools, it was normal for requests to come back to him from readers of the *Journal*, inquiring as to how these schools were conducted, what the program was like, etc. This rather wide correspondence led to the establishment of other Sunday Schools throughout England and Wales, at an ever increasing rate for several decades.

The extent of the achievement by the time of the death of Robert Raikes in 1811 is an indication of how great the need was and how the Sunday School appeared to promise the answer. Its quick success will have to be attributed to circumstances, probably even more than to Raikes' vision and hard work, i.e., to the fact that undesirable conditions existed for which the Sunday School was a very cogent and expedient answer. It is hard to conceive any other adequate explanation for the rapid growth. Remember the first little school was started in 1780, but by 1811, a mere thirty-one years later, there were nearly a half million children enrolled in these schools in the British Isles. This is a remarkable achievement, numerically at least, under any conditions. And when we also remember that the Sunday School had to live from hand to mouth, without tax funds and for the most part without organized support from the churches, it is even more remarkable that in a period of three decades a half million children came to be enrolled in Sunday Schools—an extraordinary achievement which can scarcely be attributed to anything else than that it was a timely answer to the perplexing conditions besetting the masses of the people and ensnaring them in a hopeless plight.

Opposition to the Sunday School

In spite of this very apparent success, it should be made clear however that all was not clear sailing for the Sunday School; it had many pockets of resistance to overcome, some of them deeply entrenched. For one thing, there was opposition from the churches. There were many Christian people who, not without some degree of sincerity, believed that the Sunday School was a breach of the Fourth Commandment, a desecration of the Sabbath. There were early instances in this country about which it has been reported that earnest church officials, however misguided they may have been, regarded the Sunday School as an evil institution. Some reports depict them on occasion as shaking their canes warningly at schools, calling them instruments of the devil.

There was also opposition from the aristocracy. Some representatives of the privileged classes believed that the Sunday Schools brought enlightenment to people who were not supposed to be educated and that this in turn would breed new difficulties. Give these people a little taste of education, they thought, and they would become dissatisfied with their station in life. This would be sure to confront society with new problems, probably worse than those which Raikes was trying to alleviate.

The Relation of the Sunday School and the Church

There is a strong intimation in the early story of the Sunday School that Robert Raikes had hoped that the clergy would adopt the movement and make it an integral, if not official, part of the Church. It is doubtful that modesty would be a sufficient reason for Raikes to omit himself from the publicity and give the spotlight to the clergy. You will recall that his first announcement began by saying, "Some of the clergy in different parts of the country," and then went on to tell about the Sunday School as an emerging charity-school effort. A reason more adequate than modesty can be seen for the kind of approach Raikes made to the public. This is that he wanted the clergy and the Church to take over the movement. By and large the history of the Sunday School makes clear that they did not do this. We might say that Raikes tried to throw the ball to them, but they failed to catch it; certainly they did not run with it.

We have to deal with the relation of the Sunday School movement and the Church with some particularity because there is perceptible variance in this relation between England and the United States. For both England and the United States, as well as the remainder of the world, this relationship has great significance for the Sunday Church School and indeed for Christian education generally. For one thing the nature of the relation of the Sunday School and the Church in the past is one of the reasons the educational ministry has a secondary or tertiary place in the ministry of the Church today. While it is not the only reason, the fact that the Sunday School movement was for so long outside of the Church, as it were, and conducted largely by laymen, has strengthened the attitude commonly held today that nurture is a secondary and possibly unimportant element in the life of the Church. At one stage of the game, however early, the clergy did not take over when they could well have done so; had they assumed the leadership Raikes evidently desired for them, it would be a reasonable conjecture that the history would have been quite different from that which is being reported here. But this is not to lay the blame entirely upon the ordained leadership of the Church. Unquestionably the Sunday School movement had its weaknesses and, as it actually developed, it has deserved little better recognition than it has received.

We will now be more specific concerning this relationship in England and the United States. The churches of England have scarcely adopted the Sunday School with any fullness or completeness. At the end of the nineteenth century, the Sunday Schools were not integral to the life of the church in England. They were not in the budgets of congregations; their officers were not appointed by the official bodies of the churches; their schools were not a direct responsibility of the minister. The tradition in England is still a greater separation of the Sunday School from the Church than in the United States, loose as the relationship often is here. In fact this condition was reflected in the World Council of Christian Education until very recent years. When Nelson Chappell, who is the present general secretary of the World Council of

Christian Education, was appointed to that office in 1953, he at the same time became the first lone general secretary that the World Council of Christian Education had. Previous to his appointment this was a dual office, with two separate executives of equal status, one in England and one in the United States. This reflected generally the different conceptions of Christian education held in those two leading nations. In England, Christian education has been the Sunday School; in the United States, it has quite commonly become something broader than this.

By comparison, the relationship between the Sunday School and the Church in the United States has been somewhat closer than in England. Some denominations earlier, and others later, adopted the Sunday School as an important institution by which the Church could perform its teaching task. One factor that was incidental to the time of acceptance was the attitude of the different communions toward the public school and the eventual general success of the public school in the United States. Some denominations, partly because of the social level of their constituents and partly for theological reasons, were more ready to accept the Sunday School than others. The Methodists, for example, were very early in adopting the Sunday School, as were the Baptists. The Presbyterians, by contrast, were quite late in following them, and one reason for this reluctance was that they were entertaining the academy idea, a virtual parochial school, until as late as the latter half of the nineteenth century. This communion was divided between the academy and the public school in choice of alternatives, and as long as there was some possibility that the academy could be generally established in the parishes, the Presbyterian Church was not ready to embrace the Sunday School. By the end of the nineteenth century, it was generally agreed however that the academy was no longer a possibility. This agreement may have been more a matter of expediency than principle, but it exemplifies the reasons for later acceptance of the Sunday School on the part of some denominations.[3] Although some came early and some came late, it can be seen that there were some differences between England and the United States in the relation between Sunday School and Church. Generally there has been a closer relation in

[3] See Lewis J. Sherrill, *Presbyterian Parochial Schools 1776–1870*, New Haven: Yale University Press, 1932.

the United States, but, even so, not full adoption and respect as an integral part of the Church.

The Early Movement and the Sunday School Today

Before concluding this chapter, it will be well to make some connection with the present. All that has been attempted in this chapter is a sketch of the Sunday School movement, more especially in its beginnings; more inclusive developments of which it may have been the forerunner will be considered subsequently. One line of connection between this early movement and the present can be easily suggested; this is the sequence of various associations and conventions. For the Sunday School movement in the United States and some other countries, and later at the international level, became articulate as a movement in local societies and national unions. The first of these local societies in the United States was the First Day or Sunday School Society of Philadelphia, organized in 1791 only eleven years after the first Raikes' school was established. The American Sunday School Union was formed in 1823, and its organization was followed by a series of interdenominational conventions. In 1906 the International Sunday School Association was formed, and under its banner international Sunday School conventions have been held quadrennially. It is a going institution today, closely identified with the World Council of Christian Education. In 1922 the International Council of Religious Education was formed, combining churches of Canada and the United States in one common effort and expanding the original Sunday School conception to include a great many other activities as a part of the work of Christian education in the Church. In 1950 the International Council of Religious Education became the Division of Christian Education of the National Council of Churches, when a number of other ecumenical bodies also came together to form the National Council of the Churches of Christ in the U.S.A. In this Division the old Sunday School concept, much modified, and also broadened and enriched by other conceptions concerning teaching in the Church, is still vigorously articulated as a force in the Church.

By way of conclusion two characterizations of the Sunday School can be made which are evident in its history and which may help in understanding the plight of the Sunday School today. The first of these is that the Sunday School was an interdenominational movement, although it probably was not ecumenical in any full or significant sense. And if we can read history backward with any validity, we may conclude that the Sunday School would not have come into existence on a denominational basis alone.

Somewhat different from this, but still an important characterization relating to its present status in the Church, is the fact that the Sunday School movement was a lay movement. It was largely an effort of laymen in the Church, and it has scarcely ever had the full participation of the clergy. Its leadership has been lay leadership, here and there supported, strengthened, and, more recently, guided by ordained ministers and official church bodies.

CHAPTER 5

The Psychological Movement of the Nineteenth Century

*T*he psychological movement in education began on the European continent, but it had its consequences in many parts of the world, and its influence reached into the Church rather extensively. One of its earliest achievements, in relation to religious education, was to bring graded lessons into being, shortly after the turn of the twentieth century, to supplant in part the uniform lessons which were without a competitor from 1872 to 1908. This was the first tangible influence the psychological movement had on the Sunday School. While the movement was largely of the nineteenth century, its forerunner, if not its inception, was in the thought of Rousseau who lived in the previous century. We will therefore begin this discussion of the psychological movement with Rousseau and then turn to Pestalozzi, Herbart, and Froebel, who were the leaders of the movement.

JEAN JACQUES ROUSSEAU (1712–1778)

Jean Jacques Rousseau had both Calvinistic and Roman Catholic influences in his background and associations, as will soon be evident, although neither of these affected him very deeply. He was born in Geneva, and Geneva has since honored him by a statue signaling his memory, located on a little island in the Rhone River, virtually in the center of the city. Rousseau lived in this citadel of Reformed Christianity for the first twelve years of his life; in fact it is reported that some of his forebears on his mother's side were Protestant ministers. He ran away from Geneva as a young adolescent however, allegedly in a fit of rage at the city gate-keeper who closed the door on him when he returned late from one of his excursions into the country. This made Rousseau so angry that, when he eventually got into the city, he gathered his belongings together and made a dramatic departure. From this point on for quite some years, he lived virtually as a vagrant, spending much of his time in the beautiful Savoy country of France.

However, he also became entangled in a number of attachments which did much to determine the course of his life. His first attachment was with a Madam De Warrens who lived on a pension from the government of France; eventually he became her secretary and lover. But on the occasion of his first meeting with her and visit to her home, she sent him on his way to Turin, Italy, with other travelers, for indoctrination as a Roman Catholic. At the end of his instruction by the Roman Catholic Church, he was confirmed as a Catholic and then stayed on in Turin for a time. But one of his confreres in the catechetical course apparently had the same wanderlust that possessed Rousseau, because it was not long before they were back on the road, returning to the Savoy countryside. As might be expected, Rousseau soon turned up again at the home of Madam De Warrens. From this point on, many years of his life were focused in this household as a part of the Madam's retinue. Of course, he was eventually superseded by other lovers, but for the years the liaison lasted, he lived in comparative comfort, courtesy of the French government, and was a dilettante student of astronomy and music, in his spare time. In fact, he invented a new system of notation for music which he was certain would replace the old one and which we still have! The only trouble with his new system was that it was more complicated than the old, and consequently he had little success when he tried to sell it in Paris. This little sample of the quality of Rousseau's life and interest, which could be paralleled by many others, will help to make plausible at least one conclusion we need to draw concerning Rousseau. It is that he was a romanticist who did not manage to settle down to a serious life of earnest effort until the age of forty when he first began to write.

This new turn in his life was occasioned by the announcement of an essay contest by the Academy of Dijon. The subject of the contest was this: "Has the progress of the sciences and arts contributed to corrupt or to purify morals?" Rousseau saw this announcement quite by accident, according to his own report, when on one of his vagrant wanderings, and it so impressed him that he sat down and wept for a half-hour! He says that when he resumed his journey, his shirt front was wet with his own tears! He wrote the essay issuing a resounding "No" in answer to the contest question; the advancement of the arts and sciences had not, in his judgment, improved the condition of the human race. Today's paradox of great technological achievements coupled with a threat to the very existence of the human race would seem to make Rousseau's essay prophetic. His vigorous manner in taking hold of the contest announcement indicates how much he was a man of violent emotions. His personal power, the depth or voltage of his personality, was expressed more by means of his emotions than by his intellect. Even so, this man did produce two classics which would no doubt be included in most anybody's list of great books. In spite of the fact that he was not a great intellect, he nevertheless wrote *The Social Contract*, a thesis in politics which exerted great influence both in the French Revolution and the establishment of American democracy, and the *Emile*, which was one of the strongest formative influences upon modern education.

The chief bone of contention which forced him into serious thought and writing was the unnaturalness and artificiality of society, especially as found in large cities. It is true that if Rousseau were to have been upset by any society, it would have been by his own adopted France. But this is not to say, as has often been done, that Rousseau would not regard other societies, that of the United States, for example, as equally objectionable, were he to live in their midst. We cannot neutralize Rousseau's revolt by saying that it was caused by the terrible artificialty of the French society he knew, as though it was peculiar only to France. His pointed remarks about sex-education and artificial sex-stimulations, arousing youth before they are emotionally ready for them, would be as applicable to our twentieth-century American culture as they were to the culture which occasioned his revolt. Our American movies and television would come every bit as much under his hammer as did certain aspects of his contemporary French culture.

He focused especially on the supercilious, polite, and wealthy.

One of the aggravations on which he wrote repeatedly in the *Emile*, was mothers of the privileged classes who farmed their babies out to wet nurses, thereby avoiding cuddling and nursing them themselves. He gives every appearance of having been obsessed by this subject. Nevertheless, by hindsight and after having had the benefit of psychoanalysis, we now see that there was something psychologically very sound in his complaint. So needing of reform did he consider the aristocracy that when he chose his imaginary Emile, whom he was going to educate as an example for the world, he picked him from a family of wealth. The reason was, according to his argument, that the poor are going to get a good education anyway, since they necessarily live close to Nature. Emile, however, was neglected in being sheltered from Nature and was not, therefore, going to get a good education unless someone like Rousseau came to his rescue!

The other focus of his great crusading concern was the poverty-stricken masses of people, forced to live in city slums. Rousseau had nothing to say in favor of the large city; as he put it, "men are not made to be crowded together in ant-hills."[1] It is not difficult to imagine his outcries against our vast and still growing monsters today, strips of cities stretching across entire states. The intention of the *Emile*, in opposition to the anti-nature atmosphere of Rousseau's time, was to show how education could be made natural.

In the *Emile*, first published in 1762, Rousseau adopted tutoring as his approach to teaching, rather than the class which includes several students. It may be that he did this for literary reasons, as tutoring is easier to portray than teaching in the group. Of tutoring itself he said that it is such an important profession that it requires a man's total commitment and cannot be made commensurate with any conceivable financial return. At best, tutoring is the function of the father and should not be delegated to a hired hand. Of himself, Rousseau said that he was not worthy to be a tutor, a self-appraisal which is not likely to be challenged. As generally known, he had three to five children by an illicit relationship with Therese Le Vasseur, who we are told was a stupid servant girl. Taking up with her came somewhat naturally, as Rousseau usually took the side of the outcast. Very shortly after the birth of each child,

[1] *Emile*, Everyman's Library, London: J. M. Dent, 1938, p. 26.

Rousseau placed each of his infants in a foundling home. In his later life he repented of this inhumanity and tried to find them, evidently enlisting the help of some of his friends in the effort. None of them were located, however, or else they were found in such a condition as would have been a shock to the aging Rousseau, and therefore his friends did not tell him about them. This one reflection of his character easily makes clear that Rousseau was quite right in saying that he wasn't worthy to become a tutor. But having made this self-appraisal, he tells us that he will do the next best thing, namely writing *Emile* to tell us how education should properly be conducted from birth to maturity. *Emile* is not the easiest reading in the world, not because it is so profound, but because it is poorly organized and often repetitious. Nevertheless, it has proven itself a classic.

There are two comments which are most important to make about *Emile* in relation to our immediate concern. The first of these is that Rousseau wanted his imaginary Emile to live as a child of Nature, as a little animal until twelve years of age, uncluttered by books and by book-learning. This was in part his way of getting the child away from society. In this rather vain hope he followed Plato, who in the *Republic* proposed to take the children away from their society, expurgate the literature they studied, and in them make a genuinely fresh start for the human race. However impossible this may be, we can understand both Rousseau and Plato in this hope if we observe with their eyes the way we commonly handle infants. When a new child is born into a home the relatives and friends "oh" and "ah" at it, pass it around the family, and everyone has to hold it and play with it. We make the child out to be a social being long before he is one. What he ought to be allowed to do is to lie on his back, or his belly if he wants to, and to vegetate. This premature socializing of the child was the sort of thing, symptomatically, that Rousseau was trying to eradicate. His advice was to let the child have a chance to be a vegetable and an animal first of all, not to try to make a social being out of him until he is ready to be one. More deeply, what Rousseau was opposing was the way society has of getting its tentacles around an individual and corrupting him before he knows what is happening.

Also in Rousseau there was one of the earliest genetic views of the child; that is, Rousseau thought of the child in terms of stages

72

of growth and development. These stages were very wide and in-clusive in Rousseau; we have learned sufficiently more about this today, e.g., as in the Yale Child-Study Clinic, so that we can be much more detailed and definitive about ages and stages than Rousseau was. Even so, he did not do such a bad job; he was not too far away from present thinking at least in the generalities of growth and development. His classification of ages and stages will be sketched briefly. The first stage is infancy: a child is an infant until he can walk. The next developmental period is from walking to five years of age. In his consideration of this stage, we have op-portunity to see Rousseau's concern for the child to be natural. Rousseau said that when the child starts to walk, we do not need to hover over him to prevent him from falling; he is not tall enough to fall far enough to hurt himself, so well has Nature taken care of this. Ages five to twelve constitute the third stage. The next stage following this is the period of pubescence which would be, if we are going to include both boys and girls and follow present knowl-edge and conditions of growth, ages eleven through fifteen. The final stage, in Rousseau's scheme of growth and development, is the period of youth, a time in which the study of society begins to be relevant. He did write one final chapter on the education of girls which he called "Sophy," or "Woman," which is about as conven-tional and unimaginative as the other chapters are revolutionary.

We may justifiably characterize the work of Rousseau as in large part destructive, although not without good intention and even-tually good effect. Someone like Rousseau had to tear away the artificialities of human social enclosures before others could turn constructive attention to the way a child grows and learns. While there were constructive things in Rousseau, especially in his pro-posals for education, his major function was tearing away the accumulated debris so that others could make more effective and positive starts.

JOHANN HEINRICH PESTALOZZI (1746–1827)

The first of these men to do the more constructive work was Johann Heinrich Pestalozzi; and beginning with him, the psycho-logical movement is placed in large part in the nineteenth century. Pestalozzi is less generally known than Rousseau, but is nevertheless of great importance in this movement. He was a peculiar Swiss boy who, early in life, became obsessed with the problems of the common man. It may therefore seem surprising that he had a confusing struggle in finding a profession, but this struggle was not as senseless as it appears on the surface. He was born on the borderline of genteel circumstances; his father was a physician who died young and left the boy Henry, his mother, his sister, and a servant girl with a very modest legacy with which they could manage in great frugality. Pestalozzi benefited by a privileged education; i.e., he went to a secondary school and the *Collegium Carolinum* of the higher school in Zurich. Pestalozzi could in no sense, however, be considered an intellectual. His first choice of a profession was the ministry—therefore no doubt his selection of the *Collegium Carolinum*. His grandfather was a minister and many of Henry's boyhood summers were spent visiting him. Often he accompanied his grandfather on his pastoral visits, and this was the beginning of his acquaintance with the condition of the common people and the first arousing of his great sympathy and concern for them. In his theological course at the College when he came up for his first trial sermon, he failed miserably, at least in his own eyes; he became so flustered that he couldn't even remember the Lord's Prayer. Of course this is not an unusual occurrence, but he thought he was a failure and so gave up the hope of a career in the ministry. He then turned to law which was even more a will-o'-the-wisp. His idea was that by being a lawyer he could plead the case of the common people in court. It soon became clear that he couldn't get very far with this idea because he had already been heavily influenced by the writings of Rousseau and was considered far to the left in his social theory. Consequently he soon turned to his third trial which was farming; his idea in doing this was the hope that he could help the common people by showing them more improved methods of agriculture. Even though Pestalozzi did not know much about agriculture, he managed to persuade a bank in Zurich to back him in buying the farm which he called Neuhof. He did try to farm this land for five years, by which time he failed financially, however; he did manage to keep the home proper, apart from the farmland, until his death. At the time that he started the farming project, he also prevailed upon the daughter of a Zurich banker to marry him. The father and mother were against the marriage;

74

they contended that Pestalozzi was an improvident man, and of course they were quite right. But love always prevails, and the daughter, Anna Schulthess, was willing to marry him anyway. If you want to read a classic of self-deprecation, look up Pestalozzi's letter of proposal.[2] In it Pestalozzi left nothing unsaid about his faults. He told her what a terrible provider he was and predicted correctly that he would get involved in social causes to the neglect of her comfort and well-being.

This is the kind of man who eventually embraced education as a life mission, although by apparent accident. When his farm failed, he took the buildings to which he still held title and invited under-privileged children so that he could teach them. He taught them weaving and spinning, and, at the same time that their hands were engaged in these activities, he taught them letters and number combinations. Accidental and lacking in thought as it was, even so, this was the beginning of industrial education. He continued this effort for five years and then was forced to give it up, again for financial reasons. He wisely sought rest for some time after this and devoted his efforts during this period to the writing of his first book, *Leonard and Gertrude*.[3]

Leonard and Gertrude was intended to be a novel with an educational message, and as such was not entirely unsuccessful. On first reading, especially in the early chapters, it scarcely rises above the level of melodrama. But more careful study of it yields greater respect for what Pestalozzi was trying to do in it. Published first in 1782, the book received wide circulation as a novel, but unfortunately most people did not read it for its educational message. Viewed from the twentieth century, however, the message is quite as remarkable as its melodrama is bad. It viewed home, school, church, and community as one continuous matrix in which the child lives. It conceived the school as being patterned after the healthy home, and it proposed a degree of equality in the ownership of property by the common people, a reach beyond the then still-existing remnants of feudalism.

A new chapter in Pestalozzi's life opened in 1798 when the Franco-Prussian War left in its wake a good many orphans in

[2] See Hermann Krüsi, *Pestalozzi, His Life, Work, and Influence*, New York: Wilson, Hinkle, 1875, pp. 18–19.

[3] Trans. by Eva Channing, Boston: D. C. Heath, 1901.

Switzerland. Since Pestalozzi was sympathetic to the French, who had the upper hand at the time, he agreed to take care of these orphans in a convent located in the village of Stanz, some distance to the south and east of Zurich. This benevolent project lasted for something less than a year, as the French, after some months, requisitioned the convent to be used as a hospital. Nevertheless, for this short time Pestalozzi carried on courageously; he was teacher, parent, advisor, cook, guardian, and everything else to these youngsters, with only occasional help. It was here that his beginning experiments in the psychology of education were ventured. The fact that they had no books or other school equipment with which they could work appeared to him at first to be a great disadvantage. But being in this plight, he turned to improvised means which proved to be an advantage in the end. The building being in great disrepair, he would ask these children to count the rents in the wall paper, the holes in the wall, etc., and describe them to him. As he proceeded with this feeble effort, he discovered he was dealing with the sense-perceptual problem of the child. He later became convinced that this is the foundation of the entire educational transaction.

From this brief beginning at Stanz, he went on to other schools; his most famous one was his school at Yverdon, located on the southwestern end of Lake Neuchatel and about halfway between Geneva and Berne. This school became well known all over the world and made Pestalozzi famous. Many people from all parts of Europe and America visited Pestalozzi in Yverdon. In fact Herbart, one of the greatest influences in German secondary education, went there to observe Pestalozzi's teaching. And Froebel, the founder of the kindergarten, actually took the three boys he was tutoring to Yverdon and lived together with them in the school for some time.

But what were the more significant conceptions which constituted the beginning of a psychology in Pestalozzi's work? First of all, Pestalozzi was very much aware that he was making a beginning, and he characterized himself as a man walking in the dark who constantly had to retrace his steps and start over. He was not a man of great intellect, but his modesty and humility helped to compensate a great deal for this. One of his attempts was to replace the verbalism of education. Every student must be aware that education at almost any level is a highly verbalistic affair; it has been so throughout the centuries since its ancient beginnings and, of course, will continue to be verbalistic. But yet there is a sense in which we in the schools make words our currency much more than we should. In relation to this perennial condition of the schools, Pestalozzi wanted to replace the verbalism of education with an education of realized relationship. He wanted to start with children at the point of their sense-perceptual experience and help them to find unity in this experience. At some point there comes a recognition in perception that, after all, an object is a unity, that it is one; in a manner which strongly suggests that he had read Kant, Pestalozzi pointed this out. For educational purposes Pestalozzi came to focus upon unity and number perception; if a set of perceptions are not one object, they are two, or more, or many. Of course, he also took into account qualities such as redness or hardness as well as number. A second step in Pestalozzi's thought was the associating of these percepts with words, so that the child learns the language in association with objects.

All of this can be quite well exemplified by the way in which art was taught at Yverdon. Pestalozzi found a man by the name of Johannes Buss who was quite talented as an artist, if unlearned, and gave him a teaching post at Yverdon. In preparation for this assignment, Pestalozzi taught him his own understanding of perception; as a result, Buss was eventually convinced that he knew more about art after having acquired Pestalozzi's principles, than he did before. Pestalozzi wanted, in the teaching of art to children, to help them see the object as it is and not interpose human schemata between the child and the object—e.g., supposedly showing the relative positions of viewer and object by dotted lines representing perspective. Indeed there is art instruction today which, in general, follows Pestalozzi on this point. In this theory of art instruction, it is held that we should not teach perspective until after a child has been confronted by problems of perspective and become perplexed by them, and, similarly, that we should not teach the color chart until after he is perplexed by problems of color.

Another major point in Pestalozzi was his understanding of the place of Nature in education. He insisted that education must follow the order of Nature; that is, we must find out how Nature works in order to learn how children learn. But he went on to say

77

more than this; education, he held, is an art; he referred to it as *the Art* which adds to Nature—education is an art which can lead Nature, augment it, and facilitate it. In fact Pestalozzi held that Nature is blind, whereas education sees and can shed light on human growth and learning.

A fourth educational doctrine in Pestalozzi, which is both relevant and important particularly in this book, is his doctrine of man. He held that individual man is fundamentally good, in much the same way that Rousseau did. The most famous lines of the *Emile* are the opening ones which read: "God makes all things good; man meddles with them and they become evil." Pestalozzi held much the same view of individual man as he comes from the creative hand of God. He explained the evil of man by saying that it occurs when the pathways to goodness are blocked. Society, on the other hand, is definitely bad, as in Rousseau, and has a corrupting influence on the individual. Pestalozzi's view of man is somewhat modified, however, by another figure he used in which he characterized man as a green hill, when viewed at a distance, but when seen close at hand, as rough and resistant as the rock underneath the verdure. From this we can see that Pestalozzi was not quite as romantic as he first appears and is often represented to be.

Finally, let us look at Pestalozzi's rationale for religious education, for he worked this out with some degree of definiteness. He said, first of all, that love for God is an experience resulting only from love for fellow man. This means that the child has to learn love for man before he can learn love for God; this love for man is first learned in the child's relation to his mother. Through the mother-child relationship, Pestalozzi held, the child also learns obedience, gratitude, and trust. Pestalozzi also held that love, obedience, gratitude, and trust are all fused together in the child, in due course, to become the germ of conscience. The crucial time in a child's religious life, for Pestalozzi, is when he becomes sufficiently independent that he no longer needs his mother. At this point the crucial transition in the child's religious nurture must be made, for the mother should then transfer the child's relation of dependence upon her to a dependent relation upon God. And by way of dramatizing the importance of this transition, Pestalozzi puts words in the mother's mouth. He would have her say something like this to the child: "Child, there is a God whom thou needest, who taketh thee in His arms when thou needest me no longer, when I can shelter thee no more."[4]

JOHANN FRIEDRICH HERBART (1776-1841)

The next figure, Johann Friedrich Herbart, while certainly an essential contributor in the psychological movement in education, had the least effect upon religious education of the four men considered here. This was in part because he was most concerned with the secondary school and the university. While argument could easily be advanced that this should not be the case, it nevertheless was true, because the Sunday School movement was closely identified with elementary education and the more recent religious education movement focused attention upon the child rather than the adult. By contrast with Herbart, Pestalozzi and Froebel were concerned with the young child, not the secondary school youth. It may be helpful to explain that elementary education in most European countries means the education of the common people; it is not preparatory for secondary education, as in the United States. Secondary education in most European countries is the education of the more privileged, more talented youths of a higher social rank, and it alone leads to the university. It was with this higher, more privileged education of quality that Herbart was concerned.

Marked by numerous distinctions, Herbart was a near genius intellectually. He wrote an essay on freedom of the will at the age of fourteen, a precocious achievement we would scarcely expect of Rousseau, Pestalozzi, or Froebel. He was privileged by having the best education which could be gotten in his time and was ardently sponsored in this by his mother. It is surprising that Herbart turned out as well as he did, having had so much mothering; traces of mother-attachment are not notably present in his writing. As a boy, Herbart unfortunately fell into a tub of boiling water and was badly burned, the accident apparently resulting in scar tissue over a good portion of his body. Being separated from his father, Herbart's mother gave inordinate attention to this child, even going along with him when his university studies began. She also took some courses together with him, Greek is mentioned in particular,

---

[4] *How Gertrude Teaches Her Children*, translated by Lucy E. Holland and Francis C. Turner, Syracuse: C. W. Bardeen, 1915, pp. 184-185.

and moved in polite social circles at Jena, where Herbart studied, making contacts which proved to be valuable to her son. It was by her instigation, for example, that he became the tutor for the three sons of the governor of Interlaken, Switzerland, after three years at Jena. This was an important three-year engagement in which his career in education was launched. To his credit let it be said that in teaching these three boys, he observed for himself both age-level and individual differences.

Some years later after teaching at Göttingen, he was most notably honored by being appointed successor to Immanuel Kant in the chair of philosophy at the University of Königsberg. In this chair he did a very surprising thing; he started a pedagogical seminary in connection with his chair of philosophy. It should be remembered that this was in 1809 and that there are still many institutions today in which we would scarcely expect to find an experimental or laboratory school attached to a chair of philosophy. Herbart was quite ahead of his time in trying to build a bridge between philosophy and education.

As might therefore be expected, Herbart had great influence in improving German secondary education, even in his own time. He was also a strong influence in making education in the United States content-centered up until the ascendancy of the influence of John Dewey and the coming of progressive education. In fact the National Society for the Study of Education, which is very much alive and publishes significant yearbooks on important subjects, was formerly known as the Herbartian Society. We will now take up the two major themes of Herbart as they had bearing on education. They are his conception of mind and the resultant method of teaching to which it led, and his approach to ethics and its consequent meaning for the purposes of education.

Herbart conceived of the mind as being what it contains. He was a cold, realistic intellectual for whom the mind was equal to its contents. However he had an understanding of the mind as being both conscious and subconscious, with the threshold of consciousness being a kind of gateway through which ideas have to pass as they come up from the unconscious. He even went so far as to work out a mathematical formula supposedly representing the balance of relationship between what is happening at any one moment in the stream of consciousness and the power of a cluster of ideas in the subconscious to push its way up into consciousness. For in his conception ideas as they fade from consciousness into the subconscious tend to cluster, similar ideas attracting each other. Accordingly, the larger the cluster of ideas, in comparison to other clusters, the more power it has to push back into consciousness. Nevertheless, if there is a particular idea which is the current focus of consciousness for the moment and if this event is allied with a less strong cluster of ideas in the subconscious, the larger cluster may be held down below the level of consciousness because the power of the lesser cluster is sufficiently augmented by what is going on in consciousness to gain for it the upper hand, as it were. While this conception may remind the reader of Sigmund Freud (1856–1939) and modern psychiatry, there apparently never was any connection between Freudianism and Herbartianism. Herbart came to his conception of mind philosophically, by speculation and apparently some introspection. His *Text-book in Psychology*[5] was purely speculative psychology.

It is from this conception of mind that he came to the formulation of his method of teaching, which includes the law of apperception, commonly oversimplified to the effect that we learn the new in terms of the old. First of all, the thing you have to do in any given act of teaching is to prepare the mind of the learner. What Herbart meant by this, psychologically, is that the teacher must call up into the consciousness of the student those clusters of ideas in the subconscious mind which are relevant to the subject at hand which is to be taught. The second step in this method is presentation, i.e., the presentation of the new material, for which the ideas already called up will provide an appropriate context or in Herbartian terms, an apperceptive mass. The third step is comparison or abstraction, in other words the relating of the new and the old. The fourth step is generalization or assimilation, by which is meant relating the new learning to a wide scope of knowledge. The final step is application of the new learning in practice. It so happens that Herbart did not work this all out in precisely these five steps; his original three major steps were further broken down by his followers to make the five distinct steps which have become famous. From this we can formulate a kind of guide which might be called the law of apperception. But it would not be so simple as the usual,

5 Trans. by Margaret K. Smith, New York: Appleton, 1891.

81

"we learn the new in terms of the old." It would more accurately be stated as "there is usually a context of ideas for learning within which the new learning is understood and assimilated."

To turn to the other of the two major conceptions in Herbart, it should be said that his theory of ethics was highly significant for education. Herbart held that the highest good for man, and therefore the ultimate objective of education, is moral character. But he also held that education has a more immediate objective, which is the means to the ultimate objective of character; this is many-sidedness of interest. For boys in the German secondary school, he coveted many-sidedness as the net yield of their school experience, as he believed it a stepping-stone to the achievement of character. Herbart believed that each child is born with a unique individuality which must be respected, but which also needs correction or polishing. In fact, so much did he respect individuality that he cautioned teachers not to impose their individualities on their pupils. He correctly perceived that we all have separate individualities and that no one individuality can be a norm for others. Individuality, he held, is nevertheless angular; it has its rough edges which need to be rounded off somehow, not lost but polished. And this is part of what is involved in acquiring character. Herbart believed that in some way individuality is corrected by universality, acquaintance with human experience universally. The way in which to give the student this universality of experience, he believed, is to immerse his individuality in the bath of human culture—the widest, broadest, and most inclusive human culture. Consequently, he placed great stress upon the humanities in the curriculum: history, religion as an aspect of human culture, and various sciences. But the whole point of this exposure to the humanities in broadest possible scope was to correct the angularity of individuality by as nearly a universal knowledge as possible.

This conception resulted in a movement or direction for education which has long characterized Herbart and is in sharp contrast to the voluntarism and activism of our own century. Herbart believed that education's most immediate contact with the individual is by means of the intellect. The intellect is the outside wrapping, as it were, of personality, comparable physiologically to our skin. By forming the intellect with this many-sidedness of interest, Herbart believed that in turn education can form the emotions, which are further inside, helping them to be appropriate feelings as correction of undesired ones. And these appropriate emotions, he believed, can in turn form the will, the core and center of personality, determining the will so that it becomes the right kind of will. Herbart's direction for education can be seen, then, as moving from the outside inward—intellect being on the outside, emotion an intermediary wrapping between intellect and will, and at the center or the core of the individual the will, the decisive determinant of character.

FRIEDRICH WILHELM AUGUST FROEBEL (1782–1852)

Froebel, the last to be discussed in connection with the psychological movement, became a strong influence in modern religious education by way of the kindergarten, which he founded, and because of the way in which the progressive education movement borrowed so heavily from him and religious education in turn borrowed from progressive education.

We will look at Froebel first as a man, and then turn to his educational ideas. He was born the sensitive child of an austere Lutheran manse in Germany. His mother died when he was yet an infant of nine months, a trauma which of course did much to determine the movement of his life and the quality of his own mentality. Students have sometimes asked if it is necessary to be frustrated in childhood in order to be an educator! It may not be necessary, but it does not take much reading of the history of education to discover that childhood frustrations were not uncommon among those who became leaders in education. Froebel had a very difficult time as a child. His stepmother may not have been unkind to him, as is sometimes reported, but at least both she and his father considered him a rather stupid child. His life as a child was of course unhappy, relieved at least on one occasion by an extended stay in the home of an uncle. It is not surprising that he became highly introspective and did not begin to find himself until apprenticed to a forester at the age of fifteen, an occupation with ample opportunity for full enjoyment of Nature. His father had a large Lutheran parish and practiced rigid discipline and responsibility in serving his parish. Needless to say, this made great claims upon his time and prevented him from being the kind of father this very sensitive child needed. This is not the place to discourse upon the problems which a minister's professional life may bring to his home and his children. But this difficulty is a real and perennial one; Froebel's father well exemplified it. From his autobiography we get pictures of Froebel's home which throw further light on his personality. For example, there are the inadvertent occasions, apparently a good many, when the young Froebel overheard the confessions of parishioners to his father, as they sought his counsel. This led the boy to question particularly why God ever created the institution of sex. This greatly burdened him as a child, and he was only relieved of his criticism of creation when his older brother pointed out to him that much of Nature other than man and the animal kingdom is also sexual. Also there apparently were many times when the young Froebel was a bystander as his father and older brother argued, disagreeing, apparently with violent emotions, about theological matters. The perplexing thing to this boy, as he listened to these sessions, was that he understood both his father and brother and could not decide with which one to agree.

Some major release from his difficulties began, however, with his forestry apprenticeship. Then his quiet, withdrawn, and introspective approach to life had a chance to get some objective reference in Nature. Certainly he must have drawn one of his important educational ideas from the experience of these years. He learned that when working with plants and young trees, you bring them into a place where they can be cultivated and do everything that you do with them around them and for them, not to them. Forestry is permissive and constructive; it seeks to create the conditions in which plants can grow. If you prune them, you prune them in order that their growth can be in the right direction. You do not step on them; needless to say, you do not bang them about. Surely his kindergarten idea had its earliest beginnings here. In essence it was that the right kind of a beginning in education for small children is to treat them as though they were in a garden, and the teaching is consequently a doing around them and for them, not to them.

He drew from an entirely different kind of experience for his educational thought some years later when he studied minerology, becoming especially interested in crystals. He was impressed that he always found a design in crystals, but never the same design. From this he made a kind of leap of faith to what he called a universal principle of unity. This was his basic and central idea, a mystical almost pantheistic idealism, rather vague and foggy, but nevertheless the total context for his entire educational effort. As a result he used certain symbols in education which will be alluded to later, because he believed they conveyed to the child facets of his mystical doctrine of unity.

It was quite by accident that he eventually fell into education as a profession, even more so than for Pestalozzi. Froebel really floundered in finding his mission in life, and in his several false starts no continuous theme can be found, as in Pestalozzi's career. His start in education came as an invitation to tutor three boys, similar to Herbart's first assignment. He took these boys with him to Yverdon and stayed with them in Pestalozzi's school for the better part of three years, attending classes with them. This uncertain beginning eventually became his consuming passion, and before his life was done, he started several different schools and gave birth to a number of influential educational ideas. He even thought that some of his ideas were so secretly and uniquely his own that no one else could understand or appreciate them. And it was only toward the very end of his life when his sponsor, Baroness von Bülow, had acquired sufficient esoteric insight, in his judgment, that he tried to reveal them to her. The supposed revelation must have been a disappointing one, because Froebel's ideas were never as profound nor as well-conceived as he assumed. Of course, as was the case with Pestalozzi, Froebel was not a man of great intellect. He may have been a profound spirit, and he did introduce certain innovations in education whose influence reached well into the twentieth century, touching the Sunday School and the religious education movement, but even so, he cannot be considered a great mind.

We will assume that this much acquaintance with the man himself is adequate for our purposes, and we will now turn to Froebel's major educational themes. The first of these is the kindergarten, his most famous idea, but not among his more profound ones. The idea of the kindergarten was really very simple; it was that if an educational career, for any person, is to be a good one, it must have a good beginning. This stemmed from one strain in his doctrine of man, specifically that one of the reasons that man is evil is not because he is born in that condition, but because of the kind of education he receives. While this is certainly a weak explanation, it should not be dismissed without getting the force of Froebel's argument. All educational institutions—small ones as well as big ones—elementary and secondary schools as well as institutions of higher learning—have a way of developing a mentality or climate that teaches side by side with the teaching that goes on in the class room, sometimes more eloquently, and sometimes in contradiction of what the school intends. In their poorer moments, because of this, teachers sometimes feel that they could abandon classes without its making too much difference in the life of the school. While education does not give man his depravity, as Froebel assumed, it often does very little to relieve it and on occasion nourishes the evil flower into full bloom. It was with this attitude that Froebel set himself to make the beginning in schools a good one—therefore the kindergarten and the cluster of symbols and practices which grew with it under his leadership and among his many followers.

As already suggested, Froebel's most important idea was his all-pervading principle of unity. It was a kind of mystical pantheism which is called "panentheism," the "en" inserted in the middle of the word to make clear that all is in God, and not that all is God. He did not carry this conception very far forward into a full conception. His philosophical equipment being rather limited, he apparently had little awareness of the problem of the one and the many necessarily involved in it. That is, how do men have a part in this all-pervading Unity, if It or He is one absolute Being? As a result Froebel remained fundamentally vague and overly general concerning his most central conception.

A third concern of Froebel, as with Pestalozzi from whom he learned much, was sense-perception. He believed that education, at least in its inception, should be largely sense-perceptual, and because of this he invented certain devices for guiding and development of the perceptions of young children. While this is comparable to Pestalozzi's idea that Nature needs to be guided by education and, as it were, speeded up, Froebel nevertheless carried the intention further by devising certain "gifts" and "occupations," as he called them, by which children would be helped in their perception. Examples are the cube, a symbol of stability; the ball, a symbol of mobility; and the cylinder, combining in its symbolism both stability and mobility. This same idea was practiced in another way years later by Maria Montessori, first of all with mentally retarded children and later with normal boys and girls. Today a number of these play-learning devices are mass-produced as so-called educator toys of one kind or another; one example is the now common set of telescoping blocks. Watch a child play with these blocks when you have the opportunity; there is a certain point in the perceptual development of children when those telescoped blocks make great sense to him. Previous to this point they are meaningless and later on, of course, they are too elementary; but it is interesting to watch a child at the point at which he is ready to fit those blocks into each other. This exemplifies the point at which Froebel's education becomes most relevant. It is clear psychologically that Froebel's "gifts" and "occupations" were sound. The difficulty they present is that Froebel tried to give them a symbolic meaning. It is a bit far-fetched for a ball to represent to the child either eternal unity or mobility, to cite only one example. It is no wonder that more recent educators have abandoned completely the symbolism in Froebel, at the same time that they have borrowed many other things from him.

Froebel's conception of religious education is of special interest, of course, and we will now take it up before one other final point. Like Pestalozzi, he took the Christian culture of western Europe as a matter of course. This made it possible, or at least easier, for Froebel to take psychology very seriously without experiencing any qualms about religion. Had he possessed greater penetration in either area, the development of his thought could not have sailed along as smoothly as it did. For example, there are occasions in his writing in which he expresses his loyalty to traditional Christian belief without apparently realizing that any cultural problem might conceivably be involved for society generally. In pluralistic America or secular Europe of today, it would be almost impossible to be as naïve as Froebel. He defined religion as: "The endeavor to raise into clear knowledge the feeling that originally the spiritual self of man is one with God, to realize the unity with God which is founded on this clear knowledge and to continue to live in this

87

unity with God, serene and strong, in every condition and relation to life."[6]

This makes clear that he regarded religious education as being largely an effort to awaken the awareness in the child that he is one with God. This of course ties in well with his universal principle of unity and his mysticism. Accordingly, his religious education was not so much redemptive in character, as it was a kind of reminder or reawakening, calling men to recognize the religious element in their lives. As this may imply, his religious instruction always assumed that there is some degree of religion already present in the child at birth as an original gift. In speaking about teaching religion in the schools, he generally appears to take a strongly loyal Christian position, in which, it is ventured, more christology is implicit, however good or bad, than Froebel intended. On religious instruction in the schools, he said: "Therefore, the school should first of all teach the religion of Christ; therefore, it should first of all, and above all, give instruction in the Christian religion; everywhere, and in all zones, the schools should instruct for and in this religion."[7]

Froebel's more simple situation as compared to ours today, namely, a nearly homogeneous religious culture, was possibly more his disadvantage than it was his advantage. In distinction from him, we cannot escape being critical today, because at the same time that we may have religious commitment, we are necessarily caught in a dialectical tension when we deal with the problem of religion in the schools in our pluralistic society. Although this may be our great perplexity and anguish, it is also our greater advantage, namely, that we are forced to be critical.

One or two minor things in his religious instruction may be mentioned finally. He did not believe that rewards should be used as incentives for desired action. He felt this was a corruption, placing extraneous incentives above the real inner possession of religious faith which is its own reward. He did not believe very much in memory work, holding that it should be used only when geared to the understanding of the child.

Finally we need to discuss his conception of age levels. Like

[6] *The Education of Man*, trans. by W. N. Hailmann, New York: D. Appleton, 1899, p. 140.
[7] *Ibid.*, p. 151.

Rousseau, he laid stress on growth and development. For Froebel the earliest developmental level is infancy; the second stage is childhood, and this stage refers to the child before he starts to school. Boyhood, which refers to the next stage, has the specific meaning of the child as he first begins school. Beginning with childhood, Froebel anticipated the developmental tasks idea of some contemporary psychologists.[8] The so-called developmental task of childhood in Froebel, although he didn't use this term, is externalizing the internal. What Froebel meant by this is that there is inner experience in the child which needs to be represented outwardly. This is done by play, self-expression in education which has often been exaggerated by apostles and opponents alike. It is one of the themes progressive education borrowed from Froebel. It may help to allay distortions if we understand clearly what Froebel intended. He meant that childhood is the time when we should allow and encourage the individual to get out of himself what is inside; this is all that was intended by self-expression. But for Froebel, boyhood had a virtually antithetical and corrective function, which has been almost completely forgotten by both friends and enemies of Froebel alike. It was that the boy at school is in another period, its peculiar function, or developmental task, being the internalizing of the external. This function is to recognize that there are many, many things in the objective world, knowledge of which must be gotten into the inner experience of the child. The child at school is in the period in which this is to be done, and this is not self-expression, it is instruction. In accordance with the more precise meaning of the word "instruction," it is the putting of things that are objective and external into the subjective experience of the child.

By way of concluding this discussion of the psychological movement in education and establishing some of the relevance it may have for religious education, there are some general remarks which are now in order.

Only two of these four men that we have considered here in the psychological movement were religious in any primary sense. Rousseau was a deist; this is made very clear in "The Creed of a

[8] See, for example, Robert J. Havighurst, *Human Development and Education*, New York: Longmans, Green, 1953.

Savoyard Priest."[9] Herbart considered religion a part of the culture, to be taught as one of the humanities. Pestalozzi and Froebel both assumed Christianity as the true religion, but did not go deeply into its meaning. They depended largely upon their Christian culture for their religion, and Pestalozzi, even so, refused to teach the Heidelberg catechism. He was opposed to catechetical instruction as such because he regarded it as encouraging the child to give back to the teacher words which had no meaning for him.

Although only two of these men had a considerable interest in religion, they all nevertheless influenced religious education, at least indirectly, by directing the world's attention to the child and to the need for studying the child. Because of this, their influence came to be felt in the Church in a variety of ways. It came into the Sunday School movement in the nineteenth century with teachers who were also teachers in the public schools. Strange as it may seem, Henry Barnard (1811–1900) pointed to the Sunday Schools of America as the chief source for teachers for the public schools—just the reverse of our position today!

At any rate this interest in child study was strong enough by 1908 to produce a clamor against the Uniform Lessons of the Sunday School and to instigate the development of closely graded lessons. After all, in the light of the psychological movement, how could a single common lesson be adapted to all age levels?

Now in a more general and far-reaching way this focus upon the child came into the Sunday School and into the churches by way of the religious education movement, which in turn was influenced by the nineteenth-century psychological movement. And this connection will subsequently require our attention in later chapters.

---

[9] *Emile*, Everyman's Library, pp. 228 ff.

CHAPTER 6

Horace Bushnell and Christian Nurture

*I*n turning attention now to Horace Bushnell (1802–1876) and Christian nurture, we are considering the history of thought in Christian education more than the history of events. Much of our discussion in the last four chapters has been a history of events, but the significance of Bushnell in the history of Christian education is to be found almost totally in his thought. Before looking at his thought however, we will consider him briefly as a person in relation to his work and his period.

BUSHNELL'S LIFE AND WORK

Bushnell was born in Litchfield, Connecticut, April 14, 1802. Litchfield is the New England township, famous as the home of the old Litchfield Law School which later moved to New Haven and became the Law School of Yale University. His father was a farmer and, according to Luther Weigle, also a kind of small manufacturer.[1] This possibly means that he operated a small mill or a tannery in connection with his farm. His father was a Methodist, his mother an Episcopalian. At the time of the birth of their son, Horace, however, they were both members of the Congregational Church in New Preston, Connecticut, and so Bushnell was brought up as a Congregationalist.

Bushnell was educated at Yale, entering in 1823 and graduating in 1827. After several months as associate editor of the *New York*

[1] Preface to Horace Bushnell, *Christian Nurture*, New Haven: Yale University Press, 1947, p. xxiii.

Journal of Commerce, and after trying his hand at teaching for a short time, he returned to Yale in 1829 as a tutor and began studying law. But by 1831 his religious doubts were sufficiently dispelled for him to enter Yale's Theology Department, now the Divinity School, to prepare for the ministry. He completed this course in 1833.

He held only one pastorate; this was as minister of the North Congregational Church in Hartford from 1833, when he was ordained in that Church, until 1859, when it became necessary for him to resign because of poor health. Before his resignation his work was interrupted during periods of recuperation. On one of these occasions, in 1856, he spent some time in northern California and helped found the College of California, which later became part of the University of California at Berkeley. Bushnell had touched both coasts. He was a great preacher, but not in the tradition of the pulpit orator. His preaching was powerful more because of his penetration and originality of thought than because of oratory.

BUSHNELL, THE AUTHOR

We will now look at Bushnell as an author. He wrote a number of books, one of the more famous being *Christ in Theology*[2] to which reference will be made later in another connection. He wrote this book in response to controversy which arose in the Church over some of his ideas—controversy which it is assumed did not favor his health. It is reported that he was threatened by trial for heresy, and according to one account he was saved from this only when his congregation in Hartford unanimously voted to withdraw from the "Consociation," as the association of Congregational Churches in that area was called.[3]

By all odds his most famous work is the one with which we are directly concerned, *Christian Nurture*. It was first published in full form in 1847, although some parts of it had been published earlier. It is available to our generation in a reprinted edition honoring the centennial of the first appearance of the book.[4] Luther A. Weigle,

[2] Hartford: Brown and Parsons, 1851.
[3] See *Encyclopaedia Britannica*, 1955, IV, 454.
[4] New Haven: Yale University Press, 1947.

who for many years held a professorship at Yale honoring Bushnell by its name, was the editor and prime mover in getting this edition published. Other of the better known works of Bushnell were *God in Christ*,[5] *Nature and the Supernatural*,[6] and *The Vicarious Sacrifice*.[7] It was *God in Christ* that got him into theological controversy, and *Christ in Theology* was the book that he wrote after the controversy had died down in order to make his ideas clearer. He declared in the introduction to this volume published in 1851 that his intention was not to continue or extend the controversy, but rather to explicate his position further than in the earlier book. Bushnell was quite prolific as a writer and produced a number of other works; we have chosen to mention only his more famous writings. Of course his first book, *Christian Nurture*, is the best known.

BUSHNELL'S TIMES

The next subject which should be discussed before going further is the intellectual climate in which Bushnell lived and worked. Since this is the climate to which Bushnell was responding in his thinking, preaching, and writing, an attempt will be made therefore to depict some of its features; no attempt will be made however at wholeness or completeness of detail. In the more remote background of Bushnell's setting was an influence from the previous century, that of Jonathan Edwards (1703–1758). His dependence upon the English philosopher, John Locke (1632–1704), certainly gave his thought great novelty, but it is not so clear that Edwards achieved the level of a unique American mind.[8] It was probably not the theology of Edwards that most aroused Bushnell; rather it was the preaching of Edwards, which was a part of the background of Bushnell's day, which helped stir in him the spirit of rebellion.

Edwards' sermon, "Sinners in the Hands of an Angry God,"[9] did much to perpetuate the austere Calvinism that induced revolts such as Bushnell's. Horace Mann (1796–1859), for example, suf-

[5] Hartford· Brown and Parsons, 1849.
[6] New York: Scribner, 1858.
[7] New York: Scribner, Armstrong, 1877, 2 vols.
[8] See Perry Miller, *Jonathan Edwards*, New York: William Sloane, 1949.
[9] See Vergilius Ferm, Editor, *Classics of Protestantism*, New York: Philosophical Library, 1959, pp. 180–197.

fered as a child under the preaching of Nathaniel Emmons in Franklin, Massachusetts. Dr. Emmons was a Calvinist of some repute in his time who tutored many candidates for the ministry; this was prior to the existence of many of our theological seminaries. This boyhood experience in the church together with the death, years later, of his young wife, comprised such a trauma for Horace Mann that he could only find solace and the approximation of a religious life in the transcendentalism of Ralph Waldo Emerson and the Unitarianism of William Ellery Channing.

Another less immediate strain in Bushnell's intellectual environment was the form of German idealism which gained expression both in England and the United States by means of men of letters more than in the formulations of philosophers. In England it was *Aids to Reflection* by Samuel Taylor Coleridge and the writings of Thomas Carlyle that made idealism influential. *Aids to Reflection* was edited and published in the United States in 1829 by James Marsh, who was then President of the University of Vermont. As with Horace Mann this same idealistic influence evidently touched Bushnell, bringing with it some promise of relief from the threatening austerity of New England Calvinism.

But more immediate to Bushnell was the religious revivalism of the mid-nineteenth century, and to this he responded with vigorous resistance. It was this revulsion in his life which produced in him the compulsion to write *Christian Nurture*; it is fair to say that it was a book which came out of deep struggles of his soul. The present author does not propose to add one more supporting second to the thought of Bushnell, but nevertheless it must be recognized that his book was the result of significant and courageous thought. While it may not be completely accurate for every segment of the movement, it is generally correct to observe that the revivalism of the nineteenth century against which he was reacting was not a pure expression of Calvinism and was not free from corruptions. With it, for example, went religious folkways about sin as self-indulgence, as debauchery, as the sowing of wild oats in youth, etc. These folkways of revivalism, constituting a kind of unconscious theology also made radical conversion the antidote. An example of the violent emotional upheaval which was expected may be found in the conversion of Charles G. Finney (1792–1875), one of the great evangelists of the nineteenth cen-

94

tury. He describes it fully with all the morbid details in his auto-biography.[10] Strictly speaking, in the judgment of this author, the revivalists' conceptions both of sin and salvation were far more ethical than theological.

BUSHNELL AS SPOKESMAN TO HIS TIMES

The question is now in order, What was Bushnell's intellectual response to his intellectual world? Before turning particular attention to *Christian Nurture*, let us look at some other threads of Bushnell's thought, in order to have a general context for his famous work on Christian education.

His most inclusive and general response to this intellectual environment was to put forward the thesis that both language and logic must always be suspect in matters of religion. Now this has a strangely contemporaneous flavor, for there are a growing number of thinkers today who are raising similar questions. In philosophy there are the language analysts who are trying to make words do more accurately the very thing that Bushnell did not expect of language.[11] And more especially in theology there are those who are seeing more clearly the symbolic character of language, at least when used in theology, and they show promise of extending this effort beyond anything Bushnell could envision or hope for in his time.[12] Apparently Bushnell's major thesis was that language and logic are all right in ordinary human discourse, for example, in mathematics, as he specifically mentioned calculus. But he also argued that language and logic simply are not dependable instruments in theology and religion. In fact it will be necessary for us to take this matter up in a later connection but in its contemporary form, when we talk about the Bible and nurture.[13] Language and logic are not dependable in religion, Bushnell said, because when used in theology they take human forms—including words, which

[10] *Memoirs*, New York: Fleming H. Revell, 1876.
[11] See for example John Hospers, *An Introduction to Philosophical Analysis*, Englewood Cliffs, N.J.: Prentice-Hall, 1953, and D. J. O'Connor, *An Introduction to the Philosophy of Education*, New York: Philosophical Library, 1957.
[12] See Paul Tillich, *The Dynamics of Faith*. New York: Harper, 1957; Rollo May, ed., *Symbolism in Religion and Literature*, Braziller, 1960; Roger Hazelton, *New Accents in Contemporary Theology*, New York: Harper, 1960.
[13] See Chapter 10.

are really figurative in their derivation—and apply them literally to God and to God's dealing with man. This was the heart of Bushnell's argument; it would not be fair however to say that Bushnell was anti-theological, as he did hold that there is a province for theology. His contention at the least was that theology must use words in a symbolic, not literal, manner, since words are human forms. It cannot be said with certainty that Bushnell, when he so argued, was making the idealist distinction between appearance and reality or the distinction between the idea and the thing-in-itself, but the approximation is very close here. Were this the case, he would have been saying that one reason we should not depend on language and logic in theological matters is that we live in a world of appearances behind which reality is veiled. In the use of language to state formulas or to signify objects we can deal with the appearances, but we cannot deal with reality in such a use of language. Or to take another but similar idealist tack, we can think ideas, and even use them to build systems, but we can never identify our ideas with the reality about which they speak. Again, let it be said that it is not clear that Bushnell was influenced by idealism, or if he was to what extent; but since Coleridge's *Aids to Reflection* were formative for him in some degree, it seems likely that he was touched by some measure of idealist influence.

Of course there is a mid-twentieth-century version of what Bushnell was apparently saying. The prospect now is that there will be much more discussion of a similar theme in the years just ahead. Today's more common approach is to make a distinction between a sign and a symbol.[14] Less common vocabulary is to say virtually the same thing by distinguishing between symbol and metaphor.[15] If we were to use the more common of these two vocabularies and transpose Bushnell's thesis into modern terms he would be saying: all words are signs, therefore they become inadequate in religion; rather in religious matters we must speak in symbols, because they function in a way other than being signs for things signified.

The extent to which Bushnell was influenced by the philosophy of idealism has significance for the traditions expressed in the re-

---

[14] Susanne K. Langer, *Philosophy in a New Key*, Cambridge, Mass.: Harvard University Press, 1942.
[15] Martin Foss, *Symbol and Metaphor in Human Experience*, Princeton: Princeton University Press, 1949.

ligious education movement of the twentieth century. It is possible in the light of what we have said that one tradition in religious education has been a fusion of idealism, liberal theology, and Bushnell's thought. The reason this should be pointed out is that this is a very different tradition from that of John Dewey and progressive education,[16] another strain in modern religious education that often gets the burden of blame for the mistakes and errors of the movement. It is important, and only fair, that we recognize that both of these strains have been in the religious education movement and are still present there.

Let one thing more be said. Bushnell's distrust of logic and language must have shown through in his preaching. One of his famous sermons was entitled "Unconscious Influence."[17] In this sermon he propounded the idea that it is what we are and what we do that influences others, more than what we say. This then comes very close to the central thesis of his major work, *Christian Nurture*, our primary concern in this chapter to which we will turn shortly.

BUSHNELL'S THESIS CONCERNING CHRISTIAN NURTURE

Before considering this topic, let us turn again to recall the prevailing folkways concerning conversion against which Bushnell reacted so strongly and try to see them as he must have seen them. In fact we can quote him directly regarding them. He says: "Our very theory of religion is that men are to grow up in evil, and be dragged into the church of God by conquest. The world is to lie in halves, and the kingdom of God is to stretch itself side by side with the kingdom of darkness, making sallies into it, and taking captive those who are sufficiently hardened and bronzed in guiltiness to be converted."[18] "It would not be more absurd to suppose that God has appointed church education to produce a first crop of sin, and then a crop of holiness."[19]

But this does not mean that in rejecting the revivalistic mode, Bushnell was also rejecting the Calvinistic doctrine of man. He

[16] See Chapter 7.
[17] See Horace Bushnell, *The New Life*, Edinburgh: Alexander Strahan, 1860, pp. 118–132.
[18] *Christian Nurture*, p. 27.
[19] *Ibid.*, p. 26.

accepted generally the doctrine of man held by the tradition stemming from Calvin; and here also he speaks for himself: "There are many who assume the radical goodness of human nature, and the work of Christian education is, in their view, only to educate or educe the good that is in us. . . . The natural pravity of man is plainly asserted in the Scriptures, and if it were not, the familiar laws of physiology would require us to believe what amounts to the same thing."[20]

Although he insisted that the children of Christian parents should not find it necessary to go through the violent conversion which was the mode of the revivalists, he nevertheless held that there is some kind of conversion struggle which such children will normally experience. It is difficult to argue with Bushnell as he rather carefully phrases his statement of important points; nevertheless at a later point we will take exception to a part of his proposed correction of the revivalistic mode. At the present point, however, it is important to allow Bushnell to make his point theologically as he sought to do it. It may very well be that this is the base from which his central theme was derived, however imperfectly. He further says: "The growth of Christian virtue is no vegetable process, no mere onward development. It involves a struggle with evil, a fall and a rescue. The soul becomes established in holy virtue, as a free exercise, only as it is passed round the corner of fall and redemption, ascending thus into God through a double experience, in which it learns the bitterness of evil and the worth of good, fighting its way out of one, and achieving the other as a victory."[21]

We are now ready for the main thesis of *Christian Nurture*. Bushnell italicized it in his book for all the greater emphasis. It is: *"That the child is to grow up as a Christian, and never know himself as being otherwise."*[22] He further enlarges upon this by saying, "In other words, the aim, effort, and expectation should be, not, as is commonly assumed, that the child is to grow up in sin, to be converted after he comes to mature age; but that he is to open on the world as one that is spiritually renewed, not remembering the time that he went through a technical experience, but seem-

[20] *Ibid.*, p. 15.
[21] *Ibid.*
[22] *Ibid.*, p. 4.

ing rather to have loved what is good from his earliest years."[23]

By "technical experience" it is quite clear that he means conversion as the revivalists conceived it. It is equally clear that Bushnell did believe in conversion but not according to a particular form. As we have noted, he did say that the Christian becomes a Christian by going around the corner of sin and redemption; but this is a theological statement not a description of a mode.

It must already be evident that Bushnell was speaking about the children of Christian parents; this of course limits the scope of his argument. This is also a limitation to be kept in mind today at the same time that we correctly emphasize the importance of the Christian home as the primary agency of religious nurture. His focus was upon children who in some vital sense, however unconscious, are a part of the Church by virtue of being a part of a Christian family. Except for the fact that he points to the Christian home as the agency of nurture, the study of Bushnell is a study of a chapter in the history of thought as it bears upon religious education.

Bushnell approached the nurturing function of the home in the context of a generally organismic conception of social institutions. He understood all social institutions as being virtually organisms.

The organismic conception of institutions was one of the strains in American idealism, one of its leading exponents being William T. Harris (1835–1909), onetime Superintendent of Schools of St. Louis, United States Commissioner of Education, editor of the *Journal of Speculative Philosophy*, and author of the book, *Psychologic Foundations of Education*,[24] in which the organismic conception of institutions is propounded. In fact a comparable view was also stated by Walter Rauschenbusch in his book, *Christianizing the Social Order*,[25] he may also have felt the impact of the same idealist view of society. The following is one of Bushnell's statements concerning the organismic character of society: "All society is organic—the church, the state, the school, the family; and there is a spirit in each of these organisms, peculiar to itself and more or less hostile, more or less favorable to religious character, and to some extent sovereign over the individual man."[26]

[23] *Ibid*.
[24] New York: D. Appleton, 1898.
[25] New York: Macmillan, 1926.
[26] *Christian Nurture*, p. 22.

99

It can easily be seen by this that Bushnell's understanding of the home and other social institutions was that they are essentially organisms. That the family can be an organism is not hard to perceive in a good healthy home, nor does it need to be a religious or Christian home, just a good healthy family. In fact it is hard to believe that the family is anything less than an organism psychologically and sociologically, as well as biologically. Here is a family, for example, father and mother and two sons, who took a leisurely coast-to-coast drive during the summer. The father, being the usual busy professional man, was not ordinarily in the home for many hours at a time except for sleep, as is so common these days. But the four of them, together in their car for several days continuously, found out in a healthy and wholesome way how much a part of each other they were. Commenting on this in retrospect, the father, not a man of sentiment, remarked, "The boys talked about things they had never discussed with us before and told us many things about their thoughts and experiences we had not known." For him, he said, the trip would be a cherished memory, not so much as a vacation experience, but as a rich familial oneness.

This is the kind of organismic life which Bushnell saw in the home and of which he proposed the Church make use in giving birth to Christians. Let such an organism be an instrument of the Spirit, and the child who lives in and of it, he argued, will breathe the air and eat the food of the Christian faith. This can be represented most directly and most clearly by a somewhat extended quotation from *Christian Nurture* in which Bushnell labored his argument rather heavily.

> Perhaps I shall be understood with the greatest facility if I say that the family is such a body, that a power over character is exerted therein which can not properly be called influence. . . . In maintaining the organic unity of the family, I mean to assert that a power is exerted by parents over children, not only when they teach, encourage, persuade, and govern, but without any purposed control whatever. The bond is so intimate they do it unconsciously and undesignedly—they must do it. Their character, feelings, spirit, and principles must propagate themselves, whether they will or not. However, as influence, in the sense just given, can not be *received* by childhood prior to the age of reason and deliberative choice, the control of parents, purposely expected, must be regarded, during that early period,

as an absolute force, not as influence. All such acts of control, therefore, must, in metaphysical propriety and as far as the child is concerned, be classed under the general denomination of organic causes.[27]

We see therefore that nurture for Bushnell is an organic cause in the Christian home. In this conception he appears to be adding a new catogory to Aristotle's well-known four causes: the material, the formal, the efficient, and the final causes. Bushnell here speaks of another cause, the organic.

The Christian home, Bushnell implies, is a part of the Church, a kind of cell of the Church, as it were a Christian organism. As the Church, being the body of Christ, is a kind of organism in which the Spirit of God is at work; so also the Christian home, being a part of the Church, is an organism in which the Spirit of God is at work. It is quite in order then, within his line of argument, for Bushnell to preach to Christian parents, telling them what they should hope for and anticipate in their children. And so he said to them, for example: "God does expressly lay it upon us to expect that our children will grow up in piety, under the parental nurture, and assume the possibility that such a result may ordinarily be realized."[28] By the word "ordinarily" he apparently means to say "normally"; he does not quite rule out the concept of the automatic, but more cautiously says "ordinarily" children of Christian homes will "grow up in piety."

We will take up just one more point, which is a minor theme in Bushnell's argument. It is that he does strongly imply that the Christian Church is comprised of members which are families as well as members who are individuals. And this is a conception which can bear some attention. Possibly when congregations send their annual statistics to the central offices of their denomination, they should list the number of families as well as the number of individual members, because it is possible, certainly within Bushnell's thesis, that families are members of the Church as well as individuals. In the following he speaks directly concerning this: "The Church life—that is, the Holy Spirit—collects families into a common organism, and then by sanctifying the laws of organic unity in families, extends its quickening power to the generation

[27] *Ibid.*, pp. 76–77.
[28] *Ibid.*, p. 26.

following, so as to include the future, and make it one with the past. And so the church, in all ages, becomes a body under Christ the head. . . ."[29]

COMMENTARY

By way of conclusion, what should be said today in critical evaluation of Bushnell's thesis concerning Christian nurture? Theologically sophisticated though some of us may now be, do we regard Bushnell any more critically than we have in the recent past?

It is not as easy to take Bushnell to task as it might first appear, although it is the conviction of this writer that some criticisms should be made. First of all, the acknowledgment may be necessary that a Christian parent runs the hazard of doing injustice to his own children, were he to say that Bushnell's main thesis was wrong. If they are Christians in their homes, why shouldn't Christian parents expect their children to become like them? Why should they expect them to be devils, delinquents, or hoodlums? Again why shouldn't they expect their children to be reasonably like them? This of course was Bushnell's question. Therefore the hazard in raising one's voice against Bushnell's primary assumption: does the critic show disrespect to his own children by expecting of them something less than Bushnell intended for children of Christian homes? Nevertheless, there are ways of making things right with one's children, and something does need to be said in correction of Bushnell.

Although Bushnell did not so intend it, his argument turns out actually to be more in terms of character and ethics, than it is theological and religious. It is normal that children take on the ways of their parents; but does this fact necessarily make a child of a Christian parent a Christian himself in any deeper sense than having a Christian pattern of life? Just because my child takes on my ways, does this make him a Christian in terms of his theological condition? May Bushnell's position not be the same old hazard that Christian nurture has always faced from the very beginning— namely, slipping away from the teaching of faith to the teaching of morals? The criticism made here is that although Bushnell in-

[29] *Ibid.*, p. 94.

tended to be theological in his argument, he was actually advancing an argument in ethics and morals.

The greatest concern raised by Bushnell's *Christian Nurture* is implicit in his argument rather than explicit. May not the Christian home become a shield or a protective device that shelters a child from facing his own religious and theological crises for himself? Actually the Christian home can be a disadvantage or a handicap to the child, strange as that may seem. Apparently Bushnell ignored this hazard, namely that the Christian home may give birth to second-hand Christians who never come to believe for themselves, but only by way of their parents. May not the concern to reproduce Christian character produce a generation of so-called Christians who are actually pagans although they have a "Christian" gloss? This can be so because they have the outward pattern of life of the Christian without having gone through the crisis of belief and commitment which are at the heart of being a Christian. There are some evidences today that we are now far enough beyond the theological renaissance of the twentieth century that we have students in theological seminaries who want to hold the beliefs of Karl Barth, Emil Brunner, Paul Tillich, and Reinhold or Richard Niebuhr, without going through their theological struggles. But does anyone have the right to think and believe like a Niebuhr, a Barth, or a Brunner unless he also goes through the struggles that brought them to their beliefs? Bushnell's conception of nurture has this very possibility built into it. It can make Christians who in our particular culture are Christians in appearance, but are they really Christian in the deep struggles of the soul which comprise the soil out of which genuine belief grows?

In retrospect, there is ground for fear that this is what we actually have done in the various educational efforts of the Church in recent generations. We may have produced successively a new generation of members who have followed a Christian pattern of life, but who have been religiously and theologically weak. Therefore our lack of depth of faith which some future generation must repair. By conforming to patterns of life, we have lost theological depth, and until some generation goes through the struggles required to recapture this depth, we remain in great need of a vigorous faith.

This raises of course a critical question which if we are to be responsible, should not be posed without being discussed. This we hope to do in some real measure at a later point, when we will take up successively the relation of theology and nurture and of the Bible and nurture.[30] But before these discussions two matters of history yet need our attention; they are the philosophy of John Dewey and the progressive education movement as they have influenced education in the churches, and the religious education movement of the twentieth century. To these two subjects we turn respectively in the next two chapters.

[30] See Chapters 9 and 10.

CHAPTER 7

John Dewey and Progressive Education

The educational philosophy of John Dewey and progressive education have been commonly identified as virtually one and the same thing. This is an oversimplification which needs correction. While the experimentalism of Dewey and progressive education have shared a common spirit and in frequent partnership have comprised the major influence in American education during the first half of the twentieth century, they still are distinct entities and can better be understood if their distinctness is kept clear. The first of these is a philosophy of education; the second a pattern of practice in education, in some cases having philosophic roots and in other cases not. Both the philosophy of John Dewey and progressive education must be included in an overview of the historical development of nurture in the Church, because both made a heavy impact upon the religious education movement.

First of all, some relevant chronological considerations need mention. The earliest progressive schools so-called were in England, not in the United States, as might understandably be assumed to have been the case. Abbotsholme, the first modern experimental school, was established in Derbyshire by Cecil Reddie in 1889, and Bedales, an early successor in the tradition started at Abbotsholme, was founded in 1893 by J. H. Badley, a onetime associate of Cecil Reddie. Were it warranted in relation to the task at hand, a long list of other European progressive schools could be named, ranging in founding dates from 1889 to 1915 and located in France, Germany, England, Switzerland, Holland, and even Russia. The point is that while some American progressive schools were very early, they were not the first. Through the last two decades of the nineteenth century and the first two decades of the twentieth century, progressive schools were being founded here and there both in Europe and the United States. John Dewey's famous Laboratory School in Chicago, while one of the early ones, was not started until 1896.

It is significant that it was prior to the formulation of his educational philosophy that John Dewey established the Laboratory School—significant because the Laboratory School was not an application of his fully formulated philosophy. This experimental school established by Dewey was more likely one of the means he used in finding his way toward his philosophy of education. He sought primarily to do two things in his school. First of all, he attempted to make learning literally a laboratory experience, that is he wanted it to be an experiment for the learner. Only incidentally, it might be said, was it an experiment for the teachers and for the University of Chicago, with which the school was affiliated. Dewey's second intention in his school was to try to form an education in which a strong place would be given to social awareness; Dewey himself was a responsible person socially and was involved in many social action movements. One of his dissatisfactions with education as he found it in traditional schools was that it was separate from social currents, if not actually romantic.

John Dewey's experimentalist philosophy, as over against his Laboratory School, was formed sometime between 1892 and 1916, and probably in a slow, step-by-step evolution of thought. Morton G. White, in his study of the sources of Dewey's instrumentalism, has designated the year 1892 as the time by which Dewey had definitely rejected the idealism of his own tutelage in the University of Vermont and at Johns Hopkins University.[1] In the days of his doctoral studies, as well as during his early years of teaching, his mentor was the idealist, George Sylvester Morris (1840–1889). By 1916 the new philosophy of John Dewey, taking the place of his old idealism, was sufficiently well-formulated that he could publish

[1] *The Origins of Dewey's Instrumentalism*, New York: Columbia University Press, 1943, p. 47.

his now famous book *Democracy and Education.*[2] This book was never revised, is still in print, and is surprisingly relevant even in this atomic and space age four decades later. It is evident that it was no freak of circumstance which made Dewey's thought so widely influential.

This bit of history, if not mere chronicle, has been introduced in order to indicate that there is a separateness and distinctness between the philosophy of John Dewey and the progressive education movement. Progressive education may be characterized, primarily and most correctly, not as a philosophy, but as a practice which was a revolt against formalism in education. This is one of the reasons why it arose in Europe as well as America, for there was a great deal of formalism in European education, especially, as is still true, in the secondary schools. Progressivism was a revolt against this formalism, an attempt to find an educational practice and a spirit for the school which would be less formal.

PROGRESSIVE EDUCATION CHARACTERIZED

Let us move on now from these chronological considerations to present some characterizations of progressive education. No attempt will be made here at completeness; while much more could be said, eight characteristics will be singled out for mention. First of all, progressive education tried to give the student greater freedom than he had in the older schools. This took a variety of forms and in some instances became exaggerated and extreme. Secondly, greater stress was placed on interest and less on discipline when defined as something externally imposed upon the learner. Most progressives believed that learning activities should be interesting for the student. In the third place, progressives had a reluctance about a timetable for classes such as is common in most conventional schools. They believed that the ordering of time in the school should be more flexible.

Fourth and related to this, larger units of work and study were commonly sought by most progressive teachers than can be marked out by class sessions and daily assignments. One of these schools, still thriving today, the Dalton School in New York, plans all pro-

2 New York: Macmillan.

107

grams of study by monthly assignments. Within this plan each child can work at his own pace; the only requirement is that he cannot take up a new month's work until he has finished all assignments for the previous month in his respective courses.

A fifth characterization of progressive education is that it encouraged more overt activity. In progressive schools students were evidently and openly doing things, and more often than not, doing them physically. On the occasion of one visit, the room in which the art department was housed was empty; there were no students there at all! Where were they? Out on the lawn adjacent to the building, sketching the landscape. This was understood as being in perfectly good order. Should a student want to go outside to sketch or paint on a given day, he simply reported in to this effect.

In the sixth place, progressive education has been reluctant about transmission of information. There has been a strong conviction that education should do more for and to the student than give him information. Seventh, progressive education has demonstrated greater discernment of and dependence upon the maturation of the child. Educators have been accused from time to time, and with some justification, of being afraid of the maturation process— afraid, for fear it might show them up as not doing anything to children when they teach them. Accordingly there have been some innovators who have said that we should delay the child's progress in school, instead of hurrying it up, to allow for the child's maturation to take over as a guide. As teachers we need to be humble; we need to recognize that some things do happen by maturation and that we do not bring them about. The progressives, by and large, have been more willing to give this place to maturation than some of our more formal teachers have been.

The eighth and final characteristic is the tendency of progressive education to get beyond the four walls of the school and out into the community. This is an expression of the concern that school life be as informal as possible and that it be consciously rooted in the soil of the human community.

THE PHILOSOPHY OF JOHN DEWEY

Over against progressive education as a practice, we will now set the thought of John Dewey as a philosophy of education. Of

108

course, this philosophy is both complex and profound; it therefore cannot be done justice by a brief statement. Our purpose here, however, is only to suggest its spirit and character as a philosophy of education, and thereby to distinguish it from a movement of experiment and practice such as progressive education. We will deal only with two of its leading characteristics.

First of all, in Dewey there is a redefinition of knowledge and learning. Dewey held that life is episodic; for very good reasons it moves by "flights" and "perchings." It moves by episodes because life is indeterminate and because we are constantly confronted with indeterminate situations causing these episodes to take form. In between we may be able to "perch" or be at rest for a while, depending upon how closely together the crises come.

The educational significance of this is that these episodes are the occasions for knowledge; we get knowledge by following an experimental movement in living through or working out these episodes. In other words, it is by experiment that we cope with indeterminacy. This is actually the heart of the logic of John Dewey, the point at which he made a significant contribution to modern thought. We may need to pause to make this a little clearer. The experimental movement works somewhat in this way: as you face one of these episodes, you are arrested or caught by it and have to find out what it is that is stopping you. Your first discovery is what it is that is wrong; this is the formulation of the problem at hand. Dewey says that as you face this indeterminacy and start to think about it, it begins to come into focus and to take on a definite pattern; thus you see that you have a problem and what it is. And the problem in turn becomes a pattern for further examination of the situation for relevant data of a more detailed character. This is observation of data, as the familiar jargon has made plain, but it is not roaming all over the place seeking out data, both relevant and irrelevant, because the subject is guided by the problem in observing data. The problem gives a focused pattern for the observation.

The problem definition and the data observation, when the latter has proceeded far enough, lead in turn to guesses or suggestions as to what might be a possible solution. These insights, when they emerge, are of course hypotheses to be tested, and it is by testing them that a solution is found and life is made to move smoothly again. But the solution has to meet certain requirements in order to be acceptable, it has to resolve the difficulty totally, not partially. In fact, what is happening psychologically in this movement is that the subject is delaying his response long enough to give a total response instead of a fractional one.

The other demand made by Dewey on the solution is that it must not jeopardize the next episode into which life will move; it must not mortgage the future. If I'm short a hundred dollars on this month's budget, it doesn't help me if I borrow that much money from the bank to pay this month's bills, for in doing so I give myself a handicap for the future. The solution can be neither fractional nor can it put the future at a disadvantage. This is what Dewey meant by experimental movement and also by knowledge. Knowledge and learning both have the pattern of movement just described. They are both experimental; consequently knowledge is always something which is used. In Dewey's thought, knowledge is not true; it only works truly. So much for this first main idea in Dewey, a redefinition of knowledge and learning.

The second main idea is of another sort; it is a redefinition of being. "Being," for Dewey, is not something substantial; he would say it is not "static" or "fixed." For Dewey the only kind of being there is, the background of our human existence, is a fluctuating, moving, changing flow; there are no entities in this, no things which are abiding. Now this is the background for one of the clichés to which Dewey's thought has given rise, namely that all things change. Of course it is as old as Heraclitus (c. 540–470 B.C.). Accordingly we have had a good many books in American education with titles like *Education for a Changing Civilization*.[3] However superficial his followers may have been, Dewey nevertheless faced the ontological problem and asked "What is the nature of being?" He answered this question by saying, "There is no fixed being; everything is flowing and changing." The thing that is important to get here, and which often may be naïvely overlooked, is that Dewey was nontheistic, if not antitheistic, in his ontology. Although he does use the term God in his book, *A Common Faith*,[4] it is an admitted accommodation to the emotional need for religion of many of his readers.

[3] William Heard Kilpatrick, New York: Century, 1926.
[4] New Haven: Yale University Press, 1934.

INFLUENCE ON RELIGIOUS EDUCATION

It may be well to conclude this brief discussion by commenting on the influence of John Dewey and progressive education in religious education. Of course for many years Dewey was read and heard in all quarters, which is not at all surprising. Just read *Democracy and Education*[5] or his logic,[6] and you will discover that this man was not born yesterday. He knew the history of philosophy very well, and he was fully cognizant of what he was saying in the light of it. He was not a superficial American who spoke with an ocean between himself and Europe. Yet he was even more radical and revolutionary than he appears to be on first reading. It is no accident that he was broadly read and listened to not only in the United States, but also in Japan, China, and Russia. His thought was pervasive, and its influence is still very strong, although we are passing out of the period of his ascendancy in the United States.

There were notable interpreters in religious education, as in secular education, who quite sincerely, but often naïvely, gave a confused expression to his philosophy; among these were George Albert Coe and Harrison Elliott. The influence of progressive education also came into religious education through such leaders and the new way of doing things. But in addition it was in the air; it was the spirit of the times. One aspect of this and other influences abroad in the 1920's and 1930's, believe it or not, was that professors of religious education were the top men on the totem pole in many theological seminaries. It was assumed by many that it was religious education that was going to make the new generation and thereby save the world. This was a very different world than the one we live in now, in which theology is in the ascendancy and the lowly religious educator plays second fiddle to almost everyone else. Protestantism at that time, and a good segment of Judaism, tried to be up-to-date, and this meant very largely following Dewey in thought and adoption of progressive practice insofar as it was understood.

In concluding this chapter three examples of this tendency will be given. First of all, the free use of arts and crafts in the early days

---

[5] New York: Macmillan, 1916.
[6] *Logic, The Theory of Inquiry*, New York: Henry Holt, 1938.

111

of the Vacation Church School, with little reference to what was being studied, was an early, if corrupt, adaptation of the so-called new education. A second example was the problem approach in curriculum writing. This is still practiced with a fuller rationale in some curriculums, but go back a few years and you can find all kinds of curriculum units that followed the problem approach as though it were an orthodoxy. The accepted method was to begin the unit with some problem that the children for whom the material was prepared would supposedly face, and then to turn to the Bible for the answer to the problem. It was a somewhat corrupt version of Dewey; nevertheless this was its source. The third and final example is the use of the unit and the project in building curriculum as well as in planning methods. Both the unit and the project have their values and are valid when properly used, as will be shown later;[7] therefore no deprecation of them is intended in pointing out that their source was in progressive education and the philosophy of John Dewey.

[7] See pp. 259–261.

CHAPTER *8*

The Religious Education Movement
and Its Sequels

*T*he religious education movement of the twentieth century had several antecedents, four of which will be mentioned specifically. The first was the Sunday School movement which was discussed in Chapter 4. The second was the nineteenth century psychological movement, particularly the educational theory of Pestalozzi and Froebel of which study has also been made earlier. Direct connection has already been made specifically between Pestalozzi and Froebel on the one hand, and, on the other, the accumulation of sufficient child-study interest in the Sunday School movement to bring about the clamor for closely graded lessons. The third antecedent was the thought of Horace Bushnell, more especially his famous book, *Christian Nurture*, and the liberal movement in theology of the nineteenth and early twentieth centuries. The fourth of these antecedents of the religious education movement was the philosophy of John Dewey and progressive education, discussed in the immediately preceding chapter.

THE RELIGIOUS EDUCATION ASSOCIATION

The religious education movement was in a great measure symbolized and given concreteness by the formation of the Religious Education Association and its achievement of wide acceptance and popularity among professionals and within the councils of various faiths and communions. The Religious Education Association was formed in 1903 with a no less distinguished person than William

113

Rainey Harper, onetime president of the University of Chicago, as one of its leading sponsors and founders. The original intentions of the organization were expressed as follows: "To inspire the religious forces of our country with the educational ideal; to inspire the educational forces of our country with the religious ideal; and to keep before the public mind the ideal of moral and religious education and the sense of its need and value."[1] The Association is an inter-faith organization; it is not Protestant alone, as was the case with the International Council of Religious Education and is also now the case with its successor, the Division of Christian Education of the National Council of Churches. The Religious Education Association has always had Roman Catholics and Jews among its members, and whenever it has held conventions, there have always been strong representations from Catholicism and Judaism, as well as from various Protestant denominations.

The journal of the Association is *Religious Education*. It has been published continuously for more than fifty years—a significant achievement since this journal represents the only approximation of a research journal in the field of religious education. For a number of years regular features of the journal have been résumés of significant findings and reprintings of abstracts of doctoral dissertations in religious education and associated fields. Had the Religious Education Association not done anything else during its existence since 1903, it would have been important for its contribution in the continuing publication of this journal.

The Religious Education Association has had varying fortunes through the years. The days of its beginning, just after the turn of the century, constituted of course a period of ascendancy. But all of its history has not been of this high level of strength and hope. Since World War II its major trend has been to give special attention to higher education, and it has been facilitated in this endeavor by some special grants. The Jubilee Convention held in Pittsburgh in 1953, celebrating the fiftieth anniversary of the Association, was attended by a large representation of religious leaders, and some very significant seminars constituted the major part of the program there. But the resources of the organization have always been comparatively small, and its eventual strength and his-

[1] "Purpose of the Convention," *Religious Education*, Vol. I, No. 1, (April, 1906), p. 2.

toric significance will be determined more, in all probability, by the currents of theological thought as they bear upon religious education, than by promotional efforts of the Association itself. This is indicated in part, as will be pointed out later, by the fact that the religious education movement tended for many years to gravitate away from historic religious traditions.

To take up another aspect of the religious education movement, comparable to the formation of the Religious Education Association, is to mention the ascendancy of departments of religious education in colleges and theological seminaries as an expression of the popular acceptance and growth of the movement. The great popular hope of the Protestant Church, if not also of the Synagogue, in the first three decades of the twentieth century was in making a new generation by religious education. Roman Catholicism probably was not as strongly moved by this hope, although for centuries it had placed great confidence in instruction. This was a false hope, as we can now see more clearly, but it was nevertheless the great hope of the more romantic early twentieth century. Students of the present generation may not be able to believe it, but in some of our theological seminaries during this period professors of religious education were considered the men of the hour. They were the ones who were on the wave of the future. It would be hard to say what wave they are on now, but it certainly isn't the wave of the future, so different is the picture at the present time. Wherever the stream of this particular history is flowing, it is clear that the present generation is not the early twentieth century which spawned the religious education movement.

SOME CHARACTERISTICS OF THE RELIGIOUS EDUCATION MOVEMENT

By way of indicating some of the trends which have brought us to the present situation, mention should be made of some of the distorted emphases which the religious education movement either encouraged or espoused. For example, there was the assumption that we can form the new generation of Christians or Jews by what we do in education in the Church or the Synagogue respectively. This was one of the common emphases, and it is still present, for example, in the Character Research Project. Professor Ernest Ligon,

115

a devout man of unquestioned sincerity and earnestness, has built the rather fabulous research enterprise comprising the Character Research Project with assiduous effort and heavy foundation investment over a period of more than two decades. One of the presuppositions lying beneath this project is that we can form character by a kind of refined conditioning process practiced in the home, church, synagogue, or character-building agency.

Another emphasis was an overly optimistic view about man. The religious education movement had a doctrine of man, sometimes openly stated, sometimes unconsciously assumed, which did not jibe very closely with traditional doctrines of man held by the Church. A third distortion was a lessened emphasis on the Bible. Now this had to come no doubt as a corrective of an earlier distorted emphasis on the Bible; nevertheless the lessening of emphasis was also a distortion. Extra-biblical material was often as much a source for so-called "religious teaching" as the Bible. And a fourth distortion, closely related to the third, was a lessened emphasis upon the person of Christ. Being less certain in that period concerning our beliefs about Jesus, we resorted to heavy emphasis on the teachings of Jesus and the principles of Jesus, bypassing or de-emphasizing christology. Some of these distortions, exemplified by the four just mentioned, were intentional and deliberate on the part of some leaders, but more often they were accepted as the result of a superficial followership. These were expressions of the mode of the time, and we all know how easy it is to fall into the mode when everyone else is following it. That is to say that it was with full knowledge on the part of some, but with an unperceptive followership on the part of many that these distortions became popular. It should be said that there were some—not all of them inert conservatives—who perceptively saw the trend and held back but they constituted a very small minority. It would seem that it can be said with some degree of objectivity that as the religious education movement approached the midpoint of the twentieth century, its development was such as would almost inevitably invite some reaction. To say this and enlarge upon criticism of the religious education movement is to turn from a more or less objective discussion of the movement to the expression of judgments and an assessment of the present condition of religious education today.

THE RETURN TO THEOLOGY

The correction which actually did come may be characterized as a return to theology. This is not to say that the return has been adequate, but only to indicate the direction the correction has taken. Indeed, as far as the Protestant Church is concerned, there was a return by a major segment of the Church to theology, beginning in the 1930's and influenced largely by such leaders as Karl Barth and Emil Brunner in Europe and the two Niebuhrs in this country. The return to a greater concern for theology was not as strong among religious educators as in the Church at large; nevertheless the trend was somewhat evident there too.

It is very difficult to indicate in substance, and particularly in any brief compass, what this change in religious thought was. Since the beginning of the theological revival of the twentieth century, there have been so many different voices among the theologians, disparate and at times even contradictory. Even so we will state two themes which have at least been central in the theological renaissance of this century, acknowledging that they have many variations; it is quite beyond the history being depicted in this chapter to attempt to state the latter.

The two main themes to which we refer are the doctrine of man and christology. Over against the optimism and hope of the nineteenth century and the few years of the twentieth century before the First World War, the new theology insisted upon the depravity of man, although not precisely in the formulas of the sixteenth and seventeenth centuries. Beginning most especially with Karl Barth (1886–   ), trust in man's native goodness, hope in his ability to work out his own salvation, and belief in human progress were all abandoned. The fact of sin in man and in the human predicament was again cited in this rigorous realism about man. And we were again reminded that sin is not only a psychological and sociological fact, but a deep theological disjointedness between man and God.

Also, in contrast to the vague mysticism, and even pantheism, of the idealism and liberal theology of the nineteenth and early twentieth centuries—which was accompanied by vacillation and uncertainty as to who Jesus was—the new theology reasserted the belief that Jesus was the Christ, the Living Word proclaimed in the written word of the Bible, the Son of God by whom alone God

117

can be known and apart from whom there is no knowledge of God.

To state these two major theological themes in the way it has been done here, has been actually to imply a third theme; that is the revival of the understanding of the Bible as in some way the Word of God. This did not naïvely ignore the critical and scientific study of the Bible which began seriously in the nineteenth century and continues unabated. Rather, at the same time that this critical study was still regarded with utmost seriousness, the Bible was conceived primarily as the Word of God to man, and no longer as the record of man's search for God.

To come back now from this digression, sampling some of the themes of the theological renaissance of our century, we must pick up again the last link of the primary sequence of this chapter. This is the beginning of a return to theology in the religious education movement, however feeble and fumbling, which has been one characteristic of this movement in the middle decades of the twentieth century. Possibly the first most vigorous sign of this return in religious education was the publication in 1941 of a book by H. Shelton Smith entitled *Faith and Nurture*.[2] Professor Smith had been active in the religious education movement for almost two decades before this book was published. He had been Director of Leadership Education in the International Council of Religious Education (1923–1928) before becoming a professor first at the college level and then, for most of his career, in the divinity school.[3] Early in the 1930's he experienced a crisis in his thinking as a result of serious study of John Dewey. This crisis was for him the discovery that either he must turn his back on the Church and follow the philosophy of Dewey or if he were to remain in the Church, reject Dewey's thought. He made his decision in favor of the second alternative and proceeded to rethink his entire approach to religious education in this light. Eventually this radical new departure resulted in his writing the book, *Faith and Nurture*, which criticized the religious education movement, and created a storm among his professional associates in the field. His reading public

[2] New York: Scribner's, 1941.
[3] He was associate Professor of Religious Education at Teachers College, Columbia University 1928–1929; Associate Professor of Religious Education, the Divinity School, Yale University 1929–1931; and Professor in Duke University since 1931. For a number of years previous to his retirement in 1960, he was professor of American Religious Thought and Director of Graduate Studies in Religion in Duke University.

was waiting for the constructive volume it was assumed would follow *Faith and Nurture*, and reportedly he had a standing offer from the publishers for such a volume. So far, however, it has not appeared. Nevertheless, *Faith and Nurture* was historic in that it was the first major expression of discontent with the nontheological, if not antitheological, spirit of religious education up to that point in the twentieth century.

The International Council of Religious Education set up a committee in 1944 to inquire into the educational and theological foundations of Christian education, among other circumstances of the post-war situation. This Committee made its report in 1947, much of which is included in an unofficial but quite accurate statement in the book *The Church and Christian Education*, Chapter 2, "The Foundations of Christian Education."[4] This statement was more theological than educational; if it was lacking in profoundness and penetration, this may be explained by its being a composite statement made by a group of different denominational representatives. Such statements, for expedient reasons, have to be reasonably satisfactory to all, and consequently at some points can say no more than some believe thus, while others hold different positions. Even so, this report constituted another effort on the part of religious educators to recognize some responsibility to have theological presuppositions underlying their practice.

A still further move in the direction of theological responsibility was the launching of somewhat radical new departures in the curriculum of Christian education. One matter of secondary importance, here, but something that should not be overlooked, is that these departures came denominationally and not interdenominationally. But certain denominations felt that they were ready to make the changes and fortuitously found the kind of leadership which enabled them to launch out in radically new curriculum ventures. *The Faith and Life Curriculum* of the Presbyterian Church U.S.A.[5] was the first of these ventures. Paul Calvin Payne, who was General Secretary of the Board of Christian Education of that denomination, apprised the International Council of Religious Education of the departure being made in this new curriculum to point out clearly that it was not a narrowly denominational effort

[4] Paul H. Vieth, ed., St. Louis: Bethany Press, 1947.
[5] The denomination is now the United Presbyterian Church, U.S.A.

119

which ran counter to the spirit of interdenominational cooperation and ecumenical endeavor.

The study and thought which eventually produced *The Faith and Life Curriculum* began as an intensified effort by 1940, but the curriculum did not make its appearance in print until 1948. Among other things, it was an attempt to give theological vigor and authenticity to the curriculum of Christian education in this particular denomination. Another major concern was to deal with the Bible responsibly, in the light of the critical study of the Bible which has been carried forward for a century now, but of which the Church at large has been almost completely ignorant. It also had other concerns; e.g., the hope to restore the family as an institution of Christian nurture, and the assumption that hard-back books, which could compete in the children's book market because they are of the same caliber as books being sold in the trade, are the kind of religious books that a child will want to keep. It was hoped in this connection, that instead of throwing such a book away, as often happened with the old curriculum materials even before the youngster got home from church, the child might enjoy reading these books and want to keep them. Here again, the major concerns of this curriculum comprised another sign of the times, symptomatic of a return to theology—an attempt to make a curriculum that had some real theological depth.

A second of these new departures in curriculum, followed more recently by several others, came a few years later in the Protestant Episcopal Church; it was the Seabury Curriculum, the earliest parts of which were published in 1955. This curriculum was a similar endeavor to produce study materials for the Church which were more an expression of the thought and life of the Church than were previously available. In connection with this curriculum, six background volumes[6] were published which were not an integral part of the curriculum itself but which, it was hoped, would become possessions of every home. With these volumes in every home and with the family studying to fulfill its teaching function, back-

---

[6] Robert C. Dentan, *The Holy Scriptures: A Survey*, 1949; Powell Mills Dawley, *Chapters in Church History*, 1950; James A. Pike and W. Norman Pittenger, *The Faith of the Church*, 1951; Massey H. Shepherd, Jr., *The Worship of the Church*, 1952; Powell Mills Dawley, *The Episcopal Church and Its Work*, 1955; Stephen F. Bayne, Jr., *Christian Living*, 1957; all published by Seabury Press, Greenwich, Connecticut.

ground could be provided for much that goes on in the church school and at the same time the alert layman could be given some authentic understanding of his Church and its faith.

Lastly, in trying to depict the return to theology in religious education in the recent past and the present generation, allusion will be made to some other writings expressing this trend. Randolf Crump Miller of Yale Divinity School has two such books, *The Clue to Christian Education*[7] and *Biblical Theology in Christian Education*,[8] both of which argue for more theology in the curriculum. *The Clue to Christian Education*, for example, takes up successively different doctrines of the Church and shows how they can be taught at different age-levels. James Smart, who was the first editor-in-chief of *The Faith and Life Curriculum*, published a book in 1954 entitled *The Teaching Ministry of the Church*,[9] making the case for theology with even greater vigor and emphasis. Dr. Smart argues that the issue between the theologians and religious educators will have to be more sharply drawn than it has been and theology taken more seriously by religious educators, before things can get better. He further argues in this book that Christian education should be considered a discipline of theology and that it will not come into its valid place in the life of the Church until this is the case. In the time intervening until now, a number of similar books have been coming from the presses.[10]

This chapter may be concluded, not inappropriately, by an attempt to assess the present situations in religious education. It yet remains for this generation or its successors to explore thoroughly the possible continuity between theology and nurture, building responsible theory in the light of such a continuum and putting it to work in effective practice. This is to say that the issue is not yet clearly drawn and therefore no clear resolution is yet on the horizon. The problem of the relation of theology and religious education is far more than how to put theological content into the curriculum. It is the discussion of this larger question which will be taken up in the next chapter.

[7] New York: Scribner's, 1950.
[8] New York: Scribner's, 1956.
[9] Philadelphia: Westminster.
[10] See for example Iris V. Cully, *The Dynamics of Christian Education*, Philadelphia: Westminster, 1958, and Allen O. Miller, *Invitation to Theology*, Philadelphia: Christian Education Press, 1958.

CHAPTER 9

Theology, Philosophy of Education, and Nurture

WHAT IS THEOLOGY?

*H*aving spent some time now in surveying the historical development of nurture and education in the Church, we must return to our place of beginning in the Church before carrying our thought further. We said in the first chapter that the Church in any generation is the necessary point of departure in faith. We attempted to understand the nature of the Church, and we attempted to derive an understanding of nurture from the nature of the Church. The task now is to focus upon a predominantly intellectual aspect of the Church and of faith, namely the kind of thought which is necessary both to the Church and to faith. We want to consider what this thought is—its status and its function, particularly in relation to the teaching task. This brings us to the major subject to be taken up first: what is theology?

There are at least two ways in which theology can be defined, that is, two ways contingent upon the question as to whether theology is a process or a substance. We will take up both of these definitions, but first of all the substantive definition of theology. Theology can most easily be defined as substantive; indeed it is more commonly and more popularly defined in this way. According to this definition it is a body of doctrine comprising the content of the Faith. With this substantive aspect in mind, we can say that the task of theology is to infer the explicit meaning of the Faith from the events of revelation and from the literature of revelation, the Bible. More naïvely this definition of theology can be made to mean, indeed it is commonly made to mean, that theology is a more or less fixed body of truth which is passed on from one generation of believers to the next. This is the popularly received understanding of theology; nevertheless it is only one way of looking at theology, and possibly not the primary way.

Let us change the attempt to define theology now from a substantive view of it to theology as a process or discipline. We might allude to the substantive definition of theology as dealing with theology as a noun; theology as process is to deal with it as a verb, as action or movement. This way of defining theology is to lay more weight on the function of theologizing than upon the substantive yield of this process. It is a less common definition and a somewhat more difficult and hazardous one. According to this way of defining it, theology is the thinking of the Faith. It is an intellectual discipline in which the Church must continually engage in order for the Faith to be first of all an immediate faith and not a second-hand faith. It is necessary also in order to restate, to redefine, and to defend the Faith against the characteristic forms of heresy and unbelief peculiar to particular generations. The important thing for our concern and the most relevant consideration in relation to nurture is that theology is an active discipline, an active responsibility of the Church. It is something the Church does and not just the content which the Church transmits. At this point this understanding of theology can shed a great deal of light upon the relation between theology and nurture, disclosing that it is much more than putting theological content into teaching, important as that may be. If a connection is made between the thinking responsibility of the Church and the teaching responsibility of the Church, a significantly broad spectrum is provided in which to view nurture.

Returning for a moment to the substantive aspect of theology, the definition can be made more concrete if we now indicate the kind of structure a theology commonly has. There are several major themes with which theology commonly deals, determined chiefly by the concern that theology be derived from the original events of revelation and from the Bible as the literature of revelation. While these major subjects are necessarily given an order in this presentation, no particular significance is intended by the order. Theology is of course concerned with God, the derivation of the word theology indicates this; most theologies therefore have a doctrine of God. Christ is a major concern in Christian theology, and so most Christian theologies have a Christology. Theology is also very commonly concerned with the Holy Spirit; therefore two other subjects common to it are the doctrine of the Holy Spirit and the doctrine of the Trinity. Since theology views the world or universe as a created order, not a happenstance, and man as a creature intended by a Creator, not a gratuitous accident, most theologies therefore have a doctrine of creation. Also theology regards God as somehow initiating the knowledge of himself made possible to man, in contradistinction to the idea that God is an object to be discovered, as it were, by scientific investigation; most theologies therefore have a doctrine of revelation. Since man himself is a subject with which theology is perennially concerned, there is a segment of theology known as anthropology or doctrine of man—not the science of anthropology, although there is of course a connection between the two. In fact doctrine of man, as has been noted, has been a focus of the thought that has marked the revival of theology in the last three or four decades. There has been the conviction on the part of many that the gateway to any profound theology must be an adequate and realistic doctrine of man. Doctrines of man in theology, in their turn, are commonly arrested by the sin into which man falls with such great ease, if not by a determined recalcitrance; consequently another major subject in theology is doctrine of sin. But sin must have its antidote, as theology views it, in a conquest of man's perennial predicament by the saving action of God; therefore two other major preoccupations, the doctrines of atonement and redemption. Theologies in this generation are also commonly concerned about the last things, that is about the consummation of the whole human process, and so there is the subject of eschatology. And to mention one final doctrine, in as much as there is greater realization today of the need for an adequate theology of the Church, another subject which has emerged in theology and has received great emphasis is doctrine of the Church.

We have done no more here than indicate structure and the reason for doing this, in addition to enlarging the definition of theology, is that as we turn to philosophy and philosophy of education, we have to indicate a rather different kind of structure. By focusing attention upon structure, we do not mean to lay heavier stress upon the substantive definition of theology than on the process definition; in fact the intention is to lay heavier emphasis on the process or disciplinary definition. It is also necessary in order to make a valid comparison and contrast with philosophy. Philosophy has a rather different kind of structure from theology, and this observation is not based on the common assumption that theology is theocentric and philosophy is anthropocentric. At best such an assumption is a superficial distinction, and we hope to make the comparison and contrast somewhat more adequate by indicating the different kinds of structure and the reason for the differences in the differing sources.

PHILOSOPHY AND PHILOSOPHY OF EDUCATION

Philosophy derives its nature and structure from the categories of the human mind; or stated more loosely, philosophy derives its nature and structure from the ways in which the human mind works. By contrast theology derives its nature and consequently its structure from the events of revelation and the literature of revelation, the Bible.[1] This is to say something other than that philosophy is necessarily anthropocentric and theology theocentric. Whatever the persisting questions are which the human mind must ask, these are the questions of philosophy. These questions of course are many, and they change their direction as new generations meet new conditions. The generation just now emerging may possibly

[1] Some qualification of this statement needs to be made, since it cannot be pursued further in the text. In this portion of the present chapter there is occasional reference to this characteristic of theology, namely, that it derives its structure from the events of revelation. This is not literally true historically, however urgent it is now considered as a norm for the discipline of theology. In the history of Christian thought almost up to the present time, reason and the logical constructs of ancient philosophy, particularly those of Plato and Aristotle, have played upon the Bible and the original events of revelation to yield a kind of "logical" form or system for theology. In the present century more than ever before, with partial exceptions noted for Luther and Calvin, theologians have been striving to break out of this circle of a borrowed logical system. The point of this striving is to build theology so that it does derive singularly from the events of revelation, without benefit of logical forms which are "secular" in their origins. It is therefore in the normative sense that theology ought to derive its structures from the events of revelation that the distinction made in the text should be understood more precisely. It is not a completely accurate description of what theology has actually succeeded in doing up to this time.

125

see significant changes in the direction of these questions because of the remarkably different world the electronic and space age may bring. It is not likely however that the fundamental questions will change materially; these questions, many and varied though they are, tend to cluster around three major concerns and in all likelihood will continue to do so. The first of these three major questions is, "What is reality?" This is the metaphysical question, the parent metaphysical question, around which and under which a host of other questions cluster. The second major question is, "How do I know when I know?" And this is another parent question or pole around which many others cluster. This is the question of epistemology, "How do I know when any alleged knowledge is true?" And the third of these questions is, "What is the nature of value and how are values achieved or possessed?" This has clustered about it many axiological questions and implies many fields of value—for instance, esthetics, ethics, economics in its value aspects, and similarly politics and education in addition to many other value fields. These three major questions are the parent questions in philosophy indicative of its structure. This is a clearly different structure from that of theology, which derives its nature from revelation; by contrast these questions are derived from the yearnings, the perplexities, and the speculations of the human mind.

Let us now go on to consider the structure of philosophy of education. Philosophy of education is the discipline by which philosophic penetration and responsibility are brought to bear upon education. Philosophy of education is not the application of philosophy to education—that is, as though there were certain general findings that philosophy makes and then these are worked out in education. It may be well to begin in philosophy of education as people commonly do with questions concerning educational objectives such as "What are we about in education?" Or to focus on the function of the educational institution in society, the question is commonly stated as "Why does the school exist?" But in order to blossom into a philosophy of education, this pursuit needs to follow these questions to their roots in the whole range of value theory, theory of reality, and theory of knowledge.[2] This is one

[2] See the author's book, *Four Philosophies and Their Practice in Education and Religion*, rev. ed., New York: Harper, 1957. In chap. 23, "Building a

place at which educators and religious educators do not go deeply enough; they too commonly assume that they can deal responsibly with principles of education and principles of religious education without reference to philosophy or theology. The assumption apparently made is that theology and philosophy can be screened off on one side as separate disciplines, with operation at the other side as a separate practice, and somewhere in between is a kind of twilight area which, also reasonably distinct, can be designated as the principles of education or the principles of religious education. An assumption which is more nearly correct is that there is no such intermediate area as principles of education or principles of religious education. Once we leave operation sufficiently to theorize about it or even if we theorize right in the midst of operation, there is no stopping point for responsible theory without going clear over into full fledged theoretical considerations, philosophy of education, philosophy of religious education, and theology.

But the point of the entire discussion in this section is to make a tenable distinction between theology and philosophy of education. We have stated that theology begins with revelation, not with revelation as an idea, but with the empirical historical events of revelation. As we have said, it has a certain characteristic structure which is determined by its beginning at this point. Philosophy, on the other hand, begins with the questions of the human mind and because it begins here, it also has a certain characteristic structure. Now both deal with very much the same subject matter, but they deal with it in different ways—not from different points of view so much as from different points of departure. The concern of theology with the doctrine of God or with the doctrine of the Trinity and the concern of philosophy with metaphysics, for example, are concerns which necessarily converge.

It is therefore a mistake to make the easy distinction that theology is theocentric and philosophy is anthropocentric. Theology is sometimes anthropocentric, possibly without intending to be. In a similar way biblical studies are often anthropocentric. The human categories we sometimes impose upon the Bible in the name of

---

Philosophy of Education," this argument has been stated more fully, showing how the more common questions the layman asks concerning education necessarily lead into a rather fully conceived philosophy of education if the attempt to answer these questions is thoroughly serious.

biblical studies, assuming that these categories are implicit in the biblical writings, are rather surprising. Scholarship has not reached a very high level of sophistication when it proceeds on the assumption that theology believes in revelation and philosophy does not believe in it. It may be true of course that a majority of secular philosophers do not believe in revelation. While it may be necessary for a theologian to believe in some kind of revelation, it does not follow that a philosopher, as a philosopher, does not believe in revelation. There is no reason why, in answer to some of the questions which philosophy raises, particularly the epistemological question, there cannot be recourse to revelation in making answer. There is nothing necessary in philosophy which demands the exclusion of revelation. It is a more fair and more accurate distinction, therefore, to say that these two disciplines work from different starting points—theology beginning with the events of revelation and philosophy beginning with the questions of the human mind— but that the two disciplines converge at many points in the subject matter with which they deal.

THEOLOGY IN THE CONTENT OF TEACHING IN THE CHURCH

Theology certainly has a place in the content of teaching in the Church. Primarily, the content of written curriculum and classroom teaching in the Church school should be biblical, theological, and historical. While this does not exclude so-called secular material, it does say that primarily the content should be derived from the bible, doctrine, and the history of the Church. To single out the one of these with which we are primarily concerned here, this means that in curriculum writing and in teaching, great effort must be devoted to making theological concepts meaningful to children at their respective age-levels. Within this particular and somewhat limited context, the relation of theology and the content of teaching, it is fitting to put the doctrines of the Church in such form that children of respective ages can have authentic understanding of them, however fractional this understanding may be.[3]

[3] See Randolph Crump Miller, *The Clue to Christian Education*, New York: Scribner's, 1950. Dr. Miller is quite correct in his insistence that we recognize that one of our concerns is the relation of theology and the content of teaching. The hazard is that this concern will be substituted for the larger

In this connection there are two imperatives which must be taken fully into account. The first is that we must learn as much as we can regarding the conceptual capacity of children at different age-levels and keep abreast of this knowledge. This is a point at which we must borrow from psychology. It is important that we know growth and development with sufficient precision that we can effectively take into account the conceptual capacities of children and youth at their respective levels of development.[4]

The second imperative, a counterpart to the first, is that we must study the presentation of ideas most especially at lower age-levels, to make sure that we do not water them down or rob them of their authenticity. And this is an imposingly difficult problem, one that constantly hounds the curriculum writers when they become aware of it, as many of them are.

To give examples, as is of course necessary, may be to become trite and is certainly to compound the difficulty. To make the plunge anyway, we may say that Jesus Christ as Lord does not equal Jesus the good friend, the Jesus of so many children's acquaintance. One of our editors of curriculum materials has said that Jesus the good friend is a monster; he is not to be found in the Bible. Here is the problem exemplified. How do you deal with Jesus Christ in literature for younger children so that an authentic, if not an adequate, Christology is expressed? Another example is the tragedy of the death of Christ. The tragedy of death and the glory of resurrection do not equal life without death, death without tragedy, or a resurrection which somehow bypasses this tragic element. This is easy to say, but it is another thing to translate such meanings of the Christian faith as this to the conceptual level of the small child without robbing them of their authenticity and validity.

Having said that there should be theological content in the teaching of the Church, let us go on to consider what the function of theology is in the content of teaching. Primarily there are two

---

and fuller concern for the relation of theology as such and nurture as such. This will be taken up later in the present discussion.

[4] See Chapters 13 and 14 which deal more fully with the enlightenment which the teaching ministry of the Church can gain from the science of psychology. At this point reference is made only to growth and development—in fact to only one aspect of it, namely, conceptual development.

things to be said about this. The teaching of a theological content is not to the end that the learner may have a set of intellectual formulations to which he can tie himself for life as though these formulations were absolute. This is not the primary function of theological content in the curriculum or in teaching. And because of this the teaching of a catechism may actually miscarry and not have results which are essentially harmonious with faith. Many adults have rationalized such teaching by admitting that when they learned the catechism as a child, they didn't know what it meant, but claiming that in their adult life, when problems and crises arose, their memory of the catechism gave them a ready answer to their problems, which was such a release and such a security! While there may be some value in this, it is open to suspicion. May it not reveal that they were too much the child at the time the instruction was given, and also that they may still be more a child than an adult, if the ready answer provides them with a quick way out of difficulty? Instead, should they not be showing the responsibility of making a more mature answer? Again, the primary function of theological content is not to provide a set of absolute formulations to which to tie for all time. This is at least an approximation of idolatry, not theology, and is not the basis of the Christian faith.

We have stated negatively what the function of theology is not, let us now try to state affirmatively what the function of theology is. Theological content in teaching gives the learner the symbols of the Faith, thereby enabling him to join in the thinking of the Faith with the community of Faith. In other words, by the teaching of theology, koinonia may come to have for the individual believer an intellectual aspect as well as emotional and volitional aspects. Too commonly in our Protestant Christianity here in the United States, if not in other parts of the world, we have conceived koinonia in emotional and volitional terms and have neglected, except for superficial transmission of ideas, its intellectual aspect. If the community of faith feels the Faith and acts the Faith, it must certainly also think the Faith. And the primary reason for having theological content in the curriculum is to give historic perspective for faith and the language of faith, thereby enabling people of different ages to enter into the intellectual aspect of the koinonia.

130

THE CONTINUITY BETWEEN THEOLOGY AND NURTURE

We have tried to define theology and philosophy and have discussed theology in the content of teaching, the latter subject reflecting the extent of the advance which Christian education has made in relating theology and teaching. In attempting to venture beyond this point, we would now like to consider whether there is some continuity between theology and nurture. The question we are raising is this: Is there any necessary connection between theology and nurture in the Faith apart from the reasonable requirement that the content of Christian teaching be theological? The argument which is proposed here is that there is, and we are going to attempt to show that this is a necessary interrelationship.

Theology in the active and more dynamic sense is thinking the Faith. Is this not what our forebears were doing when they gave to the Church and succeeding generations theological formulations and writings? For instance, in the early ecumenical councils of the Church, were not our ancient forebears thinking the Faith when they were writing their creeds? And in a sense was not thinking the Faith prior in their concern to giving succeeding generations a creed? Is this not what Augustine was doing when he was writing *The City of God*? Was he not thinking the Faith? Also, was this not true for Saint Thomas in writing the *Summa Theologica* and the *Summa Contra Gentiles*? May not the same be said of Calvin and his *Institutes* and of the different confessional statements of the Church such as the Westminster Standards? Are these not instances of believers seeking to be intellectually responsible and feeling some debt to the Church and some imperative for the Church, and therefore primarily thinking the Faith? Now regarding such writings as these that have gone before us, is their value for us primarily in what they say, or is their value rather in that these formulations and confessions engage us in the great theological conversation in the Church, a conversation which always points us to the living God, but never contains him in formula? This last is important, for these formulas, such as the creeds, are intended to point us to God, but they are not intended to contain God.

What has been said so far is that theology is the Church thinking the Faith. And now this statement can be paralleled by a companion statement to the effect that nurture is the Church communicating the Faith. These are companion functions, they are both active processes, and they are both focused existentially in the Faith. This is the point at which significant continuity can be found, one blending into the other. There is no communicating the Faith without thinking the Faith, and in a sense there is no thinking the Faith without communicating the Faith; they are continuous. Whenever the Church arises to its true genius, it both thinks the Faith and communicates the Faith. And in the context of this interrelationship attention is now focused on communicating the Faith.

In part and at a minimum, communicating the Faith is necessarily the passing on of a heritage or tradition of theology. The institution recorded in Deuteronomy of the fathers telling the children on feast days of past deliverances, the early Christian *Didache*, Calvin's *Instruction in the Faith*, and the different catechisms—at the minimum, and in some very essential part beyond this—all of these are the passing on of a heritage or a tradition of theology.

But is this transmission so much a matter of giving to the new generation set formulations to be implicitly accepted, as it is making available to the new generation that which is needed for believing and thinking one's belief? What is it that is needed for believing and thinking one's belief? The whole context of the thought of the Church in its historic dimension is needed. The literature of revelation, the Bible, is needed. The symbols of the conversation of faith, found in theology, are needed. And these are made available in this transmission of the theological tradition and the heritage in essence. This is not to say that this was the extent of the intention of our forebears in transmitting the heritage. As they passed on a heritage, they may have thought that this was something that was to be implicitly believed in every detail. But regardless of what they intended, even so were they not providing what is needed in order for a person to believe and in order for a person to think his belief? While we must teach content, this is a means to an end; the teaching of content can never be an end in itself. This same argument can be offered for every area of knowledge: that is, that content is never an end in itself, it is always a means to something else. And as far as the content of the Christian Faith is concerned, it is a means to the end of contemporaneous revelation. This content is the theology of past and present, true enough, but its primary intentions are that God may speak to us now and that we may theologize in the present. It may be that our predecessors did not make these their primary intentions as they built theological formulations, but in historic perspective, was not the prior intention, behind their conscious intention, that they might respond to God in their time?

We may now put what we have been saying about continuity between theology and nurture in a kind of formula by saying that revelation is revelation-to-communication, a single continuum, and similarly that theology is theology-to-nurture, also a single continuum.

PHILOSOPHY OF CHRISTIAN EDUCATION: THE NEED OF THE MINISTRY

In contending that the minister needs a philosophy of education, the reference is to the professionally trained, if not ordained, minister. The ministry is also conceived as one ministry, but as having a plurality of functions within its unity. The contention is that there is an urgent need for a unified approach to the educational task of the Church on the part of the minister. In one sense at least, the minister's theology and his philosophy are tools by which or with which he approaches his work as a minister; they are not in the first instance something which he teaches or preaches. They constitute the structure of his own ideology by which he goes about doing what he does. Actually few ministers, ministers of education, and directors of Christian education have such a unified approach. Evidence for this statement can be found in perusal of the catalogue of sermons the pulpit minister preaches over any extended period of time. They are not likely to hang together nor constitute a unity; they say a good many different things, some of which are contradictory. There should be some kind of interrelationship, however, in the different utterances made from the pulpit, although they are made at different times. Of course this should not be a closely knit unity, a superficially fabricated or meticulously rigid unity. But there should be some kind of unity, coherence, and interrelationship. The same can be said for the minister of education or the director of Christian education, regarding the different positions and approaches he takes in administrative sessions at various levels, in leadership courses, in supervisory conferences, and in public addresses. A lack of unity will be commonly found. Part of this lack of unity is the influence of various fashions of the time; another influence is the coloration taken from the different groups and contexts in which we work.

The consequences for the people are not good. They love and respect the minister or minister of education as persons, or at least because of their offices, but they do not commonly understand them, and they do not get a sense of direction from them. This statement is not intended as a caricature, but as a reasonably fair description of the situation in the churches. The absence of a unified approach or ideology results in a lack of direction for the people. There are some background aspects of this circumstance which can be mentioned. The first of these is that Protestantism has not yet achieved any explicit philosophy of education or philosophy of Christian education. There are of course some very legitimate reasons why. First of all, there cannot be a philosophy of education or a philosophy of Christian education which is acceptable to all of Protestantism because of its great variety; the legitimate pluralism of Protestant Christianity makes this an impossible task. While Roman Catholics do not agree in every particular, and while there are remarkable variations in Judaism, Protestantism by its nature is more pluralistic than these other religious communities. This makes the formulation of a philosophy of education exceedingly difficult. Consequently there has been no achievement of a philosophy of education by a Protestant or by Protestant groups which could be recognized as a Protestant philosophy, not even by a narrow spectrum of Protestantism. The peculiar circumstance is that so-called secular thinkers seem to realize this more acutely than committed Protestants. Because of this we cannot lay too heavy blame upon individual ministers and ministers of education.

Another background circumstance contributing to this problem is that theological education does not as yet commonly provide the occasion and the guidance for the theologue in integrating his thinking. Some teachers in theological schools regard this as an impossibility. Nevertheless the legitimate claim can be made that at some point in theological education the occasion and the guidance should be provided for the process of integrating and interrelating one's thinking and the various disciplines with which one has worked. This would enable the minister to emerge from his formal education with a somewhat unified thought, instead of being acutely conscious that he has made a good many beginnings, but has failed to discover how these beginnings hang together.

CHAPTER *10*

The Bible and Nurture
in the Church

*I*n taking up consideration of the Bible and nurture
in the Church, it is necessary to return again to the general context
to see relationships clearly. These major subjects—the Church and
nurture, theology and nurture, and the Bible and nurture—are not
in a straight line of sequence. Rather the consideration of the
Church and nurture is the point of departure for all other major
subjects. What we have done so far is to deal with the Church and
nurture broadly and inclusively, arguing that the character of nurture is necessarily derived from the nature of the Church. We have
dealt with the history of the development of nurture and education in the Church or in relation to it. We then studied the relation of theology, philosophy of education, and nurture. Now in
turning to a similar consideration of the Bible and nurture, we
must recall that our base is the Church as a total existential context
in which nurture goes on and of which nurture is. Chapters 2
through 8 attempted to portray a kind of historical sketch. Chapter 9 asked what the relation is between theology and nurture
within this total context of the Church. And now this chapter
raises a similar question concerning the relation of the Bible and
nurture, but also within this same total context of the Church.

Somewhat superficially we may say at the very outset that it is
imperative that we know the Bible; there is no intention in this
discussion of negating this in any way. It is indispensable that
children, youths, and adults in the Church come to know the Bible.
But this urgency in itself goes only so far and does not necessarily

raise the question as to the place and function of the Bible in nurture. Just because a person knows the Bible, there is no guarantee that he has any perception of its function. All that the urgency to know the Bible says to us is that we must be literate concerning the Bible; it may also imply something about prevailing illiteracy about the Bible. While ignorance of the Bible is to be lamented, it should nevertheless be pointed out that biblical literacy does not guarantee discernment as to what the Bible is really all about. Even the achievement of advanced philological scholarship in study of the original languages of the Bible does not guarantee this. A person may quote the Bible by the page; he may have an unfailing memory of the order of the books of the Bible; he may name all the kings of Israel in precise chronological sequence; he may count the number of recurrences of "the," "and," and "but" in passages of Scripture—he may have much of this kind of "biblical" knowledge and yet be quite unbiblical in his understanding of the Bible and its function. This brings us then to consider directly the really significant question, what is the place and function of the Bible in the Church and what does this mean for nurture?

THE FUNCTION OF THE BIBLE

The place and function of the Bible in the Church and in nurture may be approached by using two disparate figures: the blueprint and the letter.[1] Rather commonly and more popularly, whether consciously or not, we have thought of the Bible as a kind of blueprint, a blueprint of reality both celestial and terrestrial and a set of specifications for the good life. If we think of the Bible in this way, this predetermines the nature of faith and the function of nurture. According to this view of the Bible, if you want to find out what the true cosmology is you go to the Bible to find it out. If you want to find out what the good life is, then you turn to the Bible and find out what kind of a pattern it lays down for the good life. It follows that this is the standard you try to conform to, a kind of law you obey, the pattern you try to induce or condition in the young.

---

[1] See the author's *Four Philosophies*, pp. 544–546.

137

Actually Ernest Ligon's original presuppositions in the Character Research Project were not far different from this, at least in his supposing that the Sermon on the Mount gives us the traits and attitudes comprising Christian character.[2] Any approach to the Bible which treats it as though it were a blueprint is mistaken, and any education or nurture which is derived from this is also mistaken. For one thing, such an approach to the Bible virtually ignores the Church. The Church is quite incidental, apparently it just happens to be here, it is the Bible that is of overshadowing importance. Also this approach is highly individualistic, having little reference to social or corporate entities. But these are secondary concerns for us at this point. The important thing is that to look at the Bible as though it is a blueprint and a set of specifications is to misunderstand and misinterpret it. Any education and nurture which stem from this misconception, misunderstand, distort, twist, and may even pervert.

On the other hand if the Bible is a letter, it is something strikingly different. If it is a letter or message from God to man replete with all the vitality and warmth of person-to-person communication, then both the nature of faith and the character of nurture become remarkably different from what they are in the blueprint conception. Here, instead of going to the Bible to find out what reality is, we have in it instead revelation by and of him who is the only absolute One. Instead of having a blueprint or set of specifications we have the medium of the life of faith, which is a life of relationship to him who is the only absolute One. Consequently this conception of the Bible, when it is used in teaching or in nurture, is not one of giving people absolute forms and patterns, but rather leading them into an understanding of this Word which is spoken by God to man—which is spoken to them—and awakening in them a responsiveness to God.

Of course both of these ways of looking at the Bible are analogies; they are symbols for the Bible in only a very limited sense. But to the extent that they depict two approaches, does it make a difference which we choose in going at the Bible? Well, in one approach you seek such as the specifics of what the good life is; in

[2] Ligon, *The Psychology of Christian Personality*, 1935; *Their Future is Now*, 1940; *A Greater Generation*, 1948; and *Dimensions of Character*, 1956; all published by Macmillan, New York.

138

the other you approach it as a medium of revelation and of relation-ship with God. Also in the latter you approach the Bible as a medium of relationship and communication with others who are a part of the community of faith. Now the Bible as revelation is prior to the good life grown in the soil of revelation; the good life is derived from it, rather than being something primary. Religion, after all, is not primarily an affair of finding out what the Bible says about the good life and then conforming to it. These figures for the Bible, the blueprint and the message, are not only disparate, they are decisively distinct; and a person has to choose one or the other. Ministers in the churches and ministers of education have moral and educational responsibility to the members of the Church to be clear and decisive about this. We are not teaching people unless we engage them in ways which meet and possibly challenge their re-ceived conceptions of the Bible. This is one point at which new departures in curriculum materials, such as the Faith and Life Curriculum of the Presbyterian Church and the Seabury Series of the Protestant Episcopal Church, have been notably successful. They have been explicit in their assumptions about the Bible.

SYMBOLS IN COMMUNICATION

In the effort to be clear concerning the function of the Bible, we must become involved in the more general problem of the function of symbols in communication. To introduce this discussion let us turn to John P. Marquand's *Point of No Return*,[3] a novel which offers a kind of secular sermon in our time. The central character is Mr. Gray, a junior executive in an important bank in midtown New York which serves a Park Avenue clientele. He lives in a very comfortable home in a privileged Westchester suburb and belongs to all the clubs usual to his station in life. His wife also belongs to the best clubs, and his daughter and son attend esti-mable private schools. Things have been going very well for the promising Mr. Gray, and they continue to do so, but for a time his life is somewhat painfully turned in upon itself owing to the enticements of a higher position and the struggles attendant upon an impending promotion. After all, someone else might be elected vice-president.

[3] Boston: Little, Brown, 1949.

139

His problem is created for him by circumstance. One of the vice-presidents has died and, as everyone on the bank's staff knows, someone will be elected to the vacated office, probably from within the rank of executives just below the officers. Gray is among these—in the secondary defense, as it were. The boys up front in the tellers' cages, he often thinks, are on the line. The officers in the cubicles behind him are in safety position. But he and his colleagues of equivalent rank are the secondary defense. They are not in the cages, but they have not yet risen high enough to have private offices. They are in between, a rug on the floor under their feet being their chief symbol of a somewhat superior status.

Who will be the new vice-president? Gray is in line for the promotion, but there are other promising men around. One in particular, whom he does not like very much, has been showing up very well lately. He will probably be considered, and may even— God forbid!—get the nod. Which one will be elected? Himself, or his archenemy—or at least the man whom his involved thinking has made an archenemy?

For some days Gray lives in this state of suspense and uncertainty, lying between a notable rise in the ranks, on the one hand, and the frown of discouragement and disapproval by the big boss and the board of directors, on the other. He may have to leave his job at the bank, take a lesser position, sell his home for a less pretentious one, give up his clubs, put his children in less expensive schools, and so on.

This tension is finally dispelled for him at a dinner in his boss' home, at which Gray and his wife are the only guests. Everything, of course, goes according to protocol and the refined but demanding folkways of this particular caste of society. Relaxed and casual conviviality is not in order, nor, to Gray at least, is it possible in this tense silence before the disclosure which will affect the entire course of his life. Dinner over, the women and the men separate, and retire to their respective parlors. As this movement is in process, Gray hears a fragment of speech from the president—possibly not more than a sentence. The inflection of the words, or possibly the bent of his own feelings at the time the words are spoken, gives them a very clear meaning. He is not to get the job; his enemy at the adjacent desk is to be made vice-president. So, the path pointed out by the frown of his fortunes is clear; he will resign from the bank. He may be forced to a reduced income, instead of an advance; his home will go on the market, and his family will have to move to a less expensive community. The Grays' club life will have to change accordingly, and they will have to find less expensive schools for the children—but what a sense of freedom! Disappointed, yes. But what a surprising sense of freedom!

Only a few seconds are required to move from the dining room to the study where he is closeted with his superior. And the conversation he has already so fully and finally interpreted continues with scarcely a change in voice. Another sentence or two and it becomes clear, beyond any mistake, that never has the president or the board of directors considered anyone but Gray to rise to the vacated vice-presidency. The images in Gray's mind are again on the move, almost blotting out the conversation, but now in a new direction. Here is the new position, a virtual gift before his eyes. He can keep his expensive home, possibly even buy a more impressive one. Club life can continue as is, possibly enriched and made more plush. The schools and the prestige systems in which his children are moving are still protected and can remain as they are. All is saved!—But what a burden! How enslaved he is! For one instant he had been a free man, but now he is back in the system, the same old cycle of succeed and be smiled upon, and the same old hazard of losing caste.

A narrative pattern such as this uses words in a way which says something far beyond what the mere words themselves say. It catches us, ensnares us, and involves us in a life situation which we may understand in our own way. This same kind of story could be written for a good many areas in life, and indeed a number have been written. However significant, such novels deal with only one problem among many possible ones in order to focus and to see in depth. They do not preach or lecture about the problem in analytical and oratorical terms; rather they engage the reader, almost as a subject, in living through and undergoing it.

We have entered upon discussion of symbolic forms in communication by using the narrative pattern as one of these forms. We hope now to indicate something of what the nature of symbolic communication is and at this point Paul Tillich may be able to help us. Tillich distinguishes the symbol from the sign. A sign is a pointer which always represents a thing signified; H_2SO_4 points

141

to sulphuric acid; a statue of a man with a cock standing at his feet means Saint Peter. Different as these two pointers may appear to be, they are quite the same; the cock standing at the feet of a man represents Saint Peter in very much the same way that H_2SO_4 represents sulphuric acid. They are both signs, and it is very important not to confuse them with symbols, because this is to obscure the nature of communication. A sign always points to a thing signified.

The symbol is different; as in the narrative pattern it participates in the reality of that to which it points, but it does not point to something which is directly signified. It presents it or participates in quality very much like it; it speaks more indirectly, but it speaks in kind similar to that about which it speaks. For example, the Kingdom of Heaven is like a grain of mustard seed. This seed of negligible size when planted grows into a small tree in which the birds find their nesting places. Now this is not a sign; there is no way in which you are to find any direct equivalence between the mustard seed, together with the small tree that grows from it, and the Kingdom of Heaven. It is something which approaches participation in reality which involves us in qualities which become, as it were, a sample or taste of it. The symbol is indirect, a kind of presentation; whereas the sign is direct and a kind of representation. The symbol somehow participates in the quality and character of what it symbolizes, while the sign does not. The sign H_2SO_4 doesn't have anything to do with sulphuric acid except to denote it. The holes punched in the IBM cards have no connection with what they represent, except to make the representation. Let us allow this contrast and terminology of sign and symbol to stand for the time being.

To continue with Tillich, the use of symbols, as here defined, opens up levels of reality which are otherwise closed to us. The specific reference here is to reality beyond ourselves, that is to say that by means of a symbol our eyes may be opened and we may see something which we did not see before. The sign does not do this for us; it may do it quantitatively, but it does not do it qualitatively. A real work of art can do this; it can open our eyes to see something that we never saw before. In fact this is the genius of the artist, if he is a real artist; he can catch something that we know and that we have experienced and can present it to us so that when we behold it we say, "Yes, I know what this is about; I understand what this is saying. The artist has to say it for me, but I know what he is saying." The symbol opens these levels of reality, objectifies them for us—possibly we had never gotten them objectified until someone else did it for us—and thereby increases our perceptiveness in relation to reality. A counterpart to this is that the symbol also unlocks dimensions and elements of our souls which probably were not unlocked before and which correspond in depth to the dimension and new elements of reality to which our eyes are now open. The symbol as Tillich defines it opens to us both dimensions of reality and levels of our own souls which were not open before.

Remarkable as these symbols are, Tillich contends that they cannot be produced intentionally. Symbols grow, he says, out of the individual or collective unconsciousness and cannot function without being accepted by the unconscious dimension of our being. He apparently would say that when the artist succeeds in symbolic expression, he is expressing something which is deep in the unconsciousness of individual people and of society, and also that in a sense the artist is doing this unconsciously. Therefore, Tillich says, we cannot consciously and intentionally create these symbols. To the extent that the four Gospels are works of art, they may serve as an example of this. They are not just works of art, of course; they are something more than this; but they are what they are because first of all they are works of art. It is doubtful that the gospels could have been written with any effect if their writers had full anticipation of what they were doing when they wrote. If they had known that almost endless generations of people in many centuries to come would turn to them as literature of revelation, would they have been able to produce them? They did not know this, but in fact believed to the contrary because of their expectation of the immediate return of Christ. But had they so believed, they would have been hindered, inhibited, and defeated by the awesome self-consciousness of what they were about. It is providential that these simple men did not know what they were about—something which was so far bigger than they were that they could not possibly have had full self-consciousness of it.

While it may be true that most symbols to be communicative must be found in the individual or collective unconsciousness, it still seems possible that some symbols may be created by the artist, dramatist, or poet. It may be true that they are not fully conscious of all that they are doing, yet they may be intentionally creating a symbol for a purpose. A friend who before his death achieved some recognition as a water-color artist may constitute a case in point. He was very impatient with anyone who proposed to build an aesthetic theory explaining what it is that the artist does. A part of the basis of his resentment was that he could not conceptualize his achievements. He had an intuitive sense of what he did as an artist and also the bodily control or discipline by which he could perform effectively. Even so he couldn't always work at an inspired level, and even on those occasions when he did so perform, he would not venture to explain it. Yet he could express poetically and lyrically what most of us in our more pedantic, pedestrian way of life cannot express. Evidently for him there was a level of unconsciousness with which a conscious level somehow fused. Book reviews reveal that so many first novels are written with a sense of mission or message. Commonly this has the color of resentment or judgment, an attempt to get something off the author's chest. A wrong under which the author has suffered needs to be exposed and judged; there is some anguish he has endured about which complaint must be made. If this is true of the first novel and if it succeeds in making its point without direct preaching, then it constitutes more of a conscious creative effort than Tillich makes allowance for; it creates symbols or makes a creative use of borrowed symbols.

The religious symbol, Tillich says, points beyond itself while participating in that to which it points, after the same manner of other symbols. Religious symbols point to God and in some sense participate in the nature and quality of the divine. In no other way, he contends, can faith express itself adequately; the language of faith is the language of symbols. This is a broad generalization about the nature of knowledge, at least about religious knowledge. What this says is that mathematical formulas, scientific formulas, the language of signs in symbolic logic, formulas expressed in words, philosophical formulas, theological formulas, and words which are used in an expository sequence—none of these can say what symbolic forms of expression can say. If this epistemology were pushed far enough, it would set the literary and artistic mind over against the philosophical mind, implying that the literary or

144

artistic mind is able to say what the philosophical mind cannot. And there is a sense in which this is true. Literature and art as professions can never take the place of philosophy or theology as professions; the poetic and artistic can never abolish the necessity for the systematic and formulative. But even so, literary and artistic expression can say what expression in formula, either by means of words or mathematical and scientific signs, cannot say. Therefore, as Tillich claims, the enemy of a critical theology is not natural literalism, but conscious literalism. The natural literalism of children in their play of fantasy is not bad, neither is the natural literalism of unlettered and untutored adults when they take everything in religion as literal. Much they take as literal is assumed to be such because they understand their leaders to intend this meaning. Natural literalism is not the enemy of a critical theology because it can be truly symbolic expression. But conscious literalism is the enemy of critical theology because, being conscious and intended, it is necessarily comprised of sign and formula. Therefore when we refer to symbols in the Bible and assert that they are literally true we convert symbols into signs. This is one of the grave mistakes of fundamentalism, it has taken symbolic literature in the Bible and by rationalistic fiat has made it literal description or formula.[4]

SYMBOLS IN THE BIBLE

We can make this clearer and apply it somewhat by turning to some central biblical figures and asking what they say and how they say it. For example, let us take the shepherd figure. What more favorite and more popularly embraced passage of Scripture is there than the Twenty-third Psalm? Not uncommonly on pastoral calls at the hospital, at the bedside of a person who knows little about faith, but is in the midst of crisis, the minister is asked to recite the Psalm almost as a prayer. While this may represent infantilism—after all most of us revert in a crisis to the dim, half-forgotten beginnings of our childhood—it is still a witness to the importance of the shepherd figure of this Psalm in our unconscious. Here is a piece of poetry, a prayer which says something to the depth of our being. The figure came, of course, from the pastoral life of the

---

[4] The foregoing discussion is based upon Paul Tillich, *Dynamics of Faith*, New York: Harper, 1957, chap. 3.

Hebrew people, but as the psalmist used it to express man's deep trust in God, it became a religious symbol for Israel and eventually also for Christianity. Either Jesus used the symbol of himself or the author of the Fourth Gospel applied it to him. The psalmist did not mean to say that the shepherd is a sign for God, that God is a shepherd, that the shepherd figure defines God; he did not intend to tell us precisely and in formula what God is like. Rather the way of the shepherd watching over and leading his flock, providing for the needs of every sheep, even by extension of the figure, restoring their souls—this way of the shepherd tells us something about God in his relation to men. To say that God is a shepherd who restores our souls transposes the shepherd figure and makes it say something that the shepherd as a sign could not say. And this symbol has surprisingly much more meaning for us in this machine world of the twentieth century than the early pastoral figure could possibly say as a sign.

The father symbol of course strikes very much at the heart of religion as understood in the Hebrew-Christian heritage. In the Bible, especially in the New Testament, the word "father" is used to refer to God, indeed the figure is carried on into the thought of the Church in the doctrine of the Trinity, God as Father, Son, and Holy Spirit. To examine this biblical and theological symbol should not vitiate its communicative power. Although it may be pertinent to point out that the figure of the father is a human figure, this fact does not distract from the validity and power of the figure as a religious symbol. We need not be anthropomorphic when we subscribe to the theological understanding that God is our father, that in God there is One who is Father, meaning that he has a Son, and One who is Son, meaning that he has a Father. This formula has taken our human symbol of father and made it mean far more than our human concept "father" means; it has transcended the human meaning. There is no human father who could in any sense be an adequate example for God as father; in fact there are many human fathers who corrupt this symbol and render it incapable of conveying religious meaning. There are children to whom the father symbol cannot speak, because their experience of father is one who is a tyrant, one who never speaks without speaking in brutality, one who is on the street more often than at home and, in some instances, drunk more often than not. To such children this symbol

146

can scarcely speak religious truth. Acquaintance with two corrective institutions for delinquent girls has revealed how seldom the usual religious figures function in attempts at teaching. Most of these girls have come from deprived homes in which the father has abused them, taken advantage of them, and sometimes has been the primary cause of their own moral problem. The father figure gets tangled in this when it is used as a religious symbol, and it no longer functions as a symbol.

What we have been trying to say about this symbol is that although it has a human origin and context, when it is taken over in the Bible and in our theology, it may be made to say far more than the human concept "father" says in a nonreligious context. This is not intended to take away any of the good things that it does say in the context of the human filial experience.

The third figure to be examined is the servant figure. This figure is in the Old Testament, especially in the latter half of the prophecy of Isaiah. Jesus took up the figure and used it for himself. In one place he said of himself, "The Son of man also came not to be served but to serve."[5] In the story of the washing of the disciples' feet,[6] he assumed the symbol of the servant in his own action. In a status-conscious group where none would perform the duty always performed by the servant in the house, Jesus "girded himself with a towel" and washed the disciples' feet. Saint Paul uses this figure for Jesus most notably in a passage[7] which may have been a kind of hymn used in the liturgy of the Apostolic Church. It is a paean of praise about one, who though he was God, chose not to be equal with God, but became a servant and, as a servant, was born a man. In this figure we have one meaningful way in which the Primitive Church spoke symbolically of the Incarnation.

Still another figure, and the last to be taken up here by way of example, is the figure of the king and the kingdom. This is the symbol implicit in the celebration of Palm Sunday, although it is strangely fused with the servant figure. This symbol points to one who was expected to come as a king, to make an entry of triumph, liberating the people, and to set up his rule on earth. In the symbolic act of Jesus which the Church celebrates on Palm Sunday, he

[5] Mark 10:45.
[6] John 13:1–11.
[7] Philippians 2:5–11.

came into Jerusalem using the king figure, but so transposing it that it virtually meant something quite contradictory, quite the opposite of what the king figure had meant. Instead of coming in regal pomp, he came in the simple humility of one riding on an ass. Instead of coming as one who controls by fiat, by external control, he came as one who in love controls by inner bonds. What symbol was there in Jesus' time which would stand for deliverance into a new order established by God, except the kingdom figure? Yet this symbol was used in such a way and in such contexts as to give it a meaning transcending and transfiguring the human experience of king and kingdom.

What we have tried to do here is to take four figures, the shepherd, the father, the servant, the related king and kingdom figures, and have tried to recognize how they are human figures, coming necessarily from human speech, from human patterns of thought, and even from forms of social organization. But we have also endeavored to show that these figures have been made to transcend their human limitations and to say something far more than what they say as words, which only denote. Possibly, in some instances, they say something quite different from what they say as only descriptive or denotative words.

Let us turn now to consider more generally the different forms of literature in the Bible. There is much of the Bible which is figurative or symbolic discourse such as we have been discussing, and there is much which is narrative. However, there is also history, law, precept, and direct instruction. In focusing attention upon symbols, the implication is not intended that the Bible is all symbolic, that none of the historical portions of the Bible are actual history. Though some of them may have symbolic meaning, they may still also be history and therefore need to be understood on two levels. What has been said about the importance of symbols is not intended to gainsay the fact that there is direct teaching and precept in the Bible, as for example in the Sermon on the Mount and in portions of the letters of Saint Paul. Some discernment and judgment is to be used in determining how much of this precept is derived from the Faith, and therefore necessarily follows from it, and how much of it is an expression of the limited cultural background of the person writing it. A good example is the attitudes expressed concerning the status of women. Which of these are necessarily derived from the Faith, and which are reflections of the limitations of the author and his times? Some of our churches today will not ordain women as ministers, because they assume that the teachings of the Bible exclude women from this status. Some Christians take very literally the teaching that the husband is the head of the household and that the wife is somehow secondary to him and under his authority. Serious questions can at least be raised as to how authentic the particular passages are by which these attitudes are documented. How much are they the Word of God and how much did they come from the cultural limitations of the person writing? We have acknowledged that there are other kinds of literature in the Bible than the symbolic and the narrative, but we have insisted that symbolic discourse and its recognition as such is of consummate importance.

TEACHING THE BIBLE

The next significant question is, what does this mean for teaching the Bible? It means, first of all, that teaching the Bible, in some measure and at a less profound level of insight, is for its own sake. This is the immediate level at which the concern is for an acquaintance with the Bible and some degree of understanding it. This acquaintance is necessary in order that children, youths, and adults will have knowledge of the history and precept in the Bible and will also have a rich appreciation of its figures and narratives. This is the immediate level at which, in a sense, the Bible does need to be taught for its own sake, but the thesis argued here would be in great danger of gross misunderstanding were we not to hasten on to a further purpose which is far more important.

In an ultimate sense the Bible is not to be taught for its own sake, but as a means to an end, namely, as a means to revelation within the Church. It is to be taught as a record of the historic source of the Christian community and the Christian faith. We cannot deal with religion in the abstract; religions have histories, communities, and literatures. And specifically we cannot deal with the Christian faith in the abstract; it has its community, it has its history, it has its literature. The Bible is that literature, and this is not to deprecate other, subsequent writings emerging from the life and thought of the Church. The Bible is a record of the source of the community and of the Faith; this is one of the ends toward which it should be taught which is beyond itself. It is a medium of revelation to this community, and this is a function for which the Bible must be taught. The Bible is a medium of communication within this community, and to this end also it must be taught. The Bible must be taught in order to become contemporaneous revelation. More commonly than we ought, we think of revelation as in the past. It is, of course, in the past, but it is also in the present, and there is a sense in which the temporal dimension is irrelevant in revelation. The Bible does not come into its true function in the Christian community unless it becomes contemporaneous revelation, and not just a record out of the past, something that happened centuries ago.

In this connection it is relevant to make a comment about content in teaching. It is this: there is only one absolute content for Christian education, and that is the living Word, not the written Word, not the Bible, not theology. Christ is the only absolute content. While it may be beyond our concern at this point, we may speak more generally and say that this is true for all other areas of knowledge. God is the only absolute, and therefore there is no area of knowledge so-called that gives us absolute knowledge other than God as he confronts man. The living Word confronting us in the Bible is revelation by and revelation of Jesus Christ, the only absolute content. There is no other. Compared to this, the knowledge which science gives is not absolute. It is descriptive knowledge and as such is always changing, subject to modification by new investigations. We may therefore say that while science does not lie, it also does not tell the truth in any absolute sense.

BIBLICAL CONTENT IN THE TEACHING OF THE CHURCH

What is the consequence of what we have said so far in this chapter for biblical material in the curriculum literature of the Church School? By reviewing a little history let us look at some assumptions about this in the Sunday School movement. The Uniform Lessons, when they appeared in 1872, were a study literature which proposed to constitute a representative coverage of the Bible in a cycle of several years—at first in six years and later in seven. This was their chief function. They did provide order; apparently there was little orderly and sequential study before this

150

time. This order was a cycle during which it was assumed a person would get a representative acquaintance with the Bible. It was also assumed that a child living in the Church for the normal period of growth would go through at least the better part of two cycles in which he was exposed to the Bible two, two-and-a-half, or possibly three times by means of these lessons. Often the Sunday School was called, as you know, the Bible school, and this name is still not an uncommon one; it reflects the primacy given to study of the Bible. When the Vacation Church School first began, it was called the Daily Vacation Bible School, reflecting this same folkway. The folkway is still strong in our churches, so that a curriculum literature should contain and refer primarily, if not solely, to the Bible. This goes so far even still, as many can witness, that in a sizeable segment of our curriculum literature it is assumed that we need actually to reprint the sections of the Bible studied in each lesson. There are still some people who hold the material suspect if it does not have the actual portions of the Bible reprinted in the lesson for the day. These are the assumptions in practice, the folkways by which we have worked and out of which we have come.

What has been said in this chapter about the place and function of the Bible, however, points to a much less constricted view of the Bible and a much more fluid and discerning use of it in teaching. Let us make this more explicit. First of all, the Bible is a message rather than a blueprint, although these figures should not be pushed too far. Secondly, symbols of communication are not all signs for things signified. In the Bible as well as in human communication some of these figures are figures which participate in the truth they communicate and at the same time point beyond it. Immediately, or as a means, the Bible must be taught for its own sake; ultimately the Bible is to be taught that it may become a means or medium of revelation. This brings us to consider the place of biblical content in the teaching of the Church and in the teaching literature of the Church.

The amount or quantity of actual biblical material in a curriculum is virtually without significance unless it is nil or nearly so. The Faith and Life Curriculum of the United Presbyterian Church, U.S.A.[8] has been criticized on the score that it doesn't have as

---

[8] United Presbyterian Church, U.S.A., *Faith and Life Curriculum*, Philadelphia: Westminster, 1948 *et seq.*

much biblical material in it as it should have. The editors of that curriculum have preferred not to answer that criticism on the same basis on which it has been made, because this is to define the adjective "biblical" quantitatively. Nevertheless, when one analysis of the curriculum was attempted to find out how much direct or indirect reference to the Bible there was in it for a given year, it was discovered that there was a very broad and inclusive coverage of the Bible. In as much as this study was largely quantitative in character and was phrased journalistically for popular consumption, the editors prefer that this study be given no more than moderate weight.[9] Actually the amount or quantity of biblical material is really without significance unless it is absent. It is without significance because there may be an abundance of quotation from the Bible or paraphrase of the Bible, and at the same time the material can be fundamentally unbiblical and secular. There can be and is imposition of extraneous teaching upon the biblical material; contradictory teaching, and even unbiblical and secular teaching, can be the result even at the same time that biblical material is used. Possibly this is not done intentionally; more commonly it is erroneously assumed that such ideas are taught by the Bible. For example an imposing array of biblical material may be used, but used in such a way as to lay primary stress upon morality. Note the frequent use of the Proverbs, the Psalms, or the Sermon on the Mount, in this way; biblical material is used, but it is ethics rather than religion which is taught. Does this make it biblical? Is the material being used in the way it is intended if it is made to teach ethics rather than to be a medium of revelation and redemption? Biblical material can be used and a world view taught which is assumed to be biblical, but which may not be biblical at all. To cite a rather extreme example, Gordon H. Clark's book, *A Christian Philosophy of Education*,[10] is a rather clear case, although not intended as curriculum literature. While the book is admittedly not a Christian philosophy of education, Dr. Clark attempts to make a case in it for what he calls a biblical theism. He contends that education does not have a world view and that what education needs is a biblical theism. He proceeds to work out a rather ration-

[9] United Presbyterian Church, U.S.A., *Prospectus for 1952-53*, Philadelphia: Westminster, 1952.
[10] Grand Rapids, Mich.: Wm. B. Eerdmans, 1946.

alistic kind of theism, which virtually excludes the empirical situations in which revelation comes, and then proposes this as the world view presented in the Bible. This is making the Bible be something which it is not intended to be, a textbook in philosophy, and it makes the Bible teach a world view it does not contain. Similarly Sunday School literature of the fundamentalist variety tends to teach a world view which is not necessarily in the Bible and which the Bible does not necessarily intend, namely, a highly rationalistic theism.

In a similar way there is the attempt to make the Bible teach a social theory which is not in the Bible. Too commonly it is assumed in the churches that our American individualism is the right social theory. Passages from the Bible are slanted to make them teach it. Our American individualistic social theory, free enterprise, etc. are not taught in the Bible as explicitly Christian social and economic principles. There may be a sharp dialectic between a genuinely biblical outlook and our American individualism, and if so, we certainly are not being biblical, even though we use biblical material, when we make it teach our American individualism or the system of free enterprise.

In a more superficial vein we may assume that all children's stories should start from some Bible verse or some biblical setting. Then we proceed from this to hatch a story which is presented as biblical, even though it is a fabrication and many times is from our own culture and has little to do with the setting from which it allegedly proceeds. The difficulty is one which should readily evoke sympathy. Study materials are constantly in preparation, and the Bible must be brought near small children in some way. The story lends itself as one vehicle to use, but how can stories be made biblical?

The discerning test as to whether material is biblical is not whether the material comes from the Bible, although much of it will and should, but whether its spirit and intent, as used, is in harmony with the total spirit and purpose of the Bible. If this is true, then there are two curriculum norms which follow as consequences from what we have been saying, curriculum norms which, of course, pertain only to the use of the Bible. The first of these is that a literature is not necessarily nor adequately biblical just because it is comprised of material from the Bible. The second is to

RELIGIOUS EDUCATION

repeat what was just said, a literature to be biblical in any significant sense must be biblical in intent. When it uses material from the Bible, it must not make idols of biblical persons, stories, or events. Instead it must use the Bible as dynamic, so that it may become a message to those who are taught. How can this be done? This is probably easier to argue than it is to exemplify or explain. One example will be attempted, however—a lesson in a senior high school unit on Martin Luther. It starts with Martin Luther's unintended revolt emerging from his rediscovery that man is justified by faith. Proceeding backward historically, the question is raised with the students as to where and how Luther happened on to this realization about the way in which man is accepted by God. Necessarily the lesson moves back from Luther to Saint Paul and thence to the students' discovery that Saint Paul made a similar revolt against his own heritage and even against some who were supposed to be authoritative in the Apostolic Church. Rather successfully it draws some fairly good parallels between Martin Luther and Saint Paul. This leads to a narrowing of attention to the Epistle to the Romans, chapter 5, and to the theme of justification by faith, central both in Paul and in Luther. In at least one particular use of this lesson a context is provided for the effective facing of profound and alarming questions such as: "Do I believe? How am I saved? Am I saved by what I do, or am I saved by trusting God?" Inadequate and imperfect as this example is, it indicates one way among many in which the Bible can be used with a biblical intent and can be made contemporaneous; by which it can become dynamic for the learner as the medium of contemporaneous revelation for him, requiring acceptance or rejection.

154

CHAPTER 11

The Church, Nurture, and the Secular Culture

*A*s we take up the relation of the secular order and nurture in the church, it is necessary to return again to the base from which we have made our departure. In brief, nurture is in and of the Church, but even so both the Church and its nurture are affected by the secular society in which the Church is set. In this, as in psychology, we are considering a so-called secular subject. Our sequence has been this, and it may be well to review it by way of indicating where secular subjects are pertinent to the nature of the Church and its nurture. If we abide by the separation of the sacred or religious and the secular—which can be very misleading, if indeed not invalid—social science and psychology are secular subjects compared to the nature of the Church, theology and the Bible. However, in an earlier portion of this book when considering the historical development of nurture, we found it necessary to consider some influences from the development of education as a secular institution. In this history there is evidence that both the Church and its nurture has to cope with and take into account secular cultural influences.

In Chapter 9, concerned with theology, philosophy of education, and nurture, some elements of the secular were included, in that philosophy of education was brought under consideration, theology and philosophy of education being paired as related disciplines. In Chapter 10, which considered the Bible and nurture in the Church, there was a degree of secular reference in the attention given to symbols. However, it would seem preferable not to think of the symbolic transaction as in any clear sense secular, but rather as a concern which is involved both in the so-called sacred and the secular. In Chapter 13, dealing with psychology and nurture in the Church, we will again take up a subject which, in the same sense as the present subject, is one of the newer sciences which has arisen out of the human scene, not without certain influences from the Church, although it is very clearly a human discipline.

In turning to the secular community and nurture within the Church in this chapter, the discussion will focus more especially on the local community in which the local parish is set than on the culture broadly and generally conceived. This is not to imply any reflection upon the value of a broader study of the culture; it is because of the necessary limitations of this book and the need for a focus that attention is centered predominantly upon the local level. This may bring issues more to a head, because it is at the local level that the local church is concretely confronted by the secular order. In mass communication media and in general influences, the Church is, of course, confronted by the general culture, but in terms of concrete institutions, specific problems, and specific issues, the local congregation has to face them most pointedly in the local community.

WHY SHOULD THE CHURCH TAKE THE SECULAR COMMUNITY INTO ACCOUNT?

First of all it will be well to ask the question, "Why should nurture in the local church be guided by a perspective which includes the local secular community?" Or stated more broadly, "Why should the Church take the secular community into account?" Two answers to this question will be attempted: first, attention will be directed to the more general form of the question; later in the chapter we will deal more directly with the relation of the Church to the institutions of the community. The generality of the present discussion should not be interpreted, however, as detracting from its urgency or validity.

Why should the Church take the secular community into account? The first answer is that the community and its institutions provide the broad social and cultural matrix in which those whom we would teach in the Church live and grow. We cannot escape this. These people do not just live and grow in Christian homes, they do not live and grow in the Church alone; they live and grow in the secular community and the soil in which their life is set is "out there," both in a geographical sense and in a theological sense. Knowledge of people, therefore, within the walls of the local church, and even within the program of the local church, is most inadequate. We must know them as they are in the cultural soil, the human soil in which they grow and which in very great measure forms them, whether we like it or not.

The second answer to our question is that we must take the secular community into account because the Church has responsibility for it. It has responsibility for corporate society as well as for the individual men, women, and children who constitute it. In other words, the Church's responsibility is not only a responsibility for individuals; it is a responsibility for something which is larger than individuals, more inclusive than individuals, and is yet organic and corporate. In the area of this responsibility of the Church, our American individualized Christianity has made the mistake of assuming that if we reform individuals, we will reform societies. But this does not necessarily follow. There are so many corporate entanglements and entities involved in the secular order that a given society will not of necessity be changed by the religious conversion of all the individuals in it. The president of a business organization, for example, may be a leading official in a church and, from all individual standards of judgment, may be a Christian who is above reproach. Yet conceivably his company may own housing in which tenants live below subsistence levels and in the rental of which racial segregation is practiced. The president may be a genuine Christian, yet he may have a blind spot about the practices of his company, or they may be so involved that it would be difficult, if not impossible, for him to change them singlehanded. It may even be that the only point at which a theological issue could be drawn with him is whether or not Christianity should take a corporate approach to society or deal only with individuals. The most discerning of those who have studied the relation of the Church and society have correctly insisted that the Church must approach society corporately and that it cannot fulfill its evangelistic responsibility or ministry in any full sense if it approaches society only by confronting individuals, as though it were looking at a building only as a collection of individual bricks and not as a whole, with design, function, and interrelationships.

THE CHURCH IN SOCIAL ACTION

In the majority of local congregations, at least in this country, there is inertia which withholds the Church from social action. This inertia is both within the local church and in the community which it serves. The prevalent opinion is that the task of the Church is only "to preach the gospel." This very pious and supposedly authentic concept of the mission of the Church has in it the implication that proclamation and action can be separated. This prevalent opinion also contains the assumption that proclamation and action have at some time been separated, whereas in point of fact proclamation and action cannot be separated and in the authentic Christian tradition never have been separated.

More parochially, there is what might be called the preacher's fallacy, which is to the effect that when we say it, we have done it. There is so much reliance on the use of words in the Church, and actually there is so much work involved in preparing a good sermon and preaching it, that after all it is somewhat of an achievement. This fallacy is one of the less conscious sources of this prevalent opinion that the task of the Church is only to preach the gospel. But another less conscious and more dangerous source of the opinion is the attitude, of both laymen in the Church and citizens of the community, that the pulpit minister should preach the gospel "only" and stay out of public affairs. This attitude could very well be characterized by the member of a congregation who, after a sermon he didn't like, criticized the minister by saying, "Preacher, stick to your last." By this he said very pointedly, "Preacher, this is none of your business; you stay with your job in the pulpit, and out of social issues." Accordingly, the attitude toward the minister of education or director of Christian education is very much the same; in fact they are more likely to get shut up within the four walls of the church than the pulpit or pastoral minister is. The preaching minister can get confined easily enough within the routines of his parish work; even though he may be a member of one of the "service" clubs, speak occasionally at public functions, and have the illusion of being in relation to the community. But the director of Christian education or minister of education is more likely to be even more narrowly pigeon-holed and therefore more shut off from the community. We virtually say to the director of religious education, "Your job is here in the church. You will get out and call in the homes in order to get children to Church School and gain the interest of parents, but, otherwise, your work is largely here in the church building."

Even though in most of our communities the inertia is strongly on the side of withholding the church from social action, at the denominational level many churches take very positive stands on social issues. This is one of the hopeful signs of our time—that at the denominational level a number of our communions have been very articulate and very responsible in what they have attempted concerning social problems. A number of our denominations have spoken very clearly on the issue of racial segregation; some have also taken stands against nuclear warfare and the continued testing of nuclear arms, and some have even spoken in favor of federal aid to education. In addition, a number of denominations positively urge the formation of social education and action committees, or their equivalents, at the congregational level. It may not be too far from the truth to observe that although at the local congregational level the inertia is on the side of withholding the church from social action, at the denominational and ecumenical levels the Church has become a pioneer on social issues, taking clear and courageous stands. Now it may be granted that these are just pronouncements, not actions; even so, the picture is more hopeful at the denominational and ecumenical levels than at the local congregational level as we see it in our society today.

It is imperative therefore that the local congregation find ways of relating itself concretely to the local community. It has to find ways of relating to this community as it is; it cannot be visionary or idealistic, and it cannot assume that the community is something other than it is. But the congregation must also enter into the dynamics of community life in order to bring to bear upon it the demands of the Kingdom of God. In other words, the local church has at least two thrusts. The first is a kind of factualistic thrust, that of finding out what the community is and dealing with it as it is, without acquiescing in what it is. The other thrust of the church toward the community is the dynamic one of entering into

159

the structure and dynamic movement of the community, while bringing to bear on the community the normative demands of the Church.

These are imperatives which will have in them the element of judgment, of course, and which, if heeded, will lead to something more than the community is at the present—namely, the demand of the Kingdom of God on that community. Here is one of the frontiers of human life in which the Church stands at the threshold of value-realization, a threshold between what is and what ought to be. The Christian Church, at least in our generation, has not been living at this threshold as much as it should. It is not at all uncommon that community leaders are also officials in the church, yet it is very uncommon for these leaders to be anything other than factualistic in their thinking about community life. They commonly do not have a dynamic approach in thinking of what the community ought to be. Almost every decision is made on the basis of what now is and what the present weight of opinion in the community now is. Seldom is a decision made on the basis of what ought to be, until it is clear that there is a sufficient groundswell of popular opinion to make that decision safe. In the face of this condition, even among churchmen in public life, unless the church does approach its local community both factualistically and dynamically, the church will be cut to fit the community and will then cease to be the Church. In point of fact, this phenomenon is now all too common in our nation; the church is determined by the community, rather than the community being determined by the Church. And the reference here is concretely to the local congregation; it is the local community which determines the texture of the church, not the church that determines its own texture and, in turn, the texture of the local community.

This all means that there must be two major thrusts of the church toward the community: community analysis and dynamic community organization and action. The situation very commonly in our congregations is that we are not aware of what the community about as actually is. We see the community on the surface but somehow fail to get down into the basement where the substructure is plainly visible. And we do not know how to relate ourselves to this substructure which actually determines what the community is. For the most part members of our churches need guidance to find their way into the life of the community, so that they are woven, as it were, into the texture of the community, not to control it and not to represent a vested interest, but merely to exercise the responsibility of a Christian conscience as a member of the community. Social action therefore means not only public pronouncements, taking stands on social issues; it also means the less spectacular, but sometimes more hazardous, reaching out into the community and taking action, sometimes even in advance of pronouncement. It is particularly concerning the latter that we lack knowledge of the techniques and of the scientific or disciplined approaches by which this can be done. There is inertia to be overcome, but we do lack the knowledge essential to effective action.

ANALYSIS OF THE COMMUNITY

We will now take up more in detail the task of analyzing the community. Following this, we will turn to the second of the two thrusts we have mentioned, the dynamic element in community organization and action.

The Functioning Community

The concept of the functioning community is one of the first concepts we need as we seek to deal concretely with the local community in which a particular congregation is set. Much more than first meets the eye must be taken into account in defining any particular community which is a given church serves. Every church has a functioning community which is its normal parish, but this functioning community is not usually to be defined by the commonly accepted boundaries. Let us try, by way of example, to look at a prototype of a particular community, first taking the more superficial view of a visitor, short-term resident, or unperceptive citizen. Then let us take a second look, and see this prototype after some depth of acquaintance with it.

Superficially, our prototype is a quiet suburban college town, delightful and attractive as a place to live—beautiful homes, beautifully landscaped parks, the interest and attraction of a good college with accompanying cultural and sporting events. It is apparently a simple community unit, most attractive and most inviting. The somewhat more intimate view, after a little depth of acquaintance

161

and more careful analysis, reveals a rather different community. It is both suburban and rural, not so quiet as had been assumed, but with something of the movement of a busy metropolis. It is still delightful as a place to live, but there are some rather rigid separations of residential areas by economic, racial, and cultural lines. For example, the amount of money you are worth is likely to determine the section of town in which you live. With a few notable exceptions, all negroes live within a rather clearly limited, deprived, and congested section of town. There is an Italian community which also has its geographic section rather definitely marked out, though not as restricted as the negro section and broken by more exceptions. The college can exercise power in determining community policies and consequently some community decisions are made informally over the lunch table before they are publicly enacted by official bodies. Separation between town and gown is quite clear, although it is not so strong as it might have formerly appeared to be. To move from one church to another in the community is virtually to move from one level of society to another. Wealth does not count as much as academic distinction in achieving prestige, however. Municipal boundary lines are anachronistic, having been continued virtually unchanged from the previous century. A number of adjoining villages and rural areas are all served by the same hospital, the same physicians, the same shopping areas, the same theatres, the same churches, and the same high school. So much for the closer view of this imagined prototype of many American communities.

It is clear that the churches in such a community would be foolishly unrealistic were they to define their parishes according to the view of the community as it appears before analysis. For the area to be served by these churches is the functioning community as revealed by analysis, and not the more evident community marked out by governmental boundaries. Furthermore, the qualitative distinctions and separations of citizens into associative groups of their own choice will affect qualitatively the ministry of the churches. Such factors are never revealed in the visitor's view.

Factors in the Analysis of a Community

In a discerning analysis of any community, it is necessary to get beneath the surface, as the two views of our imaginary community have already suggested. If the analysis goes far enough beneath the surface to make significant difference, it may well become a painful experience. In trying to find out just what a community is, a first factor to take into account is government, especially local government. There are however some exceptions to this, for in some communities county government, and sometimes state government, will have some bearing upon the local community. This will be true of county-seats and cities which are state capitols. At a week-end retreat of youth in Washington, D.C., the first order of business, to the astonishment of the guest speaker, was for each member of the group to announce which state was his home. At first the necessity of this was not evident to the guest, but it soon became clear that no one was from Washington, D.C. They were from all parts of the United States, and they were in Washington because their fathers' employment was with the Federal Government. Needless to say, this factor deeply affected the texture of that group. In our state capitals state officials frequently "show" here and there in the gatherings of the churches. However, in most communities the primary governmental concerns will be local; so let us set our sights on local government and consider the type of knowledge of local government which is needed for the deeper view.

It will be important to know what the jurisdictional lines of the local government are, superficial as this is by itself. Sometimes the reasons for jurisdictional lines being where they are are very peculiar. Here is one jurisdictional boundary, for example, which goes along in a well-behaved straight line for a good distance; then all of a sudden, there is a little block that projects out into the next municipality; following this, the straight line proceeds as before. The reason for this peculiarity is that municipality A needed additional property for its high school, and it therefore annexed a piece of property from municipality B so that the high school would be inside its own jurisdictional boundaries. How normal are jurisdictional lines? That is, are there certain functioning or natural barriers that make it necessary that the line be where it is? What notable changes, if any, are there beyond these lines, and what significance do they have? Let us consider the example of one city in the day of its control by a powerful political boss. Corrupt though the controlling political machine was, there was one ordinance that made it illegal for there to be dancing where liquor was sold. This,

163

of course, had the effect of making night clubs illegal. The consequence, as far as the map of the city was concerned, was that just over the city line, which due to congestion and blight was virtually imperceptible, night clubs were to be found in abundance. This makes clear that there is some connection between the social and ethical concerns of the Church and knowledge of city boundary lines.

Of course, there are many other ways in which the Church need be concerned about such geographic or physical planning factors involving local government. The extent to which the controlling power is entrenched is significant, for one thing. It is a fairly safe generalization to say that there is not a balance of power in most communities. They usually have a dominant political color, and therefore, when one party is forced out of office, it is commonly because a very special effort has been made by a dissatisfied minority. It is important also to know something about the tax rate; it may not be necessary to keep up with it year by year, but there should be knowledge of what it is, how it changes, and how it compares to other similar communities. Also, what are the ratables on which the government can levy taxes? It makes a difference when the treasury must be maintained solely by taxes on residences; it may make living difficult or force unwise economies. It helps when the government can get some of its funds from taxes on industry or on the so-called non-child-bearing taxpayers. It is desirable to have such sources of funds, because schooling is one of the most expensive items that a local government has to provide. Consequently, because of the priority of our economic concern in the United States, the city fathers in most communities are usually anxious to attract industry. Communities that are primarily academic communities or exclusive residential communities sometimes find it difficult to provide and maintain the necessary public installations, pleasant and inviting as the community may be without industries. Taxes are by no means a bad thing, not even a necessary evil; they represent the responsibility of citizens for the common life of the community. Taxes may be made excessive by a corrupt government or by lack of a sufficient diversity in tax sources. But taxes may also be made too light; there is no necessary virtue in the real estate lobby's concern to keep taxes down—there is none at all in the device of developers of subdivisions who deliberately locate outside of city lines in order to advertise, "No city taxes."

There should be some knowledge of the courts of law, their quality, and how they operate. To what extent is the administration of justice in the community dependent upon a layman in the law, such as the usual justice of the peace, a political appointee, or a legal mind with a pure love for the law and for justice? For those particularly concerned with the teaching ministry of the Church, it is especially important to be acquainted with the juvenile courts and the means by which juvenile offenders are handled in the community. While there are of course different schools of thought as to how they should be treated, local church leaders should know how they are treated and be in a position to evaluate whether or not the treatment is enlightened and well-considered.

Another concern of no little importance is whether there is a planning authority in the government and of what quality it is. Is it a collection of men who are appointed in return for political favors? Is it a group of men who act as the mouthpiece of the powers that be? Or is it a body that is genuinely trying to plan and guide the physical development of the community as wisely as possible? Physical planning may appear at first to be a grossly secular and materialistic affair. The actual work of planning can make the planner feel very small and unimportant, if he thinks about it all. Here is a street being planned, for example, and streets have a long-enduring permanency; if the planner gives thought to the matter, he will realize that he is participating in the making of things which will long outlive him, because of their permanence and his own transiency. Nevertheless it is a very important function, and it may not be secular at all in the intention to which it gives expression. There are many things that happen in our towns and cities that need not happen if there is some kind of planning authority which can exercise direction and control. At the present time, for example, with the very rapid development that is going on and will continue at an even more rapid rate, there is reason to worry how we are going to preserve green spots throughout our country. Cities do not need to grow like Topsy; they do not need to spurt first here and then there, just because some developer or some corporation takes a notion to build a cluster of homes or a sprawling factory. This is cancerous growth, without order and without direction; good planning which is free from human presumption is like guiding the flow of a stream. The planner can't control it, can't hem it in, can't say it must not flow. But he can put up a little barrier here, and another one there, so that he determines in some measure where the stream flows rather than just letting things happen, as is still the case in most of our communities.

Another important cluster of community institutions is comprised by the public social agencies. Those engaged in the teaching ministry of the Church should know something about them, their quality, and the level of their performance. Since the Social Security Act of 1935, these government-suppported agencies have arisen to a new level of significance in American society. The most common agency at the local level is the assistance bureau. If a churchman is to know his community structurally, he should know what kind of job such agencies are doing. He should know the level of the personnel they employ, whether professional or untrained. Are such positions filled by people chosen because of political connections or because of their qualifications? Almost all assistance in the form of financial aid is the province of public agencies; increasingly this has been the case since the mid-thirties. In most communities a very small percentage of financial assistance, if any, is now offered by private agencies.

There are also hospitals, both public and private; the former are operated by government, whether local, state, or federal; the latter are operated by private corporations. It is well to know these more than superficially—that is, have some knowledge of their administrators, boards of managers, and professional staff-members. There are also custodial institutions, or those that are nearly so. Probably no institution consciously desires for itself a purely "custodial" function; hopefully they want to be doing more for people under their care than giving them a place to live. Nevertheless, there are a great many institutions which care for the deaf, blind, the physically handicapped, the mentally deficient, or the mentally disturbed. While it is hoped that education or healing may render some or all of these capable of becoming socially self-sustaining citizens, the custodial function is still of overshadowing proportions. In many instances, if we can trust the reports, the texture of these institutions leaves much to be desired; in any case, we should

166

know something about them, when they are located in our respective communities.

Is there a recreation authority in the community? If so, what is its program? In the younger states there are commonly recreational authorities, and some of them are supported by public tax funds. In older states, although there is often legislation permitting the establishment of such authorities, they frequently do not have a share in the use of tax funds. If there is a public health unit, acquaintance with it can be of value to the churches in a number of ways—one of the more important being occasions for referral. Public health units need a minimum population of 50,000 in the area which they serve. This of course does not mean that a municipality must have a population of 50,000 in order to have a public health center. It occasionally happens that a particular city is the center of what we have called a "functioning community" upon which there converge lines of communication for a population area of 50,000 or more. There should be concern for an interest in public clinics also. Are they free clinics? Are they open to all, whether the patients have financial means or are indigents? In many instances tumor clinics are free and open because of our great and proper concern to detect cancer at the earliest possible time. In the field of social work, there is deep concern as to whether any clinic should make distinction between those who can pay for service and those who cannot. Many people will not go to a clinic if they must declare themselves indigents, and as a result, the scope of service of many clinics is much more curtailed than it need be.

The Church must, of course, be concerned about the public schools and other day- or boarding-schools the children of the community attend. This should be a very special concern for those who teach in the Church. It would be of interest to find out something about the quality of the administration of these schools and of the education they provide their students. More particularly regarding the public schools, what is the quality of the board of education? Does it represent the best that the community can provide in this important position of leadership? Or is a post on the school board a job that goes begging, so that almost any Joe Doaks can be elected to fill a vacancy? The church has very clear responsibility about matters such as this. If the board of education is not a strong body, it is the responsibility of the church to arouse the

167

citizens so that they will see that it is made a strong body. The church has a stake in the quality of teachers employed and in the quality of the program of study offered; it is also vitally concerned, let it be said, that salaries are adequate to provide a good basis of livelihood for both administrators and teachers. This is not unrelated to a fiscal question which was discussed earlier: are the people of the community fulfilling their responsibilities in paying adequate taxes or are they escaping this responsibility? This is a Christian responsibility and should not be divorced from religion.

If there are independent schools in the community, the church should have some knowledge of them also. These are more common in the eastern part of the United States than in the Midwest and Far West. What is their standing, the quality of education offered, and the kind of life fostered by the particular schools in the community? To what extent are they exclusive? And to what extent do they attempt to carry forward significant experiments in education? In the same way, if there is a college or other institution of higher learning in the community, the church should know something about its purposes and strength. What kind of leadership does this institution exercise in the community, if any?

To turn to another aspect of community life, churchmen should know about the private social agencies and organizations in a community. What is the quality of their leadership, whether professional or volunteer? To what extent do these agencies and organizations exist to do their work, to render a service? Or to what extent do they constitute a vested interest, grasping for its rights? Unfortunately, this is a vital question, cynical though it may seem to be. For agencies and institutions, both private and public, have a way of forgetting, after a few years, the pure motives which may have produced them. More specifically, what is the peculiar service of each agency? How may it be legitimately used by the church for referral of people in need of a social service?

What are some of the private social agencies? There is the Red Cross, which is rightly known as a great human needs agency, although not as completely so as is commonly assumed. It offers many wonderful services mostly in the area of health, but it is also designated by the Federal Government as the official disaster-relief agency, and it also renders welfare and recreational services to military personnel. The Red Cross successfully utilizes many volunteer workers, and further it takes seriously having these volunteers trained for the job they are going to do. There are the YMCA and the YWCA, offering recreation and character-building services to the community. There are the family service agencies, which for the most part, in their own quiet and hard-working way, are offering vital services to the families of our communities throughout the land with as pure a motivation as will be found in any type of social agency. There are also the child-care agencies, rendering special services to children, including placement in foster homes. There are those agencies commonly known as character-building organizations, such as the Boy Scouts, the Girl Scouts, and the Camp Fire Girls. The church may be somewhat more directly concerned with these, because often they are tied in some way to the program of the local church. There are private clinics, mental health services and clinics, planned parenthood organizations and clinics, which, we should be reminded, deal with problems of the so-called sterility of childless parents, as well as with the limitation of families. There is no point in attempting to enumerate further; the point here is to indicate the types of agencies to be found in our communities and to make the plea that churchmen have a responsibility to become respectfully acquainted with them and to try to understand their character.

A new question of a rather different character probes into a difficult dimension of community life. It is this: is there a community council? That is, is there a voluntary community council, in which organizations and segments of the community, on their own, bind themselves together for planning and interrelating their common life? Commonly, communities have a council of social agencies, almost certainly a Community Chest or United Fund. The council of social agencies approximates the community council, but it is not as inclusive nor as representative of the whole community as the community council. Some of the questions which must be asked about such councils, to know a community with some degree of depth, are: How representative is the quality of its leadership? Is it professional or lay leadership? What is the quality of the executive board? To what extent does this council limit its function to fund-raising? This is a fairly well established folkway in many communities. The Community Chest was the earlier effort toward unity and totality in the services of the community, but

169

unfortunately, in very few communities, even under the title of the United Fund, has it developed very far beyond the fund-raising conception.

Churchmen should also be responsibly aware of the associative groups in the community. By associative groups is meant all of the varieties of organizations, such as women's clubs, business and professional organizations, and the like, in which people get together primarily for the associative benefits they receive themselves, and not for the performance of some service to the community. The ministry of the church should take these into account and not be blind to the powers these associative groups may wield in community affairs or to the weight of prestige they may carry. Usually, there is some particular one or two of these that does wield considerable power.

TOWARD A DYNAMIC APPROACH TO THE COMMUNITY BY THE CHURCH

Analysis of the community, finding out what it actually is, only goes so far. While fact-finding is an important part of any kind of community effort, it does not accomplish anything unless it is followed by some dynamic effort or strategy of relationships. Some dynamism of movement is essential if the church is to be effectively related to the community. This also has at least indirect bearing on the teaching that goes on within the church, because in relating to the community, the church is dealing with the soil in which its members live. There is also a direct relationship between some aspects of community life and what we do in the teaching program of the church, e.g., the schools, recreation facilities, and character-building agencies.

First, we will comment about the kind of relations that the majority of our American churches, meaning of course the local congregations, have with these communities at the present time. In the majority of our American churches, there are tendencies toward affiliation with some favored community agencies and a countertendency away from a relation with other agencies, which for some reason are not to be favored. This phenomenon greatly needs to be re-examined. What are the favored agencies to which the church commonly relates, according to our present folkways?

Unfortunately, it is necessary to name names in order to be clear in what we are saying. Commonly our churches relate to the Red Cross, to the YMCA, the YWCA, the Boy Scouts, the Girl Scouts, and, possibly a little less often, to the Camp Fire Girls. This, by stereotype, generally represents the extent of our active connection with community agencies and organizations. We relate to these agencies by giving them space in the church building for holding both regular and occasional meetings. We support financial and membership drives of the YMCA and YWCA, assuming all the while that they are "arms," as it were, of the church. We relate ourselves to the Boy Scouts by designating members of the church as Boy Scout committee members, in addition to housing the troop meetings.

The relevant question we should be asking in our churches is: why do we favor these agencies? The Red Cross is regarded as the great human needs agency, as has already been said, and for which there is some basis in fact, but it is not the only agency serving the needs of people in trouble. The YMCA and YWCA truly enough had their origins in Christian concern for youth, but today the question can be asked of them without impertinence, just how singly do they persist in this concern in their local community operations? The Boy Scouts and Girl Scouts may have a very generally religious character, but this does not make them any closer to the church than some other agencies whose concern can be characterized as "religious."

The thesis argued in this chapter is that the church has responsibility for some relation to every service agency in the community, responsibility for relation with every agency that is seeking to render some service to the general welfare. It has responsibility for relation to every one of them, not just some of them which happen to be preferred. The church has greater responsibility to them than to "associative" bodies. And here no doubt the distinction between the service agency and the associative body needs to be restated. When a group of women get together because they were classmates in high school and play bridge at regular intervals, that is an associative body. When people get together for the purpose of maintaining business or professional contacts, that is an associative body. But when there is an organization that is trying to render service to children, regardless of what their philosophy is or their

171

religious affiliation, that is a service agency. When there is an agency that is trying to minister to the needs of families, when there is an organization that is honestly seeking to deal with the character of boys and girls, these are service agencies. And our argument is that the church has a responsibility to relate itself to all of these, without distinction and without preference.

It is urgent, of course, that individual churches avoid unilateral action in relating themselves to the structure of the community. They should avoid going it alone in establishing such relations, although a given congregation or minister may have to do so in exceptional situations. For example, let us say you are the minister of a congregation in a community of 5000, in which there is no local council of churches and no association of clergymen. First of all, you should try to enlist the united action of your fellow ministers and if at all possible, build up a united approach among the churches. However, if you cannot get this kind of cooperation, you may have to resort to unilateral action. A united approach is preferable to a unilateral one for the reason that local churches as well as denominations are fragmented segments of the Church and are in desperate need of unity. Segmentation and rivalry among churches is of course well known, but their curse in relation to the problem at hand is the embarrassment of knowing that while the Church is supposed to be the Body of Christ, bringing the saving grace of reconciliation and unity to the human community, the actual church is as segmented as the human community whose divisions its mission it is to heal.

Somewhat more specifically, the churches should relate themselves as much as possible to the community council, as well as to separate agencies. In fact, this may be even more important than relating to the individual agencies; it may be that our relationship to the agencies should be primarily through the community council. If there is no community council or no council of social agencies—and by this author the former is preferred because of its greater inclusiveness—then the churches have some responsibility to bring into the life of the community the vision and the initiative that will help establish such a body. Granted even that it may be secular in character, the human secular community can and should experience a degree of wholeness, instead of continuing to be segmented and divided. The perennial human struggle of brother against brother is what we have in most of our communities, and it is a part of the mission of the Church to bring reconciliation and some degree of wholeness in its place. Helping the community establish a community council, while it is not a solution to all problems by any means, is yet one way of helping the community to realize some wholeness in its life and to transcend some of the segmentation.

There should be recognition that some secular agencies of the community are, by their nature, the more immediate concern of those who lead in an effective program of Christian education in the church. The church is most especially concerned with the day schools which its children attend, and most commonly, this means the public school. But wherever it is that children get their "secular" education, there the church must be concerned. The problem of Christian parents is to find the way by which the total education of their children becomes a Christian education. How can the total education of the child in our pluralistic society be so integrated and unified that it is a Christian education? The concern here is not for a parochial or sheltered education. Whether we like it or not, we must observe that we live in a pluralistic society, as far as religion, as well as many other aspects of life, is concerned. And it may well be that this is an advantage, rather than a disadvantage, in the nurture of a vital Christian faith. Within our society most children are going to get a total education which is Christian only in a composite of three institutions: the church, the home, and the school. The home and the church are the institutions in which nurture in the Faith must take place. The child will get his more general education, dealing with the world and the society in which he lives, in the day school. If this is the public school, as is more often the case than not, he will receive his so-called general education in the midst of many other live options which challenge the faith of his home and church. This lays a very heavy burden on the church, that is, that the church has the definite responsibility for initiating relationship with the home and the school and of integrating the total education the child receives. This is necessary to the end that the child may emerge into adulthood with a unified understanding of life—not an easy or overly simple unity, but nevertheless a kind of unity of faith and life. This can happen, and indeed does happen when a child attends

173

the public school and is nurtured in faith by his church and home. It can happen when a man or woman goes to a state university or to one of our independent colleges and his faith is kept vital by his home and his church.

Finally the church must have some concern for recreational agencies. Basically, recreation is not the task of the church, it is only in a limited and incidental way part of the life of the church. It is a limited function of the church in the sense that children, and especially adolescents, who are together in study in the church, should also have the opportunity to be together socially. Beyond this, it is not the burden of the Church to provide recreation. The mission of the Church is more generic than providing any of the services which social agencies render. There have been times in the history of the Church, and there still are occasions today in deprived areas, when the Church gives birth to such service institutions, but after these institutions have become established, it is time for apron-strings to be cut and for the new institution to be allowed to go its own way as part of the secular order so-called. This is not, however, to make a sharp distinction between the secular and the sacred.

Now, just two more things—there are character-building agencies to which the church needs to be related. Preferably, it should relate to these agencies while they have a separate existence outside the church building and program. And finally the church is concerned with summer camping programs. The Church has given birth to a good many of these and includes them as a part of its program, usually above the local congregational level. But the Church should also be concerned to relate itself to summer camps which have no official connection with its program, but to which many of its children go for summer-camping experiences.

CHAPTER 12

Parish Educational Agencies

In considering agencies of nurture in the parish, we are dealing contemporaneously with the current institutional forms of nurture, the predecessors of which we have already considered in earlier historical chapters.[1] And, in using the term, agency, we mean the local congregational institution, and not denominational or interdenominational boards and agencies.

First of all, something very general should be said concerning the social aspect of these agencies. We are not going to deal with them critically; rather we will be primarily descriptive, the intention being to inform the reader. At the same time, however, such descriptive treatment is not intended to imply that any of these agencies has permanency. Instead, they are regarded as the present picture—in the longer view, a cross section in the present of a developing process, which has changed in the past and will change in the future. For example, in the light of its history, it may be understandable to say that in a sense the Sunday school was a historic accident, and it may at some future time cease to exist as an agency of nurture in the Church. In other words, none of these agencies are regarded as here to stay or beyond reproach or criticism. They constitute the present cross section of the social or institutional structure of the Church in relation to nurture, especially of the congregation or local church. Consequently, the order followed in discussing the agencies is determined by our present American folkways and the comparative importance they

[1] See Chapters 2 through 8.

175

attribute to the respective agencies of nurture. It seems safe to say that in this order the Sunday School stands out as of greatest importance, the institution upon which the Church depends most today to perform its teaching function. The order of importance of the other agencies may not be so clear, but the structure of this chapter reveals one assessment of the value we have assigned to each, wittingly or unwittingly.

THE SUNDAY CHURCH SCHOOL

In as much as we have previously considered the history of the Sunday School, we will deal with it here as it is in the present. The Sunday Church School today is a teaching session held intentionally, but possibly not successfully, in the church on Sundays for the purpose of Christian nurture. As it actually is, it exists especially for children and youth; as it should be, if it continues to be an institution of the church, it will exist for adults of various ages, including insofar as possible the whole congregation, as well as children and youth.

In the somewhat larger churches, the Sunday Church School is commonly guided in its work by a professional, that is, by at least one person who has had some kind of training for the work beyond that of most laymen. This staff-member is commonly designated a director of religious education or director of Christian education; preferably, if there is anything in a name, the person should be known as the minister of education.[2] The Sunday Church School usually has a chief officer who is a volunteer, in the sense that he receives no remuneration for his work; usually he is known as the Superintendent of the Sunday Church School. Depending upon the polity of the respective denominations, his appointment to his office is made or confirmed by the highest official body of the congregation. Even when a congregation is large enough or can afford professional staff-members, it is still generally considered desirable that there be a layman as Superintendent of the Sunday Church School. The function of the professional staff is to give guidance and to work in the background, not to take the place of the volunteers. Except for the one-room Sunday Church Schools, of which there are many, there is usually a department superintend-

[2] See Chapter 18.

176

ent in each of the age-level departments, which will be explained later. With very few exceptions, the teachers throughout are all volunteers. The problem of qualified volunteer leadership will be taken up later,[3] but we may just note here that a very important concern of the Sunday Church School, if it is going to have any kind of effectiveness and authenticity, is the recruiting of teachers and the adequate preparation of them for their work.

By departments, to which we have already referred, we mean age-level divisions in the Sunday Church School. In the churches which are just a little bit larger, there are commonly several of these departments. There may be a nursery department for ages three and under, although it is not considered wise to have one unless a registered nurse can be on duty. This is because of all of the hygienic factors which must be taken into account in dealing with small children. Much more commonly the earliest classes for younger children are found in the kindergarten department for ages four and five. Usually there are separate classes for each of these ages. Preferably each of these classes should be five to eight members in size. The next department, to proceed upward in the age-scale, is the primary department for ages six, seven, and eight. Similarly there are commonly separate classes at each single age-level; again the size of five to eight members for each class holds as a good norm. The junior department, which is next, is for pre-adolescents, ages nine, ten, and eleven. The reason for this will soon become clear; it may be that in the ninth or tenth year some schools will wish to put boys and girls in separate classes. It is not assumed here that they necessarily should be so separated, but if they are, it will, in all probability, be wise to bring the sexes together again in mixed classes by the eleventh year. We will go into this somewhat in a subsequent discussion,[4] but it should be explained now that by this age they are getting a bit beyond the supposed rejection of one other because of sex, which is somewhat characteristic of ages eight, nine, and ten. In any case, this phenomenon is symptomatic and not a real rejection at all. Children are maturing more rapidly today; consequently, it is not too unusual for a boy, as well as a girl, to be pubescent in his eleventh year.

[3] See Chapter 18.
[4] See pp. 213–214.

Moving beyond the so-called children's division, the next department includes the early adolescents who are commonly students in junior high school. This department is given various names by the different denominations; in some cases it is known as the Junior High Department, in others it is given some euphonious designation. With ages twelve, thirteen, and fourteen, smaller class sizes are still desirable, and the boys and girls will wisely be grouped together in classes, not segregated. The department for later adolescents, also variously named, is commonly called the Senior High Department; it includes ages fifteen, sixteen, and seventeen, and possibly some beyond these ages, depending on when they graduate from high school. In addition to these more common departments or classes there are sometimes classes for college-age youth and for so-called young adults as well. Quite commonly there are adult classes, usually organized on some self-perpetuating basis and bound together by sociological factors, rather than subject-matter interests. New departures are now emerging in adult education which are much more interesting and promising; most of these newer classes are formed for limited periods for the purpose of carrying forward serious and responsible study of a chosen subject. Acknowledgment should also be made, resulting from recent developments in curriculum, of changes in age-level department structure. In some instances now, two-year departmental cycles are supplanting the three-year departmental cycle, common for many years from primary through senior high school departments.

In churches which have achieved some degree of effectiveness in over-all administration, there is an organizational tie between the Sunday Church School and the over-all educational planning of the congregation. This is provided by means of having representatives of the Sunday Church School as members of the Christian education committee, board, or council, as it is variously known in different denominations. We will deal with administration of Christian education as a total concern of the whole congregation in a later chapter.[5] At this point it is only necessary to make clear that the Sunday Church School should not be an isolated entity, a thing unto itself. It is imperative for it to be a part of the total work of the church, and it is by administrative conception and

[5] See Chapter 17.

178

vision and by administrative structure and relationship that this is brought about.

As to the time available for the weekly Sunday Church School session, it ranges from an hour to an hour-and-a-half. A number of churches are reaching toward an hour-and-forty-five minutes; very rarely is there more time than this. In some churches there is an extended session for some portions of the Sunday Church School, which is held during the regular congregational worship service in the sanctuary; although with present crowded conditions which necessitate having two or three worship services and as many sessions of the Sunday Church School, extended sessions are sometimes not possible. Serious question can be raised about this because it often places difficulty in the way of families attending corporate worship together. One-half to three-quarters of an hour is about all the churches succeed in devoting to class sessions, hopefully the occasion for serious study and instruction. The remainder of the time in the Sunday Church School is used for worship or even still for that regrettable institution known as the opening exercise.

Concerning worship in the Sunday Church School, it may be most desirable to plan departmental worship services at irregular intervals, not every Sunday, and to engage the children in planning them with guidance which will help make them dignified and significant. The corporate worship of the congregation should be jealously guarded and not taken lightly. It should not be too easily assumed that graded worship has value; it certainly cannot be an equivalent of congregational worship and should not be a substitute for it. We may be hindering the child's nurture in the faith if we fail to find ways and means by which he will regularly experience the worship of the congregation, preferably with his family.

If the Sunday School is to continue to be the main agency of nurture on which the Church depends, then it has one task to fulfill which it has scarcely envisioned as yet. This is integrating the child's total education, and helping to make it pervasively Christian. We have discussed this in connection with the community in which each church is set and the composite of institutions in which most children will receive their education.[6] In our American situation—and this situation has roots in the Reforma-

[6] See pp. 173–174.

tion—it is necessary, because we have the public school, for the children of most Christian parents to get their education in the composite of home, church, and school. This being the case, the Church has the task of somehow interrelating, integrating, and tying together the total educational experience of the child, so that it is one, and not a disconnected, conflicting mass of inconsistencies. We have scarcely dreamed of this function as yet in connection with the work of the Sunday Church School.

THE YOUTH FELLOWSHIP

The youth fellowship is an informally organized society of adolescents commonly meeting Sunday evenings. Its primary intention is that there may be opportunity within the church and under wise but permissive guidance, for expression among adolescents of Christian group-life. Its chief modes are fellowship and discussion, as distinguished from formal instruction. While the Sunday Church School may very often fail in its task of effective and authentic education in the faith in the more formal sense; nevertheless, this is the end intended. The youth fellowship has another function; it is intended to provide Christian life together among adolescents, including opportunities to express, respond, doubt, and make decisions in relation to what goes on in the Church, to its life, to its thought, and to its faith.

One of the oldest Christian youth fellowship movements in the United States is the Christian Endeavor Society, which was interdenominationally organized in a manner similar to the Sunday School. The movement was established in 1881; so it emerged almost an exact century after the Sunday School. The first effort was followed by denominational organizations formed within the respective communions, in the hope of making the youth fellowships more a part of the life of the respective denominations. Consequently, we now have Baptist youth fellowships, Methodist fellowships, Presbyterian, Congregational, etc. Some correction and modification of this segmentation came with the formation of the United Christian Youth Movement in 1934, which also introduced a more broadly ecumenical conception, as compared to the old interdenominational idea. The United Christian Youth Movement had two main themes: they were (1) the unification of all youth activities in the congregation under one program; and (2) united interdenominational efforts among youth at the local level. Many of the different denominations have adopted the pattern for youth work suggested in the first theme. For example, in a number of communions the youth departments of the Sunday Church School, the youth fellowship, sometimes youth choirs and Boy Scouts are interrelated and coordinated by a youth council, representatively organized to do this. The second theme in the United Christian Youth Movement, namely, interdenominational effort between youth of different congregations at the local level, is an endeavor toward genuine *ecumenism* among youth. Working from this motif, instead of youth groups operating unilaterally or even cooperatively, they try to approximate genuine Christian unity transcending denominational separations.

Churches which have the professional staff can provide professional guidance to youth groups in addition to the volunteer lay sponsors common to most churches. There may be one member of the staff who devotes all of his time to youth work, although there is some question as to whether the division of labor in the educational staff of the church should follow age-level lines. Commonly a man-and-wife team, who offer guidance to youth as their part in the ministry of the Church, are appointed advisors to youth groups by the official body of the church.

The pattern of organization that has been most commonly followed in more recent times is to have a fellowship society for the early adolescent ages and a fellowship for the middle and later adolescents. These have quite commonly been known as junior-high fellowships and senior-high fellowships; in some denominations other names are used which do not denote the age-levels specifically, though the organization is much the same.

The more specialized administration of the affairs of the youth fellowships, as already indicated, is commonly the youth council. In some denominations the council is related only to one age-level, so that there is a junior-high council and a senior-high council; in other denominations there is only one youth council, concerned with all youth activities in the church. We will go somewhat further into detail with the latter kind of organization, since as yet it may be somewhat less common. This youth council, in which adolescents by themselves administer all of the affairs of the youth

181

division of the church, usually has an advisor. The advisor in churches large enough to have more ramified organization is often a third advisor, in addition to the advisor to the junior-high fellowship and the advisor to the senior-high fellowship. Such an arrangement, in the experience of the author, makes for greater strength and helps to overcome discontinuities and separations. As to the make-up of the council, there should be among its members a representatitive from the junior-high department of the Sunday Church School, a representative of the senior-high department, a representative from the junior-high fellowship, and one from the senior-high fellowship, the counselors from each of the two fellowship groups, representatives from the youth choirs if there are such, representatives from the Scout organization if there are troops in the church, and the advisor to the youth council. Of course, there can well be variations on this plan; the important thing is that it represent all phases of the youth program. The great value of the youth council is that it makes it possible for the church's program of nurture for youth, which is carried forward in several different organizations, to be one interrelated program, instead of several different rings in a circus, all going on at the same time, but with little apparent relationship.

As to the timetable of the youth fellowship, it is fairly common that it will have weekly meetings of one to three hours in duration. This varies from group to group and within groups. The program of activities is often divided between serious discussion, refreshments, sometimes even supper, and recreation. It is quite common, but by no means universal practice, that the junior-high groups meet from late Sunday afternoon into early evening, sometimes closing with supper, and that the senior-high fellowships meet Sunday evenings, sometimes beginning with supper. It may be mentioned that the home not uncommonly has a problem of budgeting time because of the meeting-time of the fellowship groups. One family almost nicknamed one of its sons "Samuel," because for two or three Sundays in close succession he was in the church continuously from 9:00 in the morning until 9:00 at night! In planning youth fellowship programs, it should be recognized that there are some reasonable limits on the amount of time available; high school students have homework to do, for example, and sometimes it is a legitimately heavy burden.

The different denominations publish materials which are particularly designed for these two fellowship groups. It is the hope of the editors and writers of these publications that they will provide guidance and suggestions for the serious study in which these groups engage. It is important for those in professional training and for lay advisors to become carefully and sufficiently familiar with these publications to make critical evaluations of them and to devise ways of effectively using them.[7]

Finally, one thing should be said that is futuristic, anticipating rather generally what may emerge in the youth ministry of the Church. At the present time, a serious rethinking of the whole youth program of the Church is taking place in some quarters. One denomination has been holding youth consultations in many parts of the country to discover what the ministry of the Church *to, for,* or *with* youth should be. If we could start from scratch and forget all that has been done in the past, it has been asking, what should the youth ministry of the Church be? We have tried to explain here what it now is, but this should not deter the student from thinking into the future and accepting even radical changes, if they are indicated.

THE VACATION CHURCH SCHOOL

The Vacation Church School is a daily church school held during the summer vacation period and intended to provide a somewhat intensified period of nurture. At the same time that it does this, it seeks as a rule to fall in line with the spirit of freedom and play of the summer season. More fundamentally, however, it is occasioned by the separation of church and state and is an attempt to get more time for the program of teaching in the church than is available in the Sunday Church School. It has grown up for the most part in the twentieth century and has spread rather broadly, reminding us somewhat of the way in which the original Sunday School grew. It will be well for us to look briefly at its history.

First of all, the very first vacation schools were called Daily Vacation Bible Schools; we have already alluded to them in con-

[7] See Chapter 16.

nection with our folkways about the Bible.[8] Apparently the very first Vacation Bible School was held in 1894 in Hopedale, Illinois. Around 1900 a vacation religious day school was established in Elk Mound, Wisconsin; the founder was Howard R. Vaughn, a Congregational minister. Reportedly a number of successful schools were held in subsequent summers. However, the concerted movement began in 1901 in New York City when Dr. Robert G. Boville, the executive secretary of the New York Baptist Mission Society, launched the vacation school in such a way as later resulted in a widespread movement. In 1910 the Home Mission Board of the Presbyterian Church, U.S.A.—now the Board of National Missions of the United Presbyterian Church, U.S.A.—incorporated the Vacation Bible School as a part of its program. In 1920 the International Association of the Daily Vacation Bible School was formed, and in 1923 this was incorporated into the International Council of Religious Education, the formation of which has already been noted as one of the sequels to the Sunday School Movement.[9] At the present time there is a Vacation Church School Section within the Division of Christian Education of the National Council of Churches.

It is also germane to our discussion to indicate here something of the growth of this movement. By 1928 there were 3,595 vacation schools in the United States among fourteen different denominations; it is not clear as to how many children were involved in all of these schools. By 1929 there were 7,467 schools, more than twice as many as the previous year, and among thirty-eight different denominations, almost three times as many as the previous year. In 1930 there were 8,857 schools, and that summer there were 790,948 children enrolled in vacation schools across the United States and Canada. This growth has continued since that time, although not with as great rapidity and with some recessions. But the Vacation Church School today has a very general acceptance, as more recent figures will attest; in 1943 there were more than 3 million children in 70,000 schools, evidently a peak year, and in 1956 over 98,000 schools, but with somewhat less than a million children enrolled. No attempt is made here to assess the quality of

[8] See pp. 150–154.
[9] See pp. 66–77.

184

work done in these schools; we have only sought to report how and when the movement began and the nature of its expansion.

Most commonly, the Vacation Church School meets for two weeks. There are a very few schools which continue for a somewhat longer period, and there are a great number of one-week schools; the one-week school is especially common among those sponsored by boards of national missions of the various denominations which send seminary students barnstorming, as it were, into neglected communities to operate such schools. A newer vacation-school innovation, which is not so common, is the evening vacation school, scheduled at a time of day in which the whole family can be included, not just the children.

The program of the Vacation Church School has usually included periods for study and instruction, worship, handicrafts or other comparable activities, and recreation. In the earlier days of the school, crafts were scarcely different in function from recreation; they had no necessary connection with what the children were studying at the time. In more recent times, there has been recognition that activities should have a reason for existence, and there has consequently been greater effort to relate the activities to what is being studied. The very best vacation school, with which the writer has had direct acquaintance, and in which there was a close integration of activities and study, was devoted entirely to a study of the symbolism of the Church. It was conducted in a very inadequately equipped one-room church basement. One of the men of the church made movable screens for separating the basement into four compartments, and the children enrolled in the school accepted the suggestion that they decorate the screens by using symbols of the Church, so that the screens would say something in addition to being room dividers. The very best one was done by a class of junior girls; drawing on very good sources and using excellent designs, they wrote the Apostles' Creed, as it were, on one of the screens. It was hard work involving careful study, and it took all of their mornings for two weeks to get the job done. On the day before the closing of the school, an excursion was made by chartered bus to the Cathedral of Saint John the Divine in New York, all children and all classes included. Before the day was over, the teachers had many sober second thoughts about this particular brainstorm. But the children enjoyed it very much, and

185

they almost went wild, in a very ungodly manner, when they recognized in the Cathedral symbols they had studied and whose significance they understood.

Except for some professional direction, such as offered by seminary students on field-education tours of duty and occasionally here and there in larger churches by directors of Christian education, the leadership in the Vacation Church School is volunteer lay leadership of about the same quality as we have in our Sunday Church Schools. Usually this leadership does not compare in its preparation and qualification to the teachers which these same boys and girls have in day school during the remainder of the year. This is one place, among others, where the vacation school needs improvement.

Finally, something general should be said concerning the curriculum of the Vacation Church School. Many of the denominations are now publishing curriculum materials particularly designed for the vacation school, some of them of very good quality. Some of these study materials are cooperative texts, as has been the case for a good many years. They are known as co-operative materials because of the manner in which they have been produced, one denomination accepting the responsibility to prepare and publish a particular text for a particular age-level, while other denominations write and publish for other age-levels. Working together in this way, they can produce a total curriculum to be used in the schools of several communions without the production becoming an excessively heavy burden.

THE WEEKDAY CHURCH SCHOOL

As we now take up the discussion of still another agency, the Weekday Church School, we will first look at its history. The first date and place for the weekday school is 1914 in Gary, Indiana. Gary at that time was much less a city than it is at present; now a large and congested steel center and a part of the greater Chicago area, it is hard to realize that it was once a much smaller community, suffering year after year the growing pains of becoming a center of heavy industry. In 1914 William Wirt was the Superintendent of Schools in Gary, and he became one of the leaders who had part in creating the weekday school. As Superintendent of Schools, Wirt was also the originator of the platoon system in which multiple use was made of school buildings; by adjusting class schedules, all of the school space in Gary was in use almost all of the time. This made for necessary economies in a very difficult tax situation. Gary was growing so fast that the size of the population, and the consequent necessary expenditures, were always ahead of the community's income from taxes, which were always based on the ratables of the previous year. The platoon system was therefore devised to rotate children through schools, classrooms, gymnasiums, and such, and thereby accommodate the ever-growing school population. It is not likely that this plan was unrelated to another plan, also originating in Gary, providing for some weekday use of public school buildings for the teaching of religion.

By 1918 five Protestant denominations had joined in forming in Gary a community board of education to create a community system of weekday schools. In 1922 Gary had eight weekday schools, organized by the churches; there were six teachers and 3,100 pupils who availed themselves of the opportunities offered for weekday religious education. The weekday school spread to other centers; by 1922, eight years after the first beginnings in Gary, there were 324 weekday schools in 28 states, enrolling approximately 50,000 pupils. By 1928, 510 communities operated such schools in 37 states. We will continue to represent the character of the growth of these schools to as recent dates as possible, although this particular agency, unlike the Sunday Church School and the Vacation Church School, has been the occasion for legal problems which soon must be briefly discussed. In 1942 there were 1000 weekday schools in the United States, registering a million pupils; by 1948 there were 3000 schools in forty-six states, enrolling two million children. By 1956 an additional million children were enrolled in the weekday school, but schools were still conducted in about 3000 communities.[10]

A new chapter in the history of the weekday school began in

[10] See Irwin L. Shaver, "Remember the Weekday, to Teach Religion Thereon," Chicago: National Council of Churches, Department of Weekday Religious Education, n.d.

1927 when the church-state issue was raised, questioning the legal basis of this new institution. The earliest court case, to the knowledge of the author, was in New York State; the question at issue was whether releasing a child from his usual studies in the public school for a period of religious instruction violated the state constitutional provision forbidding the use of public property or money for maintenance of an institution under the direction of a religious denomination. This was the Lewis vs. Graves case, and on it the New York Court of Appeals in 1927 ruled that the constitutional provision was not violated by the act of releasing a child for religious teaching. In present perspective this was an unimportant decision, but it was one of the earliest expressions of public anxiety concerning the legal issue. Eventually other cases proceeded to the United States Supreme Court, and the resultant decisions may yet prove to be historically far-reaching, not only for the weekday church school, but in all areas of possible relation of church and state in education. Is it legal to use public buildings for the teaching of religion? Is it legal to permit time to be taken away from the public school for religious instruction in a facility other than those provided by tax funds?

The legal problem became really acute in Champaign, Illinois, in 1945; Champaign is one of the two adjacent communities (Urbana being the other) in which the University of Illinois is located. The weekday religious education program started in Champaign in 1940, and classes were held in public school buildings, apparently to avoid traffic hazards for the children. In 1945 Mrs. Vashti McCullum brought suit against the school authorities, claiming they had no legal right to use public school buildings for religious instruction. On January 26, 1946, the Circuit Court of Champaign County unanimously upheld the right of the school district to permit classes for religious education in the schools. But Mrs. McCullum appealed the case, and eventually it came before the United States Supreme Court. On March 8, 1948, the famous decision in which eight out of the nine justices concurred was rendered. Their decision reversed the action of the State of Illinois and asserted that public school buildings must not be used by the churches for the teaching of sectarian religion. This decision still stands, and at the present time there is no reason to believe that it will not stand as a judgment determining the course of history in this area, as the Dartmouth College Decision of 1819 did for the private college and the Kalamazoo Decision of 1872[11] did for the high school. The Champaign Decision did not bring to an end the Weekday Church School nor deter its growth materially; released time from the public school has been commonly used by weekday schools since the decision, but sessions have not been held in public school buildings. This very assumption made by this practice was confirmed legally by the United States Supreme Court in its decision on the Zorach Case[12] delivered April 28, 1952; it affirmed the constitutionality of released time. The practical result, in other words, is that the facilities of the public school may not be used for weekday religious instruction, but children may be released from public school time for religious education on other premises.

A court case often mentioned in connection with the Champaign and Zorach Decisions, but having nothing to do directly with weekday religious education, might well be mentioned here, because of the different character of the decision and the different constitutional point on which it was based. This was the Everson Case, in which the United States Supreme Court ruled in 1947 that it is constitutional for children to be transported on school buses furnished by public funds, even though the destination of such children is a nonpublic school. Whereas the Champaign and Zorach Decisions were based upon the First Amendment to the Constitution, the Everson Decision was derived from the Fourteenth Amendment, which protects the welfare of citizens and prevents them from being deprived of "life, liberty, or property" without "due process of the law."

There are various types of Weekday Church Schools. There are community or interdenominational schools; for example, in cities of 25,000 population or over, it is not uncommon for weekday church schools to be operated by the local council of churches. There may be a staff-member or several staff-members, depending

---

[11] See Stuart C. Noble, A History of Amerian Education, New York: Farrar and Rinehart, 1938, pp. 191–192 and 287–288.

[12] See Alice L. Goddard, "Weekday and Vacation Church Schools," chap. 21 in Marvin J. Taylor, ed., Religious Education, New York: Abington, 1960, p. 227.

189

upon the size of the city and the program, who are on salary and who give full time to weekday-school teaching. Secondly, there is the type of school which is interdenominationally administered, but has a denominational teaching program. That is, the child goes to his own church for a teaching program, using a curriculum favored by his denomination or his particular congregation, but the machinery of administration is set up on a community or inter-denominational basis. In the third instance, there is the parish week-day school which is completely unilateral in character. The given congregation plans the program of teaching and also works out the details for release or dismissal of children from school. It is quite common in this country—to mention a case involving so-called dismissed time rather than released time—for Jewish synagogues to offer weekday instruction toward the end of the school day after the children have been dismissed from public school.

Some general suggestions may well be offered for those students whose responsibility it may be to set up a weekday school or to teach weekday classes. However, let it be reiterated that we should be very open as to the kind of agencies we will establish or use for the program of teaching in a given parish or community. The first suggestion is that there should be a strong interdenominational base, if at all possible; as strongly urged in the preceding chapter, we should not proceed unilaterally as congregations or denomina-tions, unless it proves absolutely necessary. Secondly, there must be a strong base in congenial relation with school authorities; this is very important if there is to be any durability in whatever plan is devised. A third suggestion is that the weekday schools or classes, as the case may be, should be well planned and of a high order. There should be a responsible committee charged with administer-ing the plan, and the very best teachers should be secured; remem-ber they are going to be compared more closely to public school teachers than in almost any other agency. It is probably fair to say that teachers in the weekday school are by and large the best quali-fied teachers in the educational agencies of the Church. We should be careful to stay within legal bounds in whatever plan is de-vised; it is not genuinely Christian for us to try to see what the traffic will bear in any situation, and if we can get away with it, to circumvent the law or the established interpretations of the law. Whatever the law is, we should know it and respect it fully.

THE COMMUNICANTS CLASS

The class for those who are looking forward to membership in the Church and profession of faith is variously known in the different denominations. In the more liturgical communions it has been called the Confirmation Class. Without implying particular favor for the name over others, we will consider it under the title of the Communicants Class.

The Communicants Class is the modern equivalent of the earliest form which nurture took in the Church and which, in a sense, was the forerunner of all Christian education so-called. The Communicants Class is, strictly speaking, catechumenal instruction in the sense in which that term was used in the ancient Church; it is a class which prepares for profession of faith, for baptism in those communions practicing only believer baptism, and for membership in the Church.

As it is today, the Communicants Class has very wide acceptance; in recent years the estimate is that 97 percent of the congregations in the United Presbyterian Church, U.S.A., for example, have such classes. The usual duration of these classes is six to ten weekly sessions. Some of them meet for only two to five sessions; but by way of notable exception, there are some few churches in which the Communicants Classes continue throughout the fall, winter, and spring. The length of duration of the class reflects in some measure the degree to which it is taken seriously by the minister and the church.

Most commonly, however, the class for prospective communicants is held in the spring just before the Easter Communion. Many churches also have classes in the fall and winter, and there are even some churches which schedule a Communicants Class in the summer months. In the comparatively few churches in which classes are held throughout the major portion of the year, it is not presumed at the beginning of the course, that the child will make profession of faith; those who indicate their readiness, either by their own expression, or in consultation with their parents, or both, are culled out of the class for membership in the Church.

As would be expected, separate classes are commonly held for youths and adults in the great majority of churches. First of all, let us look at the function of the Communicants Class for youths, turning later to classes preparing adults for membership in the Church. The question of the age at which the child should be admitted to the class is increasingly a problem, since this is also the question of the age at which the child is ready to make a profession of faith, and since our folkways are also involved. The tendency in recent years, unfortunately, has been to reach down into the pre-adolescent ages for Communicant-Class members. While, of course, we should not hold to some rigid connection between age-level and readiness for membership in the Church, it can nevertheless be argued with validity that generally we should be raising the age of those who enter Communicants Classes instead of lowering it.

Especially, in regard to the youth, we should find some way around the gregarious element which has become so strong in our Communicants Classes and professions of faith. We should regard profession of faith as a decisive act for the individual, the most decisive in his life, and we should not permit it to be a step that a boy or girl takes because others of his own age or his own class are taking it. Profession of faith, although it has a legitimate social context in the family and in the corporate life of the Church, is an individual confession, involving decision and responsibility on the part of the individual. We should not permit it to become merely a social phenomenon, as though it were a puberty rite. To raise the age-level at which profession is made will not by itself correct the folkway, but it will make it possible for the person's decision to confess his faith to be based on a more mature judgment. We speak of the age of accountability in this connection, but what is the age of accountability? While no one can answer that question with any finality, and while the age will of course vary from individual to individual, we are more likely to get more accountability at a later age. It is a truism to say that when we are seeking belief in people, we are seeking belief; certainly we are not interested in merely adding names to the roll of the church—at any rate we should not be. The appeal being made here, although there is no golden age to which to return, is nevertheless for a return to the quality of decisiveness in becoming a member of the Body of Christ which was characteristic of the early Church. If independence is the focus of adolescence, as will be argued later,[13] then

[13] See Chapter 13.

doubt is an intellectual necessity in adolescence. And that means more than sophomoric doubt; it means honestly raising questions and raising them as life-and-death issues.

This, of course, is a painful thing to do and many cultural factors discourage its happening, and it is even more painful and hazardous in adulthood. A boy gets through adolescence, for example, and by favorable circumstances or his own enterprise, becomes economically established or even affluent. In the midst of affluence, phychological as well as economic, the likelihood of soul struggles is not very great. Yet struggles of the soul are very central in life and are the soil in which religious faith grows, just as independence of judgment and commitment are central in personal life and in faith. Somehow, therefore, the Communicants Class must find a way, if it is to have a reason for being, to encourage or to elicit, by the grace of God, a profession of faith which is one's own.

Regarding Communicants Classes for adults, it should be said that many churches are conducting such classes regularly. Often these classes have the meaning of the Faith as their theme; this is very good, but of course it constitutes only a small part of a full adult program. There are many churches today in which adults are not granted the privilege of membership until after they have gone through a period of preparatory instruction.

As to methods of enlistment, the common practice in relation to youth classes is to scan the church-school rolls for the purpose of singling out those whom we consider to be "about the right age." Then after conversation with both them and their parents, we usually invite them to become members of a class about to be formed. Such a procedure is of course necessary, but we should go about it in a way that will make it a meaningful experience for the child, and not merely a part of the mechanics of running a church and maintaining its membership. It might also be helpful were it clearly understood that joining the Communicants Class does not mean necessarily that the students will eventually profess faith and join the Church.

If there is no strong program of adult education in the church, it should be a part of regular procedure to call on adults in their homes and invite them to be a part of the church, and also to invite them to join a preparatory class of instruction. This is essential if they are to come to a considered judgment concerning a commit-

193

ment of faith; otherwise, if they join the church, they do it without knowing the full significance of it.

The Communicants Class is usually taught by the minister, or by one of the ministers in congregations having a multiple ministry. In the larger churches, it is not at all uncommon for the director of Christian education to be the teacher. Most generally, it is very uncommon for a layman to be designated as teacher of this course. And in relation to the question as to who should be the teacher, a suggestion may well be made, which may also imply a deeper problem. It is that if there is to be a Communicants Class, the task of teaching it should not be delegated lightly. In larger churches there may be need for sharing this responsibility among the members of the professional staff, especially since there will undoubtedly be several such classes each year. But, even so, there is reason for proposing that the senior minister, who is installed in the church with authority, be the teacher of the Communicants Class as often as it is at all possible. This proposal relates to one of the most embarrassing considerations relating to this particular agency of nurture: why perpetuate it at all?

This discussion will therefore come to a close in an attempt to look at this question to see what rationale can be found for the Communicants Class. From the vantage point of concern that people make a meaningful and decisive confession of faith, it is very clear that there should be a Communicants Class, if this is the only way this result can be guaranteed. But from the standpoint of concern for the strength of the other agencies of nurture in the Church, it is not as clear that there should be such a class. While the so-called educational ministry of the Church had as its first historical antecedent the catechumenal class, today, rightly or wrongly, there is an array of agencies all supposed to be nurturing in the faith, a part of which is preparation for membership in the Church. The question then is this: if the educational thrust of the Church in one or all of these other agencies is effective, why should there be need for a Communicants Class? Part of the answer to this question is in the judgment of each minister and his congregation, explicitly or implicitly, regarding the strength of its total church school. If it is strong, then there is little need for a Communicants Class. If it is weak, then it is reasonable that the Communicants Class should be a major concern of the minister, and accordingly be planned to run for a longer period of time than is now commonly the case. However, if the church school is weak, may the minister's efforts in the long run not be better devoted to strengthening the work of the church school throughout? It is granted that for the first two or three years of this effort, he may also need to emphasize the Communicants Class as well.

There are only two other considerations which have not yet been mentioned, one of which might possibly modify or change the proposal just made. If the Communicants Class has a unique function, and that is to evoke the decision of faith, then there may be in this a reason for its continuance as an agency of nurture. But what does such a conception do to the other agencies of nurture? It would appear to be based on the assumption that the other agencies do not function in relation to decision-making, that they inform or instruct, but do not invite decision. But is there any nurture that does not center in decision-making? Indeed, is there any learning or education, however secular it may be assumed to be, which does not require decision of its subjects? The conception of the Communicants Class, as uniquely focused in decision, for these reasons will have to be rejected.

The argument of some is that the Communicants Class is the only sustained situation in which the minister of the church can deal directly and rather intimately with individuals regarding matters of faith. The contention is that there is no other occasion, prior or subsequent to it, when he has this choice opportunity. If this is true, and it may often be the case in the larger congregation, then it would seem to constitute a rationale which can stand by itself. Admittedly, it is a mild rationale devoid of bold assumptions, but nevertheless one which argues for the continuance of this ancient form as one of the agencies of nurture in the Church.

We have discussed the parish agencies of education in this chapter according to a pattern quite common in books on religious education. What we have done here, we believe, will be helpful, if not enlightening, to the student. Yet a certain dissatisfaction needs to be expressed, together with a hope that the agencies of Christian nurture, as they may be seen within the kind of context this book seeks to provide, may be viewed in a much wider spectrum. This wider and more inclusive view of the agencies of nurture would include consideration of the family as an institution of religious nurture, the Church and public education, the Church and higher education, and the Church and theological education. For every one of these subjects refers to an agency, through which or in relation to which the Church nurtures men in the faith. Granted that they are not parish agencies and that their tie to the Church is commonly at higher levels than the local congregation—with the exception of the family and possibly the public school—nevertheless they are all a part of that aspect of the life of the Church to which we refer in this book as nurture.

CHAPTER 13

Psychology and Nurture in the Church: Personality and Growth

A s with other major steps in our argument, we must return now to our original point of departure—namely, the Church—before venturing this new step, which is the consideration of the relation of the science of psychology to nurture in the Church. If you will recall the course of our argument in broad outline, you will remember that first of all we gave attention to the nature of the Church. We next turned to survey the historical development of nurture in the Church. Then there was a consideration of theology, the intellectual discipline of the Church, and philosophy of education, as they relate to nurture. The fourth step was an attempt to understand the function of the Bible, as it also is related to nurture in the Church. A fifth step was to view the secular order as it affects the life of the Church and the nurture in the Faith the Church seeks to provide. This was followed immediately, because of the implicit connection, by a description of the parish educational agencies. We now move to a sixth step as we turn to the science of psychology as it has bearing upon nurture in the Church.

As with philosophy of education[1] and the study of the community,[2] we are considering in this and the following chapter, not an aspect of the life of the Church, but a so-called secular discipline; sharp distinctions however are not intended here between the sacred and the secular. For one reason, the rise of the science of psychology has been influenced to some degree by the concern

[1] See Chapter 9.
[2] See Chapter 11.

the Church has for people. As is quite well known, in the particular beginnings this science had in the Roman Catholic Church, the theological presuppositions of Saint Thomas Aquinas were highly determinative. Of course Roman Catholics have defined psychology somewhat differently from the secular science of psychology. Also, the nineteenth century psychological movement in education discloses that European Protestantism exerted at least a background influence upon the rise of psychology. For example, Pestalozzi's compassion for the struggling poor came directly from the Church and the assumedly Christian culture in which he lived. In Froebel there was concern as to the blocks which hinder man from being good and from rising to a sense of unity with God. This problem turned his attention to psychological considerations. We may say, therefore, that psychology has arisen largely as a secular science, but even so, the influence of the Church was not completely lacking in its emergence.

At the same time, the science of psychology has made a strong impact on the Church. This can be seen generally in the current, though waning psychological influence on preaching. More specifically we can see the influence of psychology on the Church in the borrowings which religious education has made since early in this century, and more recently in the whole counseling movement in the Church and in theological education. A playful objection was made about this a few years ago at a convention of psychiatrists in Atlantic City; somebody remarked there that ministers are trespassing in the domain of the psychiatrists. In religious education and in counseling movements, we see that psychology has made a strong impact on the Church.

It should be recognized that there is a connection between psychology and theology, even though theology is the intellectual discipline of the Church and psychology is one of the scientific disciplines. This is true because of the common subjects with which the two deal, and also because of a certain tension which commonly exists between them on account of their divergent understanding of the nature of man. Psychology and theology are concerned about man in different ways, and there is almost certain to be a tension between the approaches they frequently make.

This brings us then to the definitions by which we will work in these two chapters. They may not prove acceptable to the reader, but they will make clear some of the presuppositions implicit in the approach made here. One of these presuppositions is that science does not have a metaphysic, that it does not tell the truth in a metaphysical sense. Another is that science is primarily descriptive. Of course, the word "descriptive" is not used here in a narrow sense; science is interpretative within certain immediate limits and relationships. But its interpretation does not have a broad and inclusive scope; in this wider range it can only accurately be characterized as descriptive. We must now focus on the particular and consequent definition of psychology emphasized here; psychology is an orderly discipline of inquiry which has as its particular subjects man and the human psyche. As with science in general, it is not, therefore, a metaphysic or a theology, and it does not give us ultimate truth. It is a discipline of precise inquiry, yielding descriptions as accurate as instruments of inquiry make possible, but these descriptions are subject to modification and correction, as the inquiry moves on into new refinements.[3]

The three major subjects which we are going to consider in these two chapters, because of their relevance to nurture and to education, are personality and selfhood, growth and development, and learning theory.

PERSONALITY AND SELFHOOD

The terms "personality" and "selfhood" are most commonly used almost interchangeably in this discussion. On occasion there is this distinction: personality is the social expression of the self or of the self made socially evident, and that the self is the substantive person which has an ontological "reality" as well as a social expression or actuality. This is to assume, when the distinction is made, that the word "personality" connotes more especially a social manifestation, and does not imply anything concerning an ontological reality behind the manifestation. It is hoped that the slight variation in usage will not be confusing.

[3] For a somewhat fuller statement of this explanation, see the author's article, "Theology and Psychology, Some Points of Convergence," Encounter, Vol. XIX, No. 4 (Autumn, 1958), pp. 391–392.

The Physical Aspect of Personality

We turn first of all to the physical aspect of the self. It will be noted that we speak of "physical aspect" not the "physical basis" of personality. This is to imply that the so-called physical is not necessarily primary. It is also to assume that the personality or the self is an entity having many facets, one of which is the physical. While this may appear to beg some scientific questions, it may do far more justice to selfhood than the presupposition that the body is prior to and more fundamental than the self, and that the latter is either derived from the physical or is an accompaniment of it.

Man has long recognized a certain intimate reciprocity between soul and body; experience makes this recognition necessary. But for the Church this has been a perennial problem, because although the Bible deals with man as a unity, this unity has never been very clearly achieved in the thought of the Church, either Protestant or Roman Catholic. What we have done most commonly is to answer this problem with a somewhat superficial existential statement that somehow body and soul are one. We have not done so well in explicating the essence and integrity of the unity of one's personal being. This failure has its manifestations in programs of the Church, in which we often appear to be rather ambiguous; sometimes they seem to be designed for the body, sometimes for the soul, and sometimes for a kind of confusion of the two rather than a unity.

However, this close interrelationship or integrity of the self and the body is well exemplified for us in the matrix constituted by the functioning of the vital organs, the sympathetic nervous system, the endocrine system, and the emotions. Now to discuss this matrix may appear to be grossly physical; but seeing how the vital organs are all components of a single matrix of interrelationship helps to make evident the unity of so-called mental and physical phenomena in personality. No doubt, your previous psychological and biological studies give you basis for this discussion; if it is full enough, it may even make what is to be said here redundant and unnecessary. Each of us does have a sympathetic nervous system, made up of the nerve ganglia clustered inside the rib-cage and outside of the spinal column, a kind of secondary central nervous system. These ganglia are very sensitive and can easily become stimulated. One of the characteristics of a highly intense and complex civilization such as ours, to look at it very fractionally, is that people's sympathetic nervous systems tend to be overly active, and overly excitable. Parallel to this system, in a way, is the endocrine system which, as you know, is made up of several different ductless glands from which the blood assimilates secretions which are called hormones. Because the circulatory system does assimilate these hormones, we have to look at the blood stream in at least two ways. We can think of it in more gross physiological terms as a nutrition system which provides the cells of the body the necessary food in order for them to maintain life and to grow. But we must also look at it as a chemical bath of hormones, as it were, which is also necessary to the maintenance of normal personal life. Before going further, it may be helpful to observe that the sympathetic nervous system and the endocrine system are so closely related that an overfunctioning of certain endocrines will make the sympathetic nervous system overactive. Admittedly, this is all still on the physiological level, but the reciprocity here must be recognized.

Going further in attempting to analyze and describe this matrix, the functioning of the vital organs—the heart, the organs of digestion, and the lungs—may now be brought into the picture. These are tied up in their functioning with the endocrines and with the sympathetic nervous system. When the endocrines and the sympathetic nervous system are functioning normally, and when there is no other physiological or psychological reason for malfunction, the operation of the vital organs is normal. That is, there is a certain normal rhythm of movement, commonly below the level of consciousness—for example, the normal action of digestion, rhythmic and fluid. This goes on without our noticing it, except when attention is directed to it; it is accompanied by a feeling of well-being and may be described physiologically as normal digestion, normal circulation, and normal respiration. But if for some reason some of the endochines function either excessively or defectively, the vital organs will not function normally. If the endocrines function excessively, then the sympathetic nervous system gets excited and the normal rhythm of the vital organs is upset, the nature of the upset being different in different cases. If the function is excessive, usually the tendency is to slow down the rhythm of the digestive system, possibly even to work in reverse, which, for example, causes feelings of nausea. In such cases of excitement, the heart is speeded up and the rate of respiration is also increased.

Turning to the emotions, and becoming less physiological, a helpful distinction may be made, for the sake of discussion, between the emotions and the feelings. By the emotions we denote the more definitive, concrete, and explicit feeling experiences such as anger, revulsion, or disgust. These are so definite and concrete that they are almost as tangible as a physical object. But this is not the case with the feelings—for many of which we probably do not have names—which may never take on concreteness and definiteness and which seldom become conscious in the same way as fear, anger, and erotic love. Now this fits into the matrix about which we have been speaking. In a normal functioning of the sympathetic nervous system, of the endocrines, and of vital organs, a very concrete emotion, if we ignore ethical considerations, may arise and run its course with accompanying normal excitements. The related endocrines secrete more than at other times, the vital organs take on a changed rhythm, and the sympathetic nervous system is appropriately excited, but all in a normal way for the duration of this period of emotional excitement. This may be represented by a curve of gradual development to climax and sudden exhaustion.

In the case of the feelings it is not so easy to make this clear, because the feelings are less concretely defined. Nevertheless, there is a significant relationship; in the malfunctioning of the feelings or of the emotions, when these are inhibited from full expression by ethical restraint we can see this relationship most readily. When one of the concrete emotions, such as anger, is experienced beyond what might be called the threshold of consent, but at the same time, is held back from its climax and exhaustion, the sympathetic nervous system remains in an excited state and certain endocrines continue to be overactive, though all the while consciousness may not know why. The functioning of the vital ogans is similarly disrupted by causes of which we are not fully conscious, and so, in the case of the emotions, something which is quite nonphysical can produce malfunctioning for a temporary or a sustained period.

One of the characteristics of a highly complex civilization, such as ours, in which the pace gets more rapid all the time, is that this matrix becomes affected and there is overstimulation of the sympathetic nervous system, endocrine malfunction, and interference with the normal functioning of the vital organs. Accordingly, ulcers and heart failure become occupational disease of some people, and a good portion of the population takes barbiturates or, more recently, tranquilizers. All of this may help to suggest the nature of the matrix in which there is this close interrelationship of the physical side of personality with the mental. It may be a reminder of such telling comments on our culture as the one made by the young college graduate who said, "I don't want to be a success at forty and have ulcers!"

The Cultural Aspect of Personality

A concept necessarily involved in this discussion of personality and culture is that of a given individuality, a concept which may not be susceptible of scientific verification. Some enlargement of this will be attempted however. This assumption is that at birth we have in us more than just a general fund of potentiality which the culture of the home, for example, receives and molds. What is given is not just a general fund of potentiality, but a potentiality with certain limitations, some propensities accentuated and others present in diminished form, setting out, as it were, certain guidelines as to what a person may become; this is what is meant by a *given individuality*. It can also be stated in this way: as men have a certain broad givenness in common, to become men, so in our individuality we each have a peculiar givenness as individuals, which, while within the broad givenness of being a man, has a peculiar twist of angularity[4] of the particular individual's set of potentialities. Diagrammatically, the givenness of generic man could be represened by a circle as a kind of universal givenness. But this universal givenness, as found in every particular individual, takes on an individuated form peculiar to that individual. Both universal manhood and particular individuality are given as potentialities at birth.

We turn then to culture and personality. Culture may not, as some hold, determine personality in its entirety. Not uncommonly, social scientists presuppose that an individual simply cannot be anything that his culture does not make him. It is held that if an individual does not accept and conform to the value-system of his

4 See Johann Friedrich Herbart, *Science of Education*, trans. by Henry M. and Emmie Felkin, Boston: Heath, 1893, pp. 115–117.

culture, he either dies or leaves the culture by some other means. This is exemplified in the way in which certain primitive societies treat the individual who does not conform. In certain African communities whose sex norms are very rigid, if there is a breach of these norms by an individual, he is ostracized not only socially, but is physically forced out of the community to face the cruelty of the wilderness alone. While culture does not determine the personality entirely, it nevertheless has a large place in this determination, and it is, therefore, an aspect of personality comparable to the physical aspect. So we cannot study personality seriously without also dealing with culture. Culture is the context of personality, a matrix having a different relation to personality than the physical matrix described earlier; it is the matrix in which personality takes on its form. At the least, the culture is the sounding board against which the self tries out its potential. It bangs itself against the otherness of the culture and tries out its possibilities, experimenting with what it is to be; this sort of thing happens in the family continually.

At most the culture may determine totally what the individual person will be, but it is questionable whether this need be or should be the case. A relevant contemporary problem here in the United States is the great pressure to conformity and the apparent acquiescence to this pressure which is too common. We have always had a good bit of this pressure, and, in some sense, every community makes this demand upon its members, but even so, today's pressure to conformity is of a new and larger degree. We are conforming today as never before, and this is especially true of the present generation of students. Even the beat generation is a generation, and beatniks are beatniks in a community! A person is not a beatnik alone, he is always one in some group having folkways and mores which determine what the group does. In the American culture at least, it is difficult to be a nonconformist without conforming to some kind of nonconformity! It may be possible, for example, that the return to emphasis upon the family in the Church, the vogue of family nights, etc., may not be as hopeful as it appears. There may be in this a covert conformity, brought about by the coldness of our society and causing people to look for some place where they can find a little warmth. Accordingly, it may not mean a revival of family religion or even a revival of religion at all; it may easily be just another occasion for conformity.

At the least, whatever magnitude the impact of the culture may have, the self cannot come to self-conscious realization, nor can the personality become articulate, without a social or cultural milieu against which to set its own life or with which to interact. This is rather clearly illustrated by some of the results of personality tests. The accuracy of these tests of course varies, and their further refinement should yield greater dependability, but even so, enough experience with them has been accumulated to show something. One of the oldest tests is the Bernreuter Personality Inventory,[5] four of the six dimensions of which have been fairly well standardized. These dimensions are emotional stability, ascendence-submission, introversion-extroversion, and self-confidence. While this is now considered to be one of the less dependable tests of personality, its results cannot be dismissed as without significance. A decade of observation of the use of this test with students applying for admission to theological seminaries has revealed a regularity sufficiently marked in its results to suggest that it reflects the influence of the culture upon those tested. The general pattern of personality which this test revealed in this group of students was sufficiently clear-cut and occurred in such a high percentage of applicants that it appears to have reflected a broad and common influence such as the culture. The pattern was this: a very low score in emotional stability, indicating an almost complete absence of neurotic tendencies; a high score in self-confidence, representing a sense of self-sufficiency; a low score in extroversion, meaning a very out-going personality with little inner involvement; and a high score in ascendence-submission, suggesting distinct aggressiveness and the absence of inner complexity. It would seem safe to venture the speculation that our American boys and girls are not all born with this kind of individuality and that something is done to them to make them this way. There are probably minor influences at work, such as a common economic and social level, and the peculiar interests and attractions that certain types of institutions hold for people may give the selection of students a kind of homogeniety. While these elements may be involved, a safe guess is that, in the overall sense, the culture is re-

[5] Robert G. Bernreuter, "The Personality Inventory," Stanford, Cal.: Stanford University Press, 1935.

sponsible. American culture places a high value on extroversion; it is the common assumption that there is something wrong with us if we are introverted. Our culture places a high value upon aggressiveness; we want the dynamic man for mayor, or superintendent of schools, or even preacher. It is hardly surprising, therefore, that these value judgments implicit in the culture are reflected in this test.

Had we the knowledge or equipment enabling us to go into more precise analysis, possibly we would find a certain residue in individuality that cannot be explained by cultural influence, a certain givenness, as we have called it. One of the dimensions in the Minnesota Multiphasic Personality Inventory[6] is the masculine-feminine interest scale. Consultations with several young men having moderately high scores on this scale suggest forces other than cultural at work, or at the least, a deviation from the culture. At face value, these scores say that the man so scoring on the test has feminine interests. It may even warn, especially on higher scores, that he may be a sexual pervert. But the consultations disclosed that some of these men were interested in music, art, or poetry. When these interests are genuine, and not affectations, we are presented with the phenomenon of male students having propensities which the culture does not value for its male members and about which the culture tacitly says, "This is something which a woman does." It may very well be that in addition to singling out some men who deviate from the cultural norm, without being sex deviates, this scale also suggests, by way of example, that there are propensities in the individual which the culture does not give him. If this is so, these propensities would be part of the givenness of selfhood or individuality, a kind of angularity of personality which makes a man an individual, and not just another replica of the value-system of the culture.

The Complexity of the Self: An Inner View

The notion that the self is a simple homogeneous entity which can be easily apprehended by turning one's gaze inward is mistaken. Descartes was overly simple in his introspective observations,

[6] Starke R. Hathaway and J. Charnley McKinley, "Multiphasic Personality Inventory," New York: Psychological Corp., 1943.

and in his conclusion, "I think, therefore I am," which has determined the pattern of philosophy for two centuries. At any rate, he partially misguided us on that afternoon when, with nothing particular to do, he decided to doubt everything that he could doubt for the time being, and to see where it took him. As you no doubt know, he arrived at the point that he could not doubt that he was doubting, and so he concluded that since his doubt must be thought, he was thinking and he therefore had being. We also find this overly simple thinking about the self in some of the educators of the nineteenth century psychological movement. For example, Pestalozzi assumed that the inward gaze is a very simple one, whereas the outward gaze is very complicated. He therefore devoted his attention to bringing simplicity and unity for the child out of this complexity—the blooming and buzzing confusion, as William James called it. This became a major refrain in the psychological approach to education of nineteenth century Europe. Pestalozzi was quite right in the effort to bring simplicity out of external confusion, but he was quite wrong in assuming that the inside of the self was simple, compared to the complexity of the external world. As more recent psychology, especially depth psychology,[7] has shown, the interior of the self is very complex—as complex as the outside world, if not more so. It is not so easy therefore to make the inward gaze, probably not any easier than to make the outward one.

This mistaken oversimplification has frequently gained religious expression. In the idea of the retreat, formally practiced in Roman

[7] By the term "depth psychology," general reference is made here to the psychoanalytical movement, including its various expressions, modifications, and corrections. This movement began with Sigmund Freud (1856–1939) and was carried forward in the first instance by his two students, Carl Jung (1875–1961) and Alfred Adler (1870–1937). The psychoanalytic movement has had wide influence in the twentieth century, not only in the burgeoning of psychiatry, but in its influence on other disciplines as well. For example, strong affinities between the "new theology" and Freudianism have been commonly emphasized by theologians. Now, however, some warnings are being voiced, advising us that we have gone too far and too rapidly in these identifications. Professor O. Hobart Mowrer of the University of Illinois has been the chief spokesman of caution to date. Since this controversy is yet largely to be waged, its outcome is uncertain. The author should acknowledge, however, even though the issue of future discussions remains undecided, his own general indebtedness to depth psychology. This is most evident in the text in the present discussion on the inner complexity of the self.

Catholicism, but also "devotionally" preached in many Protestant groups, there is the mistaken presupposition that it is both possible and good to sit down and look at yourself, to find out wherein you are at fault, and to correct the error of your ways. The intention may be very good, but the self can not just sit down and look at itself. Consequently, much of our so-called religious introspection is mistaken, proceeding as it does from the assumption that the self is a simple static thing that can be isolated and observed. Instead the self is elusive of our knowledge. What we are really trying to find when we introspect is the person who is doing the looking; and there isn't anything to be found by the direct gaze but a static picture of the self. In the history of philosophy, there are at least two points of view on this problem among those who believe in the reality of the self. The one is that there is direct knowledge of the self; the other is that we can only have an indirect knowledge of it. In the latter case, the knowledge of the self can be symbolized as catching a glimpse of someone who has just passed by. It is very similar to the prophet's view of God symbolized in the Bible as the passing by of one only sensed while the eyes are covered or the face hidden, and as the movement of a rushing wind.[8]

The self is not a simple unity; the self must win such unity as it has. We all have heard about the abnormal phenomenon of the multiple self, but we do not commonly recognize that even most normal selves are more like a plurality than a unity. This can be seen clearly and very normally during adolescence, when we all engage in the playing of roles. Sometimes a girl is the sophisticated woman of the world, other times she is the pious do-gooder, then the adored belle of the ball, then the tom-boy, and then the lady bountiful. An adolescent boy may be successively the popular guy, the hot-rodder, the brain, the lady's man, etc. While there may be overlapping in these roles, there is admittedly disparity, inconsistency, and conflict. But viewed in the light of the maturing person, it may commonly be a permissible or even necessary multiplicity. When a person is growing up, he eventually has to find out who he is, and he needs understandably to experiment, to explore, to dabble in the different selves that he may become. It is a kind of psychological eclecticism, which, like philosophical eclecticism, may be a necessary stage in moving up to maturity.

[8] See Exodus 33:12–23; I Kings 19:1–12.

It may not be as understandable when adults continue to live many different lives. This would seem, at the least, to be an extension of adolescence beyond its time in a kind of unconscious refusal to be one's self. The high-powered executive acting as the man of decision can also be the doting father, the loving husband, the hail-fellow-well-met, and he may even turn up at church on Sunday with a carnation in his lapel as the pious and cordial usher. His wife may also have a comparable constellation of selves which she indwells. Regrettable as such a prolonged adolescence is—other aspects of adolescence such as its vigor and imagination might better be carried over into adult years—it can, nevertheless, be more easily countenanced than the playing of roles for the effect they will have in advancing one's cause or maintaining one's ascendancy in a power struggle. I may act the part of the firm man of decision with individual A because I know he will back down when confronted with firmness; or I may be sweet and agreeable with individual B because I know this is the best way to get around him. This may be good strategy, but it is psychological dishonesty and has in it the seeds of moral breakdown. In a day when the roles of the self are used increasingly as power devices, the conscientious teacher cannot avoid some real measure of reluctance in deciding to adopt role-playing as a method of teaching and learning.

Some clarity of approach to the multiple character of selfhood is provided by the subject-object figure. In adopting this approach for what help it may offer, it should still be remembered that subject and object concepts are no more than figures. They are borrowed from grammar, and a strictly literal use of them would make it as justifiable to refer to the verb-self as to speak of the subject-self and the object-self. Within the figure, however, it may be said that the multiple aspect of self is comprised completely of the objects which the subject-self creates. The posturing of the adolescent in different kinds of selves is a kind of thrusting out to see in what direction the self is genuinely to be committed. The "real" self is the one that makes the thrusts, not the projection which is thrown up for others to see, as an experiment or a trial or for a desired effect which it may produce. It is the subject-self which has being and is alive; the object-selves, once their moment is past, are dead. Of course the subject always needs an object through which to speak, and these objects may be very significant creations; a book, a poem, a drama, or a symphony. But significant and creative as such objects may be, even lucidly revealing the self who created them, they are the handiwork of the creating self, not the subject itself.

It remains for us to indicate what the educational significance may be of this somewhat esoteric discussion. Thus it should be pointed out that significant teaching and learning can scarcely take place when no more than one object-self meets another object-self. If the teacher is playing the role of being a teacher and the student is playing the role of some past object-self to which he is attached by fascination or even guilt, then learning is almost certain to be at a minimum. How can it be otherwise? Of course, it must be admitted that object-selves are always present in the classroom as in any other human situation. The subject always speaks through its object, but through an object-self projected in the present for the peculiar needs of the present situation, not through some past object-self, however laudable. Even though present objects are always in the situation and are the media of communication, teaching and learning at their best are characterized, in terms of the selves present, as subject meeting subject.

GROWTH AND DEVELOPMENT

Effectiveness in relating to children at various age-levels will be greatly aided by an accurate and detailed knowledge of specific ages. This involves intensive study of the rather limited literature available, and there is no intention here of representing in detail the present findings on growth and development. Instead, reference will be made to leading items in the literature of this field, and certain general concepts which may be inferred from the findings will be proposed. It is true that detailed knowledge of growth and development is easily forgotten and readily distorted by memory if the research is not frequently consulted, so the wisest counsel for the student or practitioner is to treat the literature of growth and development as reference literature and to return to it whenever necessary. He should return especially to the study of a particular age-level as this knowledge is needed for working with that particular age. With these reasons in mind, we recommend as such references the books which have come from the Yale Child Study Clinic, particularly *Infant and Child in the Culture of Today*,[9] and *The Child from Five to Ten*,[10] and *Youth, The Years from Ten to Sixteen*.[11]

A Descriptive Overview

Although in this discussion we can deal only in general concepts which seem to be valid for growth and development, we nevertheless need to emphasize our need to know specific things about specific ages. No matter how many general concepts we have, there can be no substitute for knowing particular characteristics of particular ages, especially in preparation for periods when one has responsibility for leading or teaching a specific age-group.

We are forced here to deal in growth concepts which, while they are necessarily general, can give us insights to aid our effectiveness and which can, of course, be exemplified by reference to specific ages. We will take up first of all three concepts which apply especially to childhood, but are also somewhat descriptive of pre-adolescence and adolescence. The first of these is that growth is not just a gradual and steady advance, but rather a rhythmic, undulating movement, marked by plateaus and even retrogressions, as well as advances. In the growth curve, plateaus alternate with advances, and sometimes the plateaus become retrogressive stages. One fond parent, who was also a psychologist, gave his two-year-old child the Rorschach inkblot test at five different points separated only by three months. He found, or at least he thought he found, that his child was generally better organized at the age of two than he was at two years and six months or at two years and nine months, and that his organization had come back again at three. If this individual case represents the age at all, then these findings would point to one of the growth levels at which there is an apparent marking of time in the progress of growth and at which the child may even retrogress to earlier stages of achievement.

The Gesell studies, which statistically have a broad base, generally confirm the findings of the parent just reported. The report was introduced here, however, not because it lacks particular

[9] Arnold Gesell and F. L. Ilg, New York: Harper, 1943.
[10] Arnold Gesell and F. L. Ilg, New York: Harper, 1946.
[11] Arnold Gesell, F. L. Ilg, and L. B. Ames, New York: Harper, 1956.

significance, but because it exemplifies what we are saying generally about growth as a rhythmic and undulating movement.

More specifically, the concepts of expansiveness and consolidation refer to the two aspects of the rhythm of growth which, in its undulating movement already described, alternates between expansion and consolidation. Figuratively, these concepts may be represented by the movement of an army. When in action in the field, the army makes an advance, extending its columns as far as it can, but it stops at a point before lines of communication become tenuous. It stops to consolidate, brings up reserves, and establishes new supply bases so it can move forward again. Growth proceeds in a similar way; there is a thrust outward into new and uncontrolled territory, and then a kind of halting period, apparently for catching up on resources, so that the further advance may be made.

The expansive periods of the child may be understood by the adult, if he thinks as an analogy of his own adjustment problems when he has to move to a new home and adapt his life to an entirely new environment. Periods of expansion are also somewhat like the experience of the student when he leaves home for the first time and goes to college; as many can attest, the adjustment problems incident to this transition sometimes become quite serious. Any one of these transitions or fresh starts has in it the reorganizing of loose ends which is involved in the expansive periods of growth. The Gesell studies—possibly in part because of the way the researches were designed—may have given us a more uniform picture of growth than is actually the case. But to the extent that we can be guided by these studies, the expansive ages (omitting reference to early infancy) are one-and-one-half, two-and-a-half, four, six, eight, and nine, and possibly eleven, thirteen, and fifteen. It is not uncommon, of course, for families to have youngsters in several of these age-levels at the same time. Parents of such broods deserve sympathy, although at a distance or in hindsight their situation can be rather amusing.

The consolidative periods which alternate with the expansive thrusts, and which from the adult standpoint are much more pleasant, are ages three, five, and seven, and possibly also ten, twelve, fourteen, and sixteen. Surprising as it may be—and as already noted, this may be partially due to the design of the researches—there is a fairly uniform pattern of alternation between expansion and consolidation not only in childhood, but also in pre-adolescence and adolescence.

Let us turn now to some chief characteristics of preadolescence, ages nine through eleven; these are in three areas, the physical, the intellectual, and the social.[12] The three years are unspectacular as far as physical growth is concerned, except for the early maturers who become pubescent in the late tenth year or in the eleventh. This exception may be less common for boys, but there are boys as well as girls who do begin pubescent changes in these years. For the majority of both boys and girls however, physical growth in this period is uneventful. The preadolescent is freer from sickness than he has ever been before, is very healthy, and, for the most part, has a very even balance as far as his body is concerned.

Intellectually, preadolescence is a period of realism, or to be more precise, a time of factualism. There is a strong intellectual interest in cause and effect; science becomes very attractive at this age. However, the preadolescent's comprehension of cause and effect apparently does not extend to history. He is not able, according to some reports, to get historic perspective on cause and effect —at least not without some direct help. This is quite relevant, of course, to what is attempted for the preadolescent in the Church school. We frequently try to teach him biblical history and, in some of the newer curricula, Church history. Yet because of his lack of readiness in these areas, he is going to need a great deal of help if this teaching is to be effective. This one example may suggest something more general about the use of psychology in religious education. Although we have borrowed extensively from descriptive psychology, it may still be true that we have not taken it seriously enough. We are quite ready to say what kind of program we should have in the Church for respective age-levels, but we are not very rich in knowledge about the kind of program for which the respective ages are psychologically ready.

The third characterization to be made of preadolescence is that there is an incipient, although sometimes rather explicit, emergence of independence, more especially among boys than girls. Girls seem naturally, or by acculturation, to be more conformists than

---

[12] The student's attention is especially directed to A. W. Blair and W. H. Burton, *Growth and Development of the Preadolescent*, New York: Appleton-Century-Crofts, 1951.

boys at this age. If a girl is going to revolt against adults, she is more likely to do it at a later age; if a boy is going to give his family trouble, this is the time he is more likely to do it, or at least to serve notice of impending revolt. Apparently this happens in preadolescence in our culture, at least in part because men are so little a part of the boy's world that he has a difficult time finding out how to be a boy. He doesn't yet know how a man acts, and the only way he can find out is to revolt against female influences, go off with his peers, and blunder his way, together with his cronies, into the meaning of being a man. This is probably one of the reasons that boys supposedly do not like girls in preadolescence. It is not because girls are not really attractive to them, but rather because they are rejecting the whole female species for the time being, including mothers, Sunday School teachers, and day-school teachers—all of whom are not uncommonly women. Having become more aware of this problem in recent years, there have been attempts to get more men into the elementary school as teachers, so that there can be male identification without boys having to go off in gangs to find out what a man is and how he acts. In other words, the chief reason we have this incipient revolt among boys in preadolescenec is to be found in the culture. In neighborhoods where fathers are around home more, boys and girls at the pre-adolescent level usually play together indiscriminately. At least they are not acutely aware of the fact that they are a mixed group of boys and girls playing together. In some measure this is so because the boys do not have the problem of finding out what a man is like, and consequently, they do not make the boy-girl distinction seriously.

Let us go on further now and ask what extent physical and social factors are clues to understanding adolescence. We assume correctly that adolescence is a very formative period; we also assume that it is a very difficult period for the adolescent. While adolescence does have its difficulties, we as adults may overaccentuate them. Somewhat ambivalently we also sentimentalize and romanticize adolescence. The common assumption for generations has been that adolescence is primarily a glandular affair, that adolescence is produced primarily by pubescent changes. While it would be an exaggeration to say that pubescent changes offer no clue to adolescence, nevertheless, it now appears that they are not the singular clue we had been inclined to assume earlier. Alongside this clue we must also recognize that social transaction is as much the key to adolescence as glandular change, if not more so. Pubescence is a fairly short period, and it happens in some cases very early. With girls it is usually complete by the age of thirteen; with some boys it is also complete by that age, but with the majority it is completed by fourteen or fifteen. This is a relatively short period compared to the ten or twelve years commonly assumed to be the duration of adolescence. It is granted that pubescence gives a dimension to life that life did not have before its onset, and this dimension has educational significance. It may very well be that graduation from elementary-school to secondary-school education should be determined by pubescence, regardless of the child's status in grade-level or achievement.[13] For when a child becomes pubescent, there are intellectual and emotional aspects which are likely to make him reach out for an education of different dimensions than are adequate to a child before he becomes pubescent. Certainly pubescence is not without significance, intellectual and emotional, as well as physical. But, even so, it is a comparatively short period.

In contrast to this, observe what a long period adolescence is. Rightly or wrongly, in our culture we think of adolescence as extending from its inception at age twelve or earlier to about age twenty-four. While the duration may be somewhat arbitrarily assigned by our culture, why is it such a long period? Some of the reasons are social, some are economic. A person cannot become self-supporting, nor can he maintain a home and support a family until a relatively advanced age. At any rate, the transition from the time when a child is preadolescent to that point at which he is ready to be independent of the parental home, has established the necessary economic stability, has made the love attachments essential to establishing a home, and has built a context of friends and peers in the midst of which he can live—this transition involves many subtle achievements of no mean order. This is not to say anything concerning the extended education which is involved for those who follow a career in college and possibly go on to graduate

---

[13] See Harry S. Broudy, *Building a Philosophy of Education*, New York: Prentice-Hall, 1954, pp. 244–247.

or professional school. For this considerable number of our youth there is a long period of education in which they have a kind of freedom and independence of their homes, but because of which the economic adjustment is postponed. Such considerations as these suggest that social factors are at least as significant as physical factors in making adolescence what it is. Because of them, adolescence is the growth and adjustment period in which the individual is under the necessity of building both his independence and its setting as well. For independence is not just something that exists by itself; independence has a setting, a context of relationships in which it can come into being and thrive. The reason for existence of the adolescent period of growth is this task of building a life and its setting. While the figure is extreme, adolescence is not unlike standing on the end of a diving board, bouncing up and down, getting ready to jump, and at the same time, by some magical feat, getting enough water in the pool so as to make the leap at least possibly successful. A youth has to build; his problem is not just a matter of leaving the nest; he has to build a nest into which to move. This is the problem of independence in adolescence, and it is a good bit more than growing physically through pubescent changes.

An Interpretive View

There is one subject remaining in growth and development which may be called the theological dimension of growth. To take this up is to present some concepts which may be helpful in a deeper understanding of growth or an interpretive view of it. This is to go beyond the descriptive and to approximate a kind of theology of growth.[14] In religious and Christian education we have borrowed from psychology at the descriptive level, although probably not enough and not carefully enough. We have scarcely done anything interpretively with psychology, except in a very limited way in some of the pastoral psychology and counseling areas; in relation to growth very little interpretation has been attempted. We take the descriptive evidence that people grow through characteristic stages of development, and we recognize that if we are going to teach them, we must somehow gear our teaching to

[14] See the author's "Theology and Psychology: Some Points of Convergence," *Encounter* (Autumn, 1958), Vol. XIX, No. 4, pp. 391–406.

the way we find the individual at any particular point. This, of course, has its relevance and importance, but we must go further.

For example, we must ask the questions: Why does a person need to grow? Why should there be growth at all? Why should nurture in the Church have to cope with the fact of growth? This is to raise a philosophical and theological question about the "why" of growth; the direction of its answer may be indicated in the following. The nature of selfhood, and the nature of man as a person and as a child of God made in the image of God, is such that he cannot be a person, or a self without participating in the process of becoming what he is to be. In other words, it is necessarily a contradiction to suppose that self could ever be born fully complete in one act; this is contradictory of the nature of selfhood, it can't happen. In order for a self to be a self it must participate in its own becoming. This means growth; it means development; it means some kind of early start from small beginnings—small in many ways, not just in size. These beginnings are potentialities, and as they move into the actualities they foreshadow, a self comes into being. This is the only way that one made in the image of God may become, in spite of his sinfulness, a fitting object of the love of God; this is the only way that such a being can come to be. Now this is a general answer, in sketch, to the question of why there is growth. It can and should be made much more articulate, if religious education is to make full and responsible use of the psychology of growth.

There are three dimensions evident in the "becoming" depicted in the psychological description of growth and development. The first of these dimensions is the qualitative development of knowledge. It begins in early childhood, with fantasy, moves into factualism by late childhood or preadolescence, and finally reaches into symbolic understanding by later adolescence or adulthood. Descriptively, we know that in childhood, up to at least the seventh and eighth year, the individual is interested in imaginative narratives. The child is fascinated and carried along by them, becomes involved in them; it makes no difference to him whether they are true or not. Of course, we never completely outgrow some interest in fantasy; but with the small child it is a consuming interest. As the child approaches preadolescence, his concern begins to shift to whether or not a narrative is true. And by whether or not it is

217

true, he means, "did it actually happen? Is this a fact?" The question, "Is it true?" may be asked as early as four or five, but it becomes both persistent and primary by preadolescence and is sometimes accompanied by a disdain of fantasy. This interest in what actually happens, in what actually can happen, in cause and effect begins to smack of the prosaic character of the adult world. When we give it some thought, we are inclined to wonder why it is that children so commonly lose their creative imagination before they get beyond adolescence. Yet in childhood it is so very rich; adults could well be jealous of the rich and free imaginative life of childhood. It is not clear whether this loss is natural; there is reasonable suspicion that the culture must bear a share of the blame. Even so, the beginning of interest in facts is also the beginning of responsibility; after all, there is irresponsibility in fantasy, inviting though it may be. We must deal with realities as realities and face facts as facts. This movement of change in the quality of knowledge may move on, and in some cases does so move, to a higher level of understanding at which fantasy is reinstated, as it were, by taking on meanings and conveying truths for which factual truth is a very inept medium. Our discussion is back at symbolism again. It may be that there are certain stories of the Bible that should be re-mythologized in adult life, transposing the natural literalism of childhood into a conscious symbolism, to use Tillich's terms again.[15] If this happens at the adult level, then instead of literalism becoming rigidly self-conscious and deliberate, there will be symbolic discernment, which is beyond both factualism and fantasy.

The second of these dimensions cuts across the ethical and religious realms and has to do with the individual's responsibility as an individual and with his potential for responsibility. The movement of this dimension begins in dependence, moves to independence, and then moves on to an independence based on a dependence of faith. To attempt this interpretation is first of all to recognize what has been said descriptively concerning the emergence of independence and then to go beyond description to imply its meaning. We are all born in the dependency of infancy; one of the mysteries and wonders of the Incarnation to those who believe in it, and no doubt a stumbling-block to those who do not so believe, is that God should be willing to come into the world of man in the com-

[15] See pp. 144–145.

218

plete dependency of infancy. It is into such complete dependency that every man is first born, and he remains so dependent for many years. One aspect of his growth and development as a person is to emerge from this state and become independent. It has already been implied that the keys to adolescence are cutting of the strings of dependence upon one's parents and family, and developing a new context to take the place of the parental home. It should not therefore be surprising to us that in the preadolescent ages children sometimes begin to revolt. In doing this they are trying to express their independence, even if in very immature ways. It is no wonder that this floundering independence takes extreme forms and that in adolescence it sometimes becomes a violent revolt. We should be happy rather than chagrined that adolescents revolt, because the revolt of the adolescent is the opportunity for a new lease on life for the human race. In fact, we should be more alarmed about simulated revolt in adolescence than real revolt, because a simulated revolt misses the real opportunity of adolescence and may result in sheer conformity, or the failure ever to be independent, or both.

However that may be, we do want to make clear that sheer independence, when viewed in the full span of growth, is not enough, however necessary it may be as a stage in growth. Sheer independence can be both immature and irresponsible; theologically, it can also be the primary and fundamental revolt of complete autonomy, setting one's self up as God instead of acquiescing to be a man. There is a quality of personal life beyond sheer independence which, while it may be very uncommon, is much to be desired; it is independence founded upon the dependence of faith in God. Genuine independence among men, apart from genuine and pure religious faith, is very rare. At this point, Martin Luther may represent for us real independence; independence based on faith, which says in action more than in words, "Here I stand; I cannot do otherwise; God help me!" This is still independence; but it is something other than presumptuous revolt, it is something other than a godless autonomy. This is independence which can stand and which does stand when the crisis is on, because it is a stand taken humbly in the prophetic faith that God will support the venture.

So much for another one of the interpretive dimensions of growth: first complete dependence; then independence; and finally independence based on faith in God. How many of us ever come to that final level of maturity is another question.

The third and last of the dimensions of growth we will venture here is social and religious. This is the movement from community to individuality and then, beyond this, to individuality in community. We all know that we are born in community, that birth is a social process, and that the small child has, as a rule, a very healthy sense of community. The small child can say "we," with meaning, long before he can say "I," with equal meaning. He cannot at first distinguish between himself and his mother, or sometimes even between himself and his father, or himself and his family. Being born in community is a very healthy condition and, no doubt, the basis of much of the happiness and contentment of a healthy childhood.

Maturation, however, causes us to move from this consciousness of community into individuality, and we find our individuality by a kind of conversation or reciprocity with the community into which we are born. This reciprocity, in which community is the sounding board, is parallel to what was said earlier in this chapter about personality coming into existence only as it interacts with its culture. Individuality, of course, is always implicitly present, but a child doesn't begin with a conscious or articulated individuality. George Herbert Meade, among many others, has pointed out that much of the child's play is an attempt, however unconscious, to find his individuality. For example, he will write a letter, go to the mailbox and mail it, be the postman who delivers it, assume the part of the person who receives it, and finally sit down to read the letter he has received. He goes through this imaginary acting, playing different roles by way of finding out who he is; it is a search for his individuality. While this kind of play usually takes place earlier, in later childhood, and certainly in pre-adolescence, the articulation of individuality is a counterpart of the emergence of independence. This development continues until there is a self-consciously distinct individuality, as over against the community. This individuality may, of course, have its aberrations in the desire for complete autonomy, rugged individualism, or a destructive attitude toward the community. There is relief, however, in the fact that there is a level of maturity beyond this, to which we will now turn in completing the individual-community cycle.

This level beyond is that one at which we self-consciously and deliberately recognize that individuality has its matrix and its home, as it were, within community. In a sense, this is a return to the healthy "we-feeling" of early childhood, but at a higher level, with all of the intricacies and ramifications of adult experience woven into it. This has great significance for nurture, for religious belief, and for theological understanding. It even has implicit in it the how of discerning the Word of God in the Bible. The individual is consciously in and of community; he knows that he can never be separate from community. Although the community cannot exercise an arbitrary and blind control over him, at a deeper level there is a kind of inner control the community exercises over the individual as he participates in and partakes of its life. Although possibly of secondary importance, this is another reason for beginning, as we have done in this book, with the actuality of the Church. This is where we must begin, not only because this is where we are, but because here the individual is healthfully within community, because he is both subject and object in this community, and because it is this community in which the Word of God is revealed.

CHAPTER *14*

Psychology and Nurture in the Church: Learning Theory

A s we continue our consideration of the science of psychology, now giving consideration to the theory of learning, we will first of all make two general observations regarding learning, neither of which reflects a particular point of view. The first of these observations has almost become a cliché among educators: that the whole person is engaged when learning takes place. John Dewey used to observe that teachers would be happier if Johnny could leave his body at home and not bring it to school; school-keeping would be so much easier that way. This remark indicates the narrow and constricted view both of learning and the learner which was current then and which is still not uncommon. We do not just learn with the mind; when we learn, all aspects of the person are involved, the body, the emotions, volition—the whole person.

The second observation is that the situation in which the learning goes on is also involved in the learning and provides a context which cannot be disregarded. Fond parents often discover this in an obverse way when their children are supposed to perform for relatives or guests. Here is a baby, two or three months old, who is about to be fed some cereal by her mother in the presence of company. The child has already achieved admirable proficiency in this new stage of eating. The mother sits down with the baby, each duly aproned and bibbed, and proceeds with the operation in full expectation of success and the admiring approval of the guests.

But, no, the infant forces every spoonful out with his tongue and refuses to eat anything! The mother moans, "This would happen now!" What is so easily missed is that the reason it did happen was that guests were present, and the context was different from what it usually is. The child is usually fed without benefit of inquisitive observers, and this is why the newly learned skill in eating didn't appear. It is so easy for us to overlook the context, but the context is part of the learning, and we can never define learning, or adequately guide learning, if we try to do it independently of the context. Again, this has its connection with what we have been saying about religious nurture; we cannot separate nurture from its context, which is the Church.

LEARNING THEORIES

We will now take up successively five conceptions of learning, the last of which is the author's attempt at an inclusive theory of learning which is both psychologically creditable and in harmony with the purpose and character of nurture in the Church. They are presented here in a manner somewhat less than technical, but not, it is hoped, with the inaccuracies of a popular presentation.

Learning as Transmission

The first of these theories is that learning is the receiving of that which is transmitted. This will be recognized readily as a very popular assumption about education, and a very little study of history will disclose that it is an extremely old conception. While there is a legitimate place for the kind of learning which is the receiving of content transmitted, there is danger that this conception will imply that there is no other kind of learning. In fact, many of our current criticisms of education, justified as they may often be, still very commonly imply that if education is to be solid, it must be largely, if not entirely, the acquisition of knowledge. Whether the valued body of knowledge is science, culture, or religion, we very commonly equate learning entirely with the acquiring of this body of content. With respect to teaching in the Church, it should be forthrightly stated that it is important that each new generation should come to possess accurate knowledge of the Bible and authoritative knowledge of doctrine. It is recognized here that there is a transmissive element in this; but this is a minimal level of learning, not the maximal. This is an acquisition of the necessary currency of the Christian faith and of the Christian community. It is not, however, an end-product, it cannot be all of nurture. How this minimal content is acquired and how far reaching its significance is will be determined by the spirit of the teaching. Is it enough, for example, for such knowledge to be gotten as a predominantly intellectual process, as is sometimes the case? It is not intellectual in the sense that it is assumed to be solely a matter of the mind, but as though, according to this assumption, we could and do know about this minimal content more than we could feel about it—more than we could have it affect either the will or the whole person. Is knowledge of the Bible or knowledge of doctrine likely to have significance for the totality of life if it is gotten in this kind of dry and limited teaching? If it comes only by an intellectual process, however unrefined or unsophisticated, how much significance can the message of the Bible and the thought of the Church have for life? Will it necessarily follow from such a purely intellectual approach that there will be transfer into Christian life and action?

We have long lamented the separation of Sunday church-going and weekday living. We have long complained that people fail to live their religion. This is also an old problem in psychology, namely, the problem of transfer of training. How do you guarantee a transfer of what is learned from the situation in which it is taught to other situations in which it is to be practiced? Now, it would seem that such a content-centered approach, which is an almost purely mental and intellectual affair, although not very highly refined, misses the point of transfer of learning almost entirely. It misses the point of the carry-over into life, and we therefore have to turn to other conceptions of learning to get some adequate recognition of the problem of transfer. Even though we have usually had little sections at the end of the Sunday School lesson on application to everyday living, in all probability there has more often been failure to transfer than not. We turn, therefore, to a second conception of learning which proposes to give more attention to transfer.

Learning as Conditioning
or Training

A disparity between learning as transmission and learning as training should be recognized at the outset. As theories they cannot be set against each other as clearly competitive, because in some real measure they deal with different kinds of learning. Transmission is especially concerned with ideas, whereas training is more likely to be concerned with desired ways of acting.

There is a legitimate place for learning which is the training of action until it is acceptable, although such learning has its limits. There is also the danger that this kind of learning will be mistakenly identified with the whole of learning, when it is only a part. Learning as training or conditioning can readily be observed in the unexamined practice of parents. After all, children, especially small children, cannot be left completely free to do what they wish; they are born into a community, and there must be a degree of conformity if, to put it bluntly, chaos is to be avoided. Now this is the level at which the community, unconscious though it may be of it, places its demands on individual members. In this light we can see that a modicum of conformity is justified by necessity. This statement needs to be circumscribed by many cautions, for it may be that the only justification of conformity and the conditioning which produces it lies in the partial justification of the child's need for security. If we allow a child complete and uninhibited freedom, not only does it lead to chaos, but it leaves the child without a framework in which to operate. It is like opening to him a highway with no traffic lanes, signs, or signals. It is hazardous and it makes the smaller child insecure because he does not have the experience or the patterns of action for using such freedom. However, this is not to justify the blind gropings for order commonly made by parents and teachers alike. Nor is it to justify their indulgence in disciplinary practices just because the child gets security out of direction and even, up to a certain minimal level, out of punishment. Herbert Spencer was quite right in referring to the unexamined action of parents in relation to their children as the snapping and snarling of animals at their cubs! This well describes a good bit of unexamined parental action, even among supposedly enlightened people. That there is a normal place for training and

225

conditioning does not mean parents and teachers have license in its use.

Nevertheless, this kind of learning does try to get at the problem of transfer of training more than the transmissive conception. What it asks by way of presupposition is, "How do you know how a child is going to act when he is not at home and when he is not in school? Is there any way that learning can guarantee or pre-determine his conduct?" By way of answer to these questions, it is assumed that we cannot be too sure that the content we teach is going to have a controlling effect. It is also assumed that by the process of training it may be possible so to condition the child to act in an appropriate way, that when he gets into other situations it will be virtually impossible for him to act in any way other than that in which he has been conditioned.

This is the idea of character education; put in an exaggeratedly crude and grotesque form, character education is the conditioning of the child's conduct so that he cannot act otherwise, whatever the change in situation. While this is a forthright and direct at-tempt to get at transfer from one situation—and in terms of religion to try to guarantee that weekday living is going to have some kind of resemblance to Sunday religion—the difficulty remains that we cannot anticipate situations other than the learning situation specifically enough in order to condition for them. John Dewey took quite some care to point this out. We simply cannot be sure that the mechanisms of response we provide are going to be ade-quate to the situations the child will have to face.

If this is put on a broad social basis, as some earlier philosophers of education attempted, it places upon educators the heavy burden of blueprinting the future society. If conditioning is to be devised which will produce the proper kind of mechanisms of response, people will need to meet society so blueprinted. The trouble with this grandiose theory is that we are unable to blueprint the future of society; we cannot even blueprint the future of the individual, not even one's own future.[1] As Dewey properly pointed out, there are so many exigencies that cannot be anticipated, that what we are likely to be doing, when we condition a child, is habituating him in too rigid mechanisms which will not only be inadequate in

[1] See Ross L. Finney, A Sociological Philosophy of Education, New York: Macmillan, 1928.

future situations, but which will also handicap and inhibit him, making him more inept in meeting new situations than if we had not conditioned him at all. Therefore, although we must recognize a certain minimal place for conditioning and understand that there is a legitimate minimal control which the community exercises over the individual, at least at lower levels of maturity, the conditioning concept of learning is, nevertheless, quite inadequate for a total conception of nurture. Because of this, we turn to yet another learning theory for further light.

Learning as Having Its Clue in Insight

Indeed, a good bit of light has come in recent years from those who insist on the centrality of "insight" in learning. This theory of learning, to the extent that it is a theory, has arisen as a result of Gestalt and Field psychological theories. It frankly assumes that learning is not a mechanical affair, not a matter of accumulating a number of associations, and not simple trial-and-error. There are times, it is argued, when trial-and-error and association are bypassed by a perception which suddenly enters the learner's view of the situation and causes otherwise mechanical items or associative connections to fall into a meaningful pattern. With comparative suddenness the learner jumps from a low level of experience, at which a great deal more trial-and-error would be needed to achieve the meaningful pattern to the point at which things hang together, so that there is control, achievement, and completion of a connection which makes sense in that situation. This is not the whole of learning, but it is a very important part of it, the perceiving of connections by which suddenly there is a rapid advance, a rapid achievement in comparison to what has gone before. This may be reflected in many learning curves, even in mechanical-learning curves, such as in learning to use the typewriter. Very early in the game there is a sudden increase in control, although true enough, this level may often recede before there can be other advances. Later similar sharp advances occur, after there is a fund of experience or practice on which they can be built.

One helpful analysis of the steps by which insight emerges is included in the book, *Introductory Psychology for Students of Education* by Edmund S. Conklin and Frank S. Freeman.[2] Ac-

2 New York: Henry Holt, 1939, chap. 9, pp. 229–268.

227

cording to these authors, the first approach we make to any situation is one of viewing it as an undifferentiated whole. We face a new situation in which something new is to be learned, and the first impression we have is that of a whole in which no details stand out clearly for us, or at most very few. Now there is value in this early stage of acquaintance, even though it may exemplify lack of insight. The value is the sense of the whole, diffuse and undifferentiated though it may be. Often in serious study of a book (if freedom from deadlines will permit it) a valuable first step is just to read the book as casually as possible, almost the way you would read a novel, without a pencil ready to mark every line which is supposedly important. For it is by discovering the whole book first that you will gain the context in which you can later determine which points are important and which are secondary.

The second step in the emergence of insight, after the sense of the undifferentiated whole, is differentiation or analysis, in which parts are brought into focus, e.g., taking pencil in hand and marking the book so as to make details stand out. There is danger of getting lost in this process of differentiation, although it is less likely if preceded by the sense of the undifferentiated whole. The second stage moves into analysis, although the learner may lose view of the whole, he still knows that he is analyzing something that is a totality. This analysis may have to go on for some time, depending upon the complexity of the situation or subject and the ability level of the learner.

Then after analysis has run its course and differentiations have been adequately made, learning moves on to the third step, which is consideration of the whole as differentiated. This is not, of course, consciously and deliberately intended by the learner; he does not say, "First I will look at the whole; then I am going to analyze; and after I have finished analyzing, I will synthesize." Rather, according to this conception of learning, this is the way the mind tends to work; it is not a consciously formulated plan of attack. Some of us have a greater penchant for detail, and we tend to get lost in detail at the expense of not seeing the whole; others of us have a greater interest in the whole and tend to neglect detail as a result. Whatever the individual propensities may be, the learner returns to the differentiated whole and looks at the whole again after analysis, with a new richness of recognition of it as a whole with parts, and of the parts as lending their peculiar quality to the whole. There is a difference, for example, between the person who first hears a symphony without any previous knowledge of it and the person who hears it with a detailed knowledge of its various themes and the total character of the work. The latter person represents this more advanced and richer stage of insight beyond the two previous levels.

There is a fourth level of insight beyond these three and which learning may only rarely achieve; it is the level known as redefinition or reconstruction. At this consummate level, a new organization of parts is made, which is other than the pattern of the present whole being studied, for which there is no precedent, and of which there is no previous knowledge, at least for the learner. This is the inventive and creative level of knowledge and learning, at which the human race makes all of its advances whenever they are made. Examples can even be found in animal life however. One of the apes in Kohler's experiments tried to "redefine" when confronted with a problem which was too difficult. Hanging high in his cage were bananas, which he wanted very much. The rope holding them was on a pulley, and the knot which was within his reach was too complex to untie. He fussed about getting them for a while, but eventually a brainstorm hit him, and he ran back to his quarters, returned with his blanket, and tried to flick the bananas with it so they would fall. Whether he was successful or not this was redefinition, a rather high achievement. A blanket is something you sleep on and not something with which to retrieve unreachable bananas, at least not ordinarily.[3] The child, when he takes his telescoped blocks and makes a platform out of them by which he can climb out of his playpen, is making a redefinition. The musician who finds some new chord combination or resolution is making a redefinition. The story is told that as Edvard Grieg was playing a new composition for his old master, Franz Liszt, he came to a certain resolution in the harmony which was new and different; Liszt exclaimed, "Yes, why not!" Why not this new harmonic sequence! This again is redefinition. It may be that one of the reasons we now have modern music, with its frequent dissonances, and progressive jazz with its fluid freedom from rhythmic structure, is that conventional melodic forms and rhyth-

[3] See Conklin and Freeman, op. cit., p. 256.

mic "beats" have been rather fully explored. To find a new and fresh musical expression, some have turned to dissonance and to unfamiliar rhythms which at times seem to have no beat at all. This also is redefinition.

We now turn to another and more common treatment of the learning process, for which this review of the four levels of insight in the field theory of learning may partially prepare the way.

Learning as Problem-Solving

Learning as the solving of problems is a theory that was created almost single-handedly by John Dewey, although some of his followers may have worked out significant elaborations and variations. It may be the most commonly accepted theory of learning today among those who think critically about the learning process; it has exerted considerable influence in educational psychology. This conception, as indicated earlier, came over into religious education by way of progressive education and the experimentalist educational philosophy.

This theory is that we always learn in a problematic situation. Accordingly, the experience of each individual focuses successively in the problems that he faces; so entirely is this the case that the individual truly thinks only when he is confronted by a problem, and only then does he learn. This is true both for individual experience and for social experience. This goes clearly beyond the conceptions of learning as transmission or conditioning; the theory forthrightly assumes that life is fluid, that it moves by unanticipated episodes, which in great measure it is not possible to anticipate, and that these episodes focus in, and are caused by, some kind of block in experience which dams it up and prevents it from flowing smoothly until the block is removed.

In the more ramified treatment in his *Logic*,[4] Dewey says that these blocks emerge incipiently in experience as indeterminacies. This theory has a significant advantage over mere transmissiveness, because it is assumed that any knowledge or information that is carried over from past experience, whether of the human race, of a group, or of one's own experience, must always be tailor-made for the particular situation at hand. Nothing can be taken over ready-made from one situation to another; always such borrowings have

[4] John Dewey, *Logic, The Theory of Inquiry*, New York: Henry Holt, 1938.

to be adapted and particularized for each situation. Furthermore, it is not possible to apply the fixed patterns of action in which one is conditioned in some previous experience; if we are to be successful, we must adjust to the situation at hand and recognize that just as there is no information that precisely fits that situation, so also there is no ready-made action that fits. There will, of course, be both information and previous actions which are comparable—in fact, that is what we look for when we are seeking possible solutions to a present problem. That is the reason, by way of an important example, that we go to history—we are seeking possible solutions for present difficulties. Accordingly, Dewey held that the best way to teach history is to teach it backwards; move from the present, and go to the library of history to pull books from the shelves which give us approximations of the particular answers we need in the present. Such an approach certainly makes history come alive. How much history we could all learn were we to turn seriously to the past to find out why we have the massive stalemate between the East and the West, which keeps the world from moving on to other more interesting and fruitful endeavors. However valuable history or any other subject may be, we cannot bring information effectively to a particular situation without adapting it, nor can we bring over patterns of action wholesale, if this theory is correct. We must always hold both patterns of action and information in abeyance, and make them fit the new situation. This, of course, means that learning is fundamentally neither transmission nor conditioning. It is something more flexible and fluid than either of these.

This conception of learning, even so, has a definite pattern, and because of this pattern an orthodoxy has grown up among the followers of John Dewey, some of whom fail to preserve the richness and freedom of his thought. If we are to keep it authentic, the pattern cannot be quite so easily frozen as it occasionally is, in spite of its definiteness and very clear direction. The first phase of this direction has already been indicated, namely, the arresting of experience by a blockage and the accompanying consciousness that something is wrong somewhere.

The second stage is the focusing of attention upon the indeterminacy, in the attempt to define it and to see clearly what it is that is wrong. Viewed psychologically, the flow of experience is

231

held up in order that action can be a total, rather than a blind response to a stimulus. In this second step, while experience is at a kind of standstill, the indeterminacy tends to become more clear, and eventually, if the subject is successful, it becomes defined as a rather fully delineated problem.

This step of defining the problem then grows into a new and third phase, which is the observation of all relevant data pertaining to the problem. At a later phase of the movement, the focus of attention will enlarge to include all resources and information which may suggest possible solutions, but at this third step attention is limited to analyzing the problem and the context in which it has arisen. In other words, this entire movement of learning can be thought of as an ever-widening focus of attention, starting with the indeterminacy, widening out to definition of the problem, then enlarging to observing the situation, and finally including resources outside the situation in which the material for solutions may be found. It will be well to observe at this point that Dewey's logic of both thought and learning is a great advance over sheer induction as first formulated by Francis Bacon in his *Novum Organum*. Induction essentially tells us to observe and get the facts. This in itself was very cogent advice which had far reaching influence, but it offered no pattern, direction, or focus for observation. This is one of the most significant advances in Dewey's thought; it offers focus and direction to the inductive process.

As the focus of learning widens out to include consideration of sources of possible solution outside the situation, as already noted for example in history, it moves into a fourth phase in which the suggestion of hypotheses may occur. To enter this phase is for the learner to rise to the level of redefinition or reconstruction in his thinking, the rare achievement already described in our treatment of the Field theory of learning. Problem-solving as a theory of learning virtually demands of the learner that he always rise to the level of redefinition.

The fifth and final step in the movement of learning comes after hypotheses are at hand which promise solution to the problem. It is a natural or normal succession to move on to the testing of these hypotheses to see which, if any, is the best solution. There are two norms by which an hypothesis must be judged in this theory before it can be accepted as a solution: (1) it must meet all the demands of the situation in which the problem arose, i.e., be a total solution; and (2) it must not handicap or borrow from the future in any way, it must leave it free and unencumbered. When a hypothesis passes these two tests, it may be accepted as the re-definition or reconstruction for the situation, by which experience may flow freely again until a new block stands in the way. This is the problem-solving pattern of learning; of course, it may be—and often has been—reduced to an arid orthodoxy, but if it is under-stood and practiced to the fullness of its possible nuances, it makes much more sense than mere transmission or conditioning.

What this learning theory has meant when it has been taken over bodily into religious education is that the approach to lessons is through problems which are real and present in the experience of pupils. What it has meant more particularly in curriculum is that curriculum units are written with a problem or life-situation as the focus.

Enlightening and practicable as this theory of learning is, ques-tion must be raised concerning its central assumption. This is that there is no thinking or learning unless the subject is forced to it by an indeterminacy in which circumstances ensnare him. Is this actually the only occasion for learning? Or do we learn because of internal compulsions to apply ourselves to some task because we want to? Is it only problematic circumstances on the "outside," which force us to apply ourselves? It is submitted here that people can and do think and learn without being forced to it by a prob-lem, although it may not as commonly be the case. There are occasions when at least some students think because of some inner urge and move out into creative achievement, even to the very rare level of redefinition.

Harry Broudy has criticized this theory from another legitimate standpoint which deserves careful consideration.[5] He has taken the exponents of this theory to task because of their emphasis upon "felt needs." He argues that to give exclusive focus to a felt need or problem may well be to miss the real need, which may not be felt and to knowledge of which we may need to be awakened.

[5] See *Building a Philosophy of Education*, New York: Prentice-Hall, 1954, pp. 56–62; 151–156.

Toward an Inclusive Theory of Learning

Having now presented four conceptions of learning, it remains to raise the question of whether there can be some inclusive conception of learning—or therefore, of nurture in the Church—more adequate than any one of these four by itself. Such a theory to be acceptable has to give due place for the minimal transmission and training which the heritage and the Christian community respectively would require, but in a valid way. It must be realistic concerning the pressure of problems in experience and as timely occasions for learning. It must give full recognition to the Christian community as the dynamic and more-than-human context in which each individual, and each new generation, somehow comes into possession of and participation in the Christian faith, when and if he does rise to faith. We will propose such a theory of learning, difficult though the endeavor is and in spite of the certainty that it will be incomplete.

First of all, the context of that learning which is nurture in the Faith, is the living dynamic community within which the learner is born, or at least of which he is a member. This is to say that learning always has a context and that for nurture in the Faith it is the Church. We are at least attempting to say more here than is said in the problem-solving theory. The context in the problem-solving theory always has the very narrow focus of the problem, so much so, that there is scarcely any background. In trying to sense the context of learning, it is necessary to discern many fluid factors in the experience of learners; this discernment approximates what the Field psychologists refer to as a field. It would be very foolish to assume that an appointed hour, a particular time schedule, and a particular subject of study constitute a field or context. What is involved for a child and his family in getting to Sunday Church School on time, for example? What is the next thing facing him after this particular class session? What demands or indulgent laissez faire will he meet when he returns home? These may exemplify the less tangible and more fluid factors, nevertheless real, that have to be taken into account in perceiving the immediate context of a given teaching-learning act.

There is also a broad and more inclusive over-all context. For so-called secular learning, this broad and inclusive context is the culture—possibly the whole world-culture, certainly the local or regional culture, hopefully, also world-wide culture and history-long culture. In Christian education this more inclusive context is the Church—the Church not only in the present, but the Church in its historic dimension as well. And more immediately—especially for the small child, but for all of us in some real measure—the Christian family is the mediator of the Church as context.

Secondly, the form or pattern of learning must approximate the forms and patterns of the experience of the learner. As indicated earlier, the effective guidance of learning has to be based on a perception of the intangibles comprising the movement of life, as it is flowing and moving now; it cannot be determined by the more arbitrary patterns of subject-matter areas, schedules of classes, arrangement of courses in the curriculum, etc., logical and valid as they may be academically. The latter are forms that are probably necessary in some measure to order and organization, but they very often get in the way of learning. This is one of the reasons that some institutions are trying to cut across disciplinary fields in course offerings, sometimes offering fewer courses embracing larger blocks of time and material. The attempt to dissolve somewhat these formal structures is an expression of the discernment that the forms to which learning must be adapted are the less tangible elements, most of which are in motion all of the time, and are components of the learner's experience.

In this context, comprised more of intangibles than tangibles, to take up the third point, a number of happenings will transpire to constitute learning. There will be transmission of subject-matter, because the community believes that it has something to communicate to the learner and because it has a language by which to communicate it. This transmissive element will be minimal, however, for by no means is it the totality of teaching and learning. Specifically in nurture in the Church there will be acquisition of knowledge of the Bible, doctrine, and history. There will also be training, not so much for the community to lay its demands for conformity upon the individual, except at very low levels of maturity, but in order that the individual may become part of the community and may participate in the corporate life of the community. This conditioning or discipline is not so much a factor by which the community requires conformity as it is a dynamic overture from community to individual, resulting in reciprocity between the individual and the community. It is a two-way affair in which on occasion the individual brings change into the community.

Specifically, in Christian nurture, character and conduct will be determined by the community at lower age-levels, to avoid chaotic determinations by the learner. At later levels of maturity, however, this will be superseded by critical and individuated responses to the community, even to the point at which prophecy can come out of this reciprocity. At this high level, the individual may stand over against the church and may even speak in terms of judgment to the church. The crux and center of this theory of learning or nurture will be confrontation of the learner in such a way that he faces necessary alternatives of judgment or action, although this may seem to constrict learning to a gateway which is too narrow. Between these alternatives there will necessarily be tension, tension which can only be resolved by the learner's decision, and not by the decision of anyone else. It may be that this needs some elaboration, especially since it is the central pivot in the theory being proposed here. This is unashamedly a dialectical conception of learning, and it may not be without connection with a dialectical theology. It is to say that, instead of having its turning point only in a block, as in the problem-solving treatment of learning, the pivot of learning is a forking of the ways at which a decision must be made. There is a necessary tension between the alternatives, of which there may be several, and the only way in which that tension can be resolved is by an act of decision.

Decision-making, of course, has its maturity levels which must be fully taken into account. At lower levels decisions will have to be gauged so as to be of a simpler order; at higher levels they can be—indeed, will have to be—of quite another magnitude. Furthermore, this resolution of tension is a resolution which only the learner himself can make; no one else can make it for him. This is also to acknowledge that decision-making permeates the entire process of education and nurture. Never is there any learning without decision; for us to make artificial separations, as we have commonly done at least in the Church, that on certain days in the year we learn and then on some particular day we make decisions, is most radically mistaken. It is to separate nurture and evangelism, with the implication that there is no decision in learning, and possibly also that there is no learning in evangelism. There is not even a secular theory of learning, having any scholarly weight, that does not include the element of decision at its heart.

As the learner faces these alternatives between which he must make a decision, in order to resolve the tension, the wise teacher must be his guide in such a delicate way that the subject's powers of insight and the revelation of God may meet—by the grace of God. While the teacher or parent must be cautious in keeping the tension from being too great for the child or youth to bear at the time, he must, nevertheless, be sure that he is never so protective as to shield the learner from his own crises and thereby prevent him from making his own decisions. Risks are necessarily involved. For the crises children and youths face are common to the human race; all men have to face them and each must face them for himself. This is essential to first-hand faith, and there can be no second-hand faith. With the Christian community as the context, the Bible and Christian doctrine as the intellectual media of communication, the essence of nurture becomes *contemporaneous revelation*—revelation in which the Living Word speaks to the learner and to which the learner is therefore in a position to respond, decide for, believe in, and live in commitment to.

While this theory, now stated at least in outline, does not take into account all of the many nuances and technical precisions of a full-fledged theory of learning, it is submitted as offering the right direction for Christian nurture and not being without some degree of theological integrity.

CHAPTER *15*

Nurture in the Church and Method

*M*ethod, like curriculum, cannot be dealt with concretely and realistically by means of written discourse. As effective study of curriculum must turn to actual literature and must analyze the attempts that have been made in it to provide an organized and intentional curriculum; so also in method, if it is to be brought to effective focus, it is necessary to deal with actual methods in operation. This cannot be done by discussing it nearly so well as in the guided practice of method.

Here is a small class, for example, of only five members. They are studying teaching method and have gone over many of the matters we will consider in this chapter. But by way of becoming concrete and operational in their study, they constitute themselves as a teaching seminar in which they take turns teaching each other. They select as their object of study, but not by unanimous choice, Dietrich Bonhoeffer's *Life Together*.[1] Their plan is to teach each other, not imaginatively as though they were an adult group in the church, but realistically as peers studying together in a theological seminary. Their plan includes a teaching session, recorded on tape, and a criticism session, for each section of the book selected for study. With the teaching session recorded, the session of criticism can be the whole class listening to itself as objectively and critically as possible.

As might be expected, this class made some rather surprising discoveries. For example, in one session there was a period of five

[1] Trans. by John W. Doberstern, New York: Harper, 1954.

minutes taken up by a conversation between two members of the class, the other three members remaining completely silent. On another occasion, they noted that after the teacher had asked one general question, his voice was not heard again for about fifteen minutes. By such an operational device as this, necessitating rather small groups, method can be studied in practice as well as in theory, although responsible and fully conceived theory of method should by no means be deprecated.

Excellent as such a procedure as this may prove to be, and important as it may be as a supplement to a chapter such as this, there are, nevertheless, some very relevant matters concerning teaching method which can be taken up in a chapter on method. The following considerations will comprise this examination of method. First, we will discuss somewhat generally the psychological and sociological roots of method. These discussions may give some continuity between this chapter and Chapters 11, 13, and 14. Following these more general approaches, we will then take up for specific consideration some staples, as it were, of methodology: discussion; the question; lecture or direct instruction; story-telling; and the unit of study.

PSYCHOLOGICAL ASPECTS OF METHOD

While detailed discussion of the psychological roots of method cannot be attempted here, it is well at least to recognize that each individual in a class brings with him psychological conditions and motifs which bear upon method. These relate to matters we have discussed generally in the chapters on psychology, such as the nature of personality, growth and development, and theory of learning. To be effective as a teacher, without assuming that anyone ever achieves the level of the so-called master teacher, or that to do so is desirable, one must take into account the psychological angles presented by each individual in his classroom.

For example, a teacher should be sufficiently perceptive of individual students to know whether the self which is presented in the classroom by each particular student is his real self, whether it is the genuine expression of the self or some ficticious facade. Teachers are a bit deluded, if not actually stupid, if they accept that self the student wants to appear to be as his real person. A part of the task of the teacher is to look behind, as it were, to see what is going on in a person's mind, seeing through to his real motivations, insofar as possible. Method, rightly conceived, is a means of getting at the real person, not being artificial ourselves as teachers and not permitting our students to be artificial. The overtures of the teacher to all the members of his class should be genuine and sincere, evoking honesty and forthrightness from the student, not self-deceit. Even at our best, all of us have self-deceit in us; we certainly should not encourage or indulge it in our teaching, wittingly or unwittingly.

GROUP LIFE

Comparable to this psychological aspect of method is group process, which also must be taken fully into account. As teachers need to be perceptive concerning the psychology of each individual, they also need to discern the corporate aspect of the class, which will have an equally important bearing upon method. There is a sociology of method just as there is a psychology of method; this is not to imply, however, that all psychology involved in method is individual psychology. Much of the sociology of a learning group may be both innocent and free from complexity, as in the case of the class in method already cited. But this is by no means always or entirely the case; often the sociology is much more complicated than this. For example, if it is agreed that a teacher or leader must recognize the natural or cultural limitations of the group with which he is dealing, but that he must also lead its members to reach beyond these limitations, then there will necessarily be times when he will place a heavy strain on his own relation with the group; he may even run the hazard of breaking this relation and losing the confidence of those he is trying to help. Going beyond the level of innocence and considering the guile present in most every group, we must recognize such unmentionables as "hidden agendas," cliques, status-seeking, power struggles, and just plain politics!

On occasion a good teacher may have to ask himself, "To what extent is there a hidden agenda in this group?" Not uncommonly, there are two agendas in a class or group: the agenda the teacher or leader intends and the agenda the students are tacitly willing to follow. There are also mixed agendas, what student A would really like to see happen and what student B really wants, for example. And most likely they are in conflict. The strange thing about hidden agendas is that only rarely can they be brought out into the open. Most commonly we must deal with them through and by means of the public agenda. This is to say that the group works at the things which are openly before it, but in working at these, it gets at the hidden agendas indirectly. It is less frequent that the leader will be able to bring covert intentions out in the open and challenge them directly.

Having looked briefly at these two general aspects of method, we will now discuss teaching methods more specifically. There will be no attempt to be inclusive in this treatment; we will consider especially those methods which must be the stock-in-trade of every effective teacher, almost without regard to the variations which may be made on them or their context in some larger methodological movement, such as the unit of study or the workshop.

DISCUSSION

Discussion is one of the "regulars" of teaching method, especially with the preadolescent age-level and beyond. Higher and graduate education may be an exception to this statement, because at these levels lecture is predominant—although this may be little more than a cultural or academic habit-pattern. It may be that in addition to having a psychological basis from preadolescence on, because of the propensities of these ages, discussion has a very real sociological basis as well because it is a natural and normal expression of group-life. As a staple of classroom activity, it often provides much of the background or setting in which other kinds of activity go on. A teacher may tell a story, deliver a lecture, or guide the class in carrying forward a unit or project, for example, but notice how much discussion is the connecting link, the means of assimilation, as in the story or lecture, or a mode of action, as in the unit of study.

Good discussions are planned, yet in a sense they also just happen. They come along normally in the flow of teaching and learning, true enough, and often it can be observed that discussions are not deliberately intended at the precise time when they occur.

What are analogies of this, where human intercourse is very informal and occurs unintended, though to very good effect? Think of play, for example; some of the play in which children engage is so much a matter of course that, when it happens at its most enjoyable, it is often not intended. Think of the mode of jazz artists in the so-called jam session. It is reported that the expensive and tightly programmed television hour involves necessary restrictions which make it too formal and rigid for the jazz idiom to get expressed at its free and spontaneous best. Good discussion is like this; when it happens there is an almost unintended freedom and flow continuous with the normal course of events.

Further, discussion may follow very normally from the study of content, especially after analysis, when evaluation and application are attempted. An adult class in the church may be seriously studying one of the Synoptic Gospels, for example, with a teacher who guides in a careful way and depends upon sound scholarship. Following the analysis of a particular passage, when the members of the class are trying to say what the passage means for them and what its significance is for life today, the mode most naturally becomes discussion.

Discussion is very likely to be an outgrowth of good questions, especially when the questions are designed to elicit evaluation and judgment. Discussion may also follow a story to very good effect, provided it is not used to the end of moralizing. When the story has relevance to the teaching at hand and when it is told so as to evoke judgment and decision, moralizing is both pointless and in bad taste.

Discussion has peculiar significance for teaching in the Church. There is increasing awareness of the phenomenon of group-life in the Church and of the value of working in sufficiently small groups that they can become articulate. At the same time, this is not to confuse the human phenomenon of group-life with Christian community, just because it is within the church as an institution. The distinction between the erotic community, however warm and secure, and the authentic Christian community must always be kept in mind.[2] There are instances, it should be pointed out, in which groups are therapeutic to the individual member. When a group is small enough to draw out and invite expression from the individ-

[2] See Bonhoeffer, op. cit., chap. 1, "Community."

ual who may have psychological problems, or maybe only make him feel accepted and socially at home, the group can actually exert a healing influence. Since discussion is so predominantly the mode of intercourse in groups, again we see that it has a most significant place in the teaching function of the Church. A second reason for this peculiar significance, entirely cultural though its roots may be, is that youth groups in the Church have relied heavily on expression rather than instruction for decades now. And when the order of the day is expression, this almost necessarily means discussion—partially, if not totally. An expressional society will do other things besides talk, but discussion will be dominant in its activity.

How to Select a Subject for Discussion

It may now be well to consider some of the requirements of a good subject for discussion. This brings us close to operation, the setting up and carrying forward of a deliberately intended discussion. A good subject will be significant to the group. It must touch some real need of those who are to be engaged in the discussion; it cannot be chosen arbitrarily without reference to the concerns or interests of the group.

Secondly, it will be sufficiently open to allow room for genuine difference of opinion. This is a somewhat touchy qualification in church groups because of our tendency to assume fallaciously that all the important questions have been answered. When this is the hidden assumption in a discussion, the members of the group go through the motions of finding the answers that have already been given, in a kind of play-acting. Actually, our situation in the Church is much more free than this. There are all kinds of questions that are still open questions; there are all kinds of answers that have to be revised and rethought. Therefore, when a leader goes into a youth group, for example, with a subject for discussion, it can very validly be a subject on which there may be honest and responsible differences of judgment and opinion.

Thirdly, a subject for discussion should not make possible a contest between differing sets of facts. The question of whether this or that is the fact in the matter at hand is foolish as far as discussion is concerned. It is a very good question in relation to research and exploration, but not as the focus for a discussion. Regarding questions of fact, we should follow Francis Bacon's advice, simply look at the facts and let them speak for themselves, as it were; their existence or non-existence is not amenable to discussion. This is not, however, to overlook the frequent points in a discussion at which information concerning certain pertinent facts must be supplied.

The last qualification to be mentioned is that the subject of a discussion should be sufficiently specific and limited as to be capable of adequate treatment in the time provided for it. The tendency almost invariably will be to take up questions so big that the most that can be done in the time available is to sort out the sub-questions involved in them or to recognize the areas in which more information is needed. Since the time limits are usually forty-five minutes to an hour, it is necessary to make the subject quite specific, except in the case of an introductory session which is to be followed by a series of meetings dealing with specific problems implicit in a general question.

How to Lead a Discussion

First of all, extraneous as it may seem, the physical setting for the discussion meeting may be quite important. Too commonly we overlook this; it is secondary, of course, but it needs due attention. For one thing, the meeting room should be adapted to the size of the group. It would be unwise to have a group of five meeting in a room which will accommodate fifty. The tendency of the group under these conditions would be to feel lost and possibly also to surmise that the members of the group and what they are doing are not very important. Indeed, in the formal class set-up of college or university, it is often difficult for a faculty member to overcome the impression that a small enrollment in his course means that it is not of good standing. Size of enrollment in elective courses may reflect on the quality of the course, but such is not necessarily the case. A small class may be every bit as important as a large one, and possibly even greater in its opportunity; and the physical setting should not suggest otherwise. Ventilation and lighting need to be taken into account, as well as arrangement of chairs. The last should not be overemphasized, but some informal arrangement is almost always preferable to the fixed row-by-row seating of the lecture hall. Somehow it is easier for the members of a smaller group to work together when they are seated about a table facing each other. The location of the leader is quite important also; he should be where he can most easily be seen, though not in a position which suggests a higher status. Sometimes it may be better for the chairman of the discussion to sit on a side of the table, rather than at the end—especially if others have to look into the light to see him, as, for example, when he is in front of a window. It is almost always desirable to have a blackboard at hand.

The problem of intrusion of outsiders is another matter of real concern in protecting the conditions favoring a good discussion. It is very difficult, if not impossible, to have a free and honest discussion if some paternalistic brother, official or self-appointed, presents himself at youth-fellowship meetings, for example, and takes part in the discussion or tacitly controls it by his presence. Any visitor, other than another peer, is bound to be a foreigner, for all practical purposes. The teacher or advisor has enough of a problem at this point, without complicating it further. And ministers will have to be sensitive as to how they can sit in with a class or fellowship-group without being an external controlling influence. On the occasion of a visit of a half-dozen theological students to an ethics class in a very fine secondary school, the teacher handled this problem beautifully. As the visiting firemen entered the room, they found about thirty senior boys and girls sitting on sofas and chairs against the walls of the room, and some of the boys sitting on the floor. The teacher sat, smoking his pipe, at the side of a desk which was placed toward one side of the room. He began the class session by saying, "Now this is where we were discussing last time. . . . We would like to pick up the discussion at this point." He also said, "We have guests today, as you can see," and turning to the visitors, he continued, "Will you please jump right into the discussion with us when you are so inclined?" The members of the class resumed the sequence from the last session with no apparent difficulty, the visitors spoke up occasionally, and the experience was genuinely satisfactory. Not a small by-product was the inspiring demonstration the session became for the young theologues.

Functions of the Leader

The leader of the discussion is necessarily an important figure; therefore, something should be said about his function. The negro minstrel show, lacking in honor though it may be, offers a helpful symbol for the leader of the discussion in the interlocutor. The interlocutor in the ministrel show stands in the middle and has the job of being a kind of straight man for the end men in the show. He asks the end men questions and their answers get the laughs. Although the object is not to get laughs, the figure does not do badly in suggesting the function of the leader of a discussion. He is the interlocutor, and accordingly, he has the function of keeping the show moving, not upstaging or competing with the other performers for applause.

He should continually try to draw others out and get expression from them, not expound his own ideas. It is wise for him to postpone taking sides in the discussion until all points of view have been elicited from those present. If he does not exercise this self-control, there may be a number of consequences which can prevent a good discussion from developing. There is danger that the discussion will become a conversation between the leader and one or two members of the group, thus excluding others and reducing them to the status of observers. Something will be said later about the place of the leader's point of view; at this point, the only argument is that the leader should delay expressing it until the point is reached in the thinking of the group at which it will not be given a value it does not deserve.

The leader should get the dialectic of discussion going by releasing into expression members of the group who actually hold opposing points of view on the question at hand. The only justification for his expressing a point of view sooner rather than later would be that there is some important view that has not yet been expressed and which needs to be brought in. However that may be, it is important that he find the poles of disagreement within the group, if at all possible. This is much better than assuming the role of antagonist or protagonist himself, although on occasion this may become a necessity.

By all means, the leader should let his own point of view be known; he should not try to hide it or pretend that he is neutral. His viewpoint should not limit discussion; it should become part of the data with which the group works, one element among others to be taken into account. The leader's position should be stated with conviction; yet it should be introduced only as one of the elements of the discussion, not as the dominant theme by which

246

the discussion is controlled. Nor should it be the hidden secret which, when brought to light, will be the answer everyone has been seeking. This is the danger in suppressing the leader's ideas; they can dominate by the halo of secrecy, so that when they are revealed, they seem to be the *real* answer.

It is also the part of wisdom for the leader to practice for himself and to inspire in others the grace to respect and accept another person even when there is disagreement. When you take into account all the personal and psychological elements involved in this kind of acceptance and respect, it is scarcely less than a Christian grace. It is hard to believe that there is much of this respect and acceptance in the world, except in the non-erotic community which Bonhoeffer contrasts with the human community,[3] a community in which you can disagree even violently, but never have a thought of exclusion or rejection. Rare though it may be and difficult of achievement, we should cultivate this kind of mutual respect and freedom in discussion—certainly in the Church, but elsewhere as well.

To turn to another point, it is possible to prepare a group for a discussion without so tightly predetermining it in advance that a "canned" discussion results. Such planning must leave arrangements sufficiently open that discussion may flow freely, and full allowance must be made for unpredictable elements to emerge. Some members of the group may be asked to be prepared to speak briefly on some particular phase of the subject at hand, and other members of the group may be prepared to bring in accurate information which may be needed at certain points for an informed discussion, but this preparation should not be formal. All preparation for a discussion, as far as the group is concerned, should be loose, tentative, and open-ended. The discussion itself should be the thing; all preparation should be toward this end and not in hindrance of it.

Let us now consider the possible stages through which a discussion may move. They, of course, cannot be stereotyped since there are so many different ways a discussion may move. However, we may look at one possible movement as an example. First of all, the leader will in most cases make the question for discussion both

[3] *Op. cit.*, chap. 1.

explicit and clear and will indicate its significance without making a speech. Just a very few moments are needed to state the question clearly. The second step may be to get an expression, insofar as possible, of all the different viewpoints and attitudes toward the question honestly held by various members of the group. The next step is not so easily timed or put in a sequence; it may happen earlier, it may be appropriate later. It is the introduction of information as needed. There is not much point in discussing in ignorance; we should have information available when it is needed, or we should terminate that particular part of the discussion until the necessary facts can be supplied. A fourth possible step is to establish relationships between ideas expressed. For example, there may be in the group some honest points of disagreement and a disposition to argue about them. It is well to recognize these openly and to guide the contentions of opposing sides so as to preserve the spirit of searching for the truth, rather than defeating an opponent. There may also be some syntheses of opposing positions to be worked out; but if this is the case, these syntheses certainly should not be forced or artificial, nor should a consensus shared equally by all members of the group be expected. An artificial synthesis or conclusion is worse than none at all, and the members of the group will recognize this, even if the leader doesn't. A fifth point—more a characteristic of the whole discussion than a step in the movement—is that we should permit the members of the group to think without pressure. This may mean that any conclusions which emerge from the discussion will not be the conclusions for every member of the group, but only of some of them. When the attempt is made to sum things up, let us not assume that the conclusion is the conclusion of every member. We should not push for decision at the time; in fact, it is doubtful that satisfactory decisions can be made under pressure. Compulsion toward decision and judgment should be an inner compulsion and not the result of pressure.

Hazards of Formalized Patterns of Discussion

There are two formalized patterns of discussion which are worthy of mention because they are rather frequently used and because they have built-in hazards.

The first of these is debate. It is not uncommon in one of our fellowship-groups to set up a debate on some question of supposed interest. If it does not become too argumentative in spirit, this may possibly be helpful. The problem debate presents, however, is that while a discussion should be striving for the truth, the debate easily gets perverted by the desire to win. Discussion is not to be held merely for the sake of discussion; nor is its purpose to provide the occasion for sharpening our competitive wits. Discussion is for the sake of truth; it is honest and responsible thinking together, which, within the life of the Church—it is to be hoped—may become serious theologizing. To the extent to which debate may get in the way of this, we should be wary of it.

The other, even more common formal pattern is the panel discussion. This is a familiar form which doubtless needs very little description. Commonly a table is set before the group, possibly on a rostrum, if the group is large enough or if this is necessary in order for all to see. There is a chairman of the discussion, commonly moderating from the center of the table; sitting with him on either side are the members of the panel, possibly as many as four, and sometimes even more. The idea, at its best, is that the members are supposed to speak to each other and to the audience: the audience, in turn, is supposed to respond to the panel. Of course, it takes a great deal of skill on the part of the chairman to make a good job of this arrangement. The skill needed is the art of maintaining a vital discussion and avoiding a self-conscious exercise of some kind. Too often panel discussions are occasions at which four people make speeches, while standing behind the same table at which their alleged co-discussants are seated. This need not happen if the chairman and the members of the panel meet in advance and clear their plans with one another. When this happens, the chairman can truly act as an interlocutor, plying the individual members of the panel with questions and almost imperceptibly drawing the rest of the group in, so that the separation between panel and audience virtually disappears. The panel discussion when used should be a real means to a real end, not a novel pattern introducing change into the routine of a group.

THE QUESTION

We will now consider the question as a mode in the teaching-learning act comparable in importance to discussion. There is, however, a significant difference between the two; while discussion is a kind of background music which runs throughout most all good teaching and in which other teaching forms have their context, the question is an auxiliary in discussion and in other movements of teaching which serves to pin down, as it were, the perchings which must punctuate the flights of the learning process.

The question cannot properly be the continuing background movement of learning, as the discussion may very commonly be, or as, at higher levels of education, the lecture often is. This is true unless we think of learning in the old sense of recitation, in which the class moves along with the teacher asking questions in a sequence and the students reciting the answers in reply. It is hopefully assumed here that this kind of teaching is on the wane, but this assumption may be premature. Inadequate, routine, and lacking in imagination though it may be, when the recitation is the main background movement of teaching, the question is no longer an auxiliary method, but the means of the primary movement of teaching and learning. Assuming, however, that the question should be largely auxiliary, let us examine some of the uses to which the question may be put in teaching.

Functions of the Question

First of all, the question may be used to get before the class the material studied in preparation for the class session. While this may appear to approximate rather closely the recitation idea, yet it has some validity. This function has the added virtue of assuming that people have studied the material; too commonly in our Church-School classes, our teachers do not have basis for this assumption. Were we to presume that preparation has been made and stick by the presumption in class, we might get more serious study. A second function of the question is to examine the class orally as to knowledge and achievement and as a basis for judgment; the oral examination is an example of this function. A third use of the question is to stimulate and guide thinking, and here is where questions, carefully thought out in sequence, can be valuable.

In the fourth place, the question can be used to guide the student in making judgments, evaluations, and decisions. In performing this function, the question is not directed to the content of material the class has studied; it is used rather to evoke from the student his value judgments concerning that material. Sometimes it may help to specify, e.g., "What is your judgment about this? Is it this or is it this?" But this must be done with care, so that the inflection of voice does not indicate a preferred answer. Of course, several alternatives may be proposed in the question, not just two. Such questions must be fitted to the student's level of comprehension; sometimes students feel the need for alternatives in order to have something to get hold of. Generally the opportunity for openness of thought is greater if possible answers are not suggested in the use of alternatives. Very often questions are made so specific that they clip the wings of imagination and prevent flights of the mind into free and creative thought. This is especially true of examination questions. More often than not it is the fault of the teacher, and not the student, that an examination gives back what the teacher has said or what has been read in a book, with nothing of the student's own thought added. Questions which are too specific will garner this kind of yield; if we must sin, we should sin on the side of generality in asking such questions.

Precautions in the Use of Questions

Questions are by no means foolproof, therefore precautions must be kept in mind in using them for teaching purposes. We will mention a few of these which seem most pertinent. First, the teacher should not spring unfair surprises in asking questions. While this may seem to make for an unnecessarily soft pedagogy, it is only ethical, fair, and respectful. The teacher's side of the desk does not enjoy the breadth of license often assumed.

Secondly, a teacher should not imply a censorious attitude by the way in which he asks a question, unless there is a disciplinary situation prompting it and fully justifying it. The classroom is not a courtroom and the teacher is not a prosecuting attorney. In the third place, it is better not to ask leading questions implying the desired answer. In fact, it is a bit childish to have specifically worded answers in mind when a question is asked. Teaching and learning should always be more than a guessing game, in which the students try to discover what "precious" answer the teacher has in his head.

A fourth precaution is that many questions are usually not

needed. A few central questions are all that is necessary to guide a teaching session, even if it is to be of the old recitation type. It is entirely possible to build a very good class session around only two or three good questions. It is not uncommon for the inexperienced or inept teacher, in a little fit of panic about his preparation, to come to class with a list of ten or twelve questions. He does it because it makes him feel that he is prepared, armed for the hour that he has to get through somehow. When things get embarrassingly silent, he can bring up another question. But this spreading out over many foci may defeat the purpose entirely, and accomplish nothing. If a teacher can just relax in the possession of a modicum of security rather than an elaborate plan, he is more likely to keep attention focused on the few central points, to get the "feel" of normal classroom give-and-take, and, along with his students, to enjoy the session fully.

A fifth precaution, and the last to be proposed here, is to point out that it is self-evident that questions which can be answered by "Yes" or "No" are not of much value, unless they further evoke the answer, "Yes, but" or "No, but," which necessarily must be explained. There are yes-and-no questions which have the necessary innuendo to elicit such further qualification in the answers, but without such innuendoes this kind of question is pointless.

How to Ask Questions

To be somewhat more positive, we may venture to make some proposals concerning acceptable ways of asking questions. The first suggestion is that a question should be an invitation to response, showing empathy for the student, unless it is asked in a disciplinary context which requires some degree of sternness. The assumption here is that most teaching situations are not of this character, yet how often questions are asked as though the third degree were being administered.

Some feel that it is desirable to state a question generally to the whole class before calling on a particular person to answer. The reason for this, in its less dignified version, is that if one person is called by name before a question is asked, everybody else can go off wool-gathering while the teacher and one student engage in repartee. And contrariwise, if the question is asked first, so that everybody sits in fear of having to give the answer, then all members of the class are on their toes throughout the question-and-answer sequence. As though students are just normally uninterested and perverse, and therefore need to be kept in a state of suspense by a clever and crafty teacher! It's enough to make Socrates regret ever starting the question on its way in a noble tradition! Certainly favorable attitudes can be engendered in a class so that the climate is one of wanting to learn; and when this is done, it doesn't make any difference whether a student's name is called before or after a question is asked. The mistake to be avoided is that the sequence in which questions are asked, will become set by habit and allow for no deviations. There is danger, however, in not having some deliberate sequence, the danger that the teacher will not deal with all the members of the class, but will favor some and neglect others. In such a case, although it may not be intended, the more vocal members of the class will get the lion's share of attention, while some very capable but recessive members may be neglected and remain undiscovered by the teacher.

Another suggestion, which should not need mention, is that questions should be thought out clearly and asked quite deliberately. Oftentimes the faulty or overly involved grammar used in a question indicates that it has not been thought out as carefully as it should be. An appropriate casualness is a very good thing and need not detract anything from the deliberateness of intent in the question asked. One good reason for avoiding formality by this appropriate casualness is that formalism in the classroom may give the unfortunate impression that something is being acted out which was previously rehearsed. The answer, of course, is for the teacher to be himself as much as he possibly can be, without becoming overly familiar or acting the part of a buddy. This is not as easy as it may appear and harks back to some of the things we were saying earlier in opposition to the playing of roles in the classroom.[4] We should have enough faith and trust in facing the present situation to be just what we are at that time and in that situation. In the same context, it should be said that we need to suit our questions to the capacities of the students, to special

[4] See pp. 206–210.

interests and needs, as they can be recognized. And this again relates to what was said earlier about discerning the student as he is and not just as he appears to be.[5]

Reversing the Question Movement

It may be well to consider the possibility of the teacher, on occasion, being the one who is questioned, rather than the one who asks questions. Surely he should stand ready to answer questions, and he should not take advantage of the occasion for a lecturing spree. As long as this does not happen, the Socratic method in reverse can sometimes be very helpful. This may be true, especially, after the student has spent several sessions studying difficult material. By making available to him the opportunity to ask questions which are real and perplexing, he can assimilate what he has learned and be made ready for further advance.

Types of Questions

In earlier days, pedagogues used to be quite stereotyped in their classification of questions by types. While this is no longer possible, something of a less formal character may offer some light concerning the different forms or purposes which questions may assume. Some questions may serve the minor purpose of establishing relationship between teacher and class at the beginning of a session and starting things in motion. "What was the chief impression you gained in reading this chapter?" is a good example, however trite. Another kind of question may be the searching question, more central in the teaching act. It is designed to help the student dig into his own thinking or study and come up with something really significant. It may be used to draw from the student his command and comprehension of material or his critical judgment regarding it. There is, of course, also the review question. It is hoped that it would be used not just to elicit a repetition of something previously learned, but rather to help the learner to attain a new perspective on past learning from the subject at hand or in the context of the whole. Finally, there is the follow-up question or a series of questions, in which some logical sequence is used to make a significant point. This can be seen in consummate form in the *Dialogues* of Plato, almost all of which depict an informal dialectic.

[5] See pp. 239–240.

By means of the question, Socrates again and again pushes his antagonist until he moves full circle from the position he assumed at the beginning of the questioning to its embarrassingly exact opposite at the end.

THE LECTURE

We turn now to lecture or direct instruction. Lecture is the common term for higher levels of formal education; at lower levels of school and Church School, direct instruction is probably a better term, because of its less sustained character. The temptation of most teachers at all levels is to make their teaching an act of telling. It is easier for the teacher than less direct methods, which have to plan for and elicit student participation. Also, the act of telling often gives the teacher a sense of accomplishment which less direct methods do not. With telling, or the formal lecture, the teacher can always reassure himself with, "Well, at least we covered so much material today." But this sense of accomplishment can be illusory. Yes, the teacher has gone through the process of telling the students a certain amount of "stuff," but that does not mean that learning has necessarily taken place. At the same time that we criticize the lecture, we must not forget that it is possible, indeed very common, to lecture against the lecture method!

Teaching should not be primarily an act of telling, particularly at lower levels. At later levels, lecture may very well be used with great frequency, provided its purpose is thought out and it is well executed in harmony with the conceived purpose. Certainly direct instruction should not be arbitrarily excluded as old hat. One of the foibles of education is that it is an affair of words; all of us, especially the students, know that education is very wordy. One of the things that progressive education was trying to get beyond was the verbalism of formal education. In fact, there is a sizable percentage of educators, who would not at all consider themselves progressives, but who would yet say that they would like students to learn to do things with their hands as well as their mouths. In the arts there are those who believe that a man cannot create with his mind unless he can also do something with his hands. Much of the agitation against and criticism of the lecture method has been prompted by the desire to correct and balance our verbalism.

Instead of thinking of the lecture as an evil to be excluded from the classroom, we should look at it in terms of the kinds of teaching situations in which it is justified as an effective instrument. Considering lecture first of all as exposition, it is a valid teaching procedure only when the material of the lecture has not been written for duplication or publication by the lecturer, and therefore is unavailable to the student in print. If the student can read this very same material from the lecturer's pen, there is no justification for the lecture. If the material is already in print by the hand of another author in an acceptable and readable form, it is doubtful that the lecture will add much to the student's education, unless there is a particular organization or interpretation the teacher wishes to give to the subject.

Of course, there are other kinds of lecturing besides exposition. It is hard to give this kind of lecture a name; it might be characterized as inspirational, but to do so suggests a stronger dose of sentiment than is desirable. It may be preferable to call it a power-lecture, although this may imply a master teacher at work—a manipulator or a promoter with something to sell—and this may be giving persuasion the ascendancy over honest inquiry. By whatever name we may denote this kind of lecture, it is not primarily the presentation of information. At its best, it is a consummate communicative work of art, designed to challenge the student and send him on his way to independent study for himself. Since such quality of lecture is possible, although not common, there is good reason for not dismissing the lecture easily, although it is not sanctioned as a habit-pattern to be followed blindly at the higher levels of education.

This may directly pertain to the heart and core of the educative transaction. The whole point of education is for the teacher to multiply his efforts by as many people as he is dealing with at any one time, not to be a channel of information from which others will all receive. His job is to bring students to that point from which they move under their own power and on their own initiative, doing their own work with a minimum of dependence upon the teacher—eventually with none at all. The power-lecture, or whatever else it may more properly be called, challenges the student to this very end. At first it may provoke the student, even arousing anger, although it should be hoped that this anger will not be excessive nor overly frequent. Later it may give a new perspective and invite to a new level of understanding. In such a lecture there may result a face-to-face encounter between teacher and taught, for which there can be no substitute. Out of this person-to-person meeting there can issue for the student initiative, action, power, and commitment. This commitment need not necessarily or particularly be religious commitment, although that is certainly not excluded; what we have more especially in mind here is commitment to a job to be done.

If the reports are all accurate, one of the best examples of this kind of lecturing was to be found in the Danish Folk High Schools in the period of their ascendancy in the nineteenth century. The idea of these schools, originating under the influence of Bishop N. F. S. Grundtvig (1783–1872) and Christen Kold (1816–1870), was to take boys and girls in late adolescence and early adulthood, in the winter when work on the farms was at a low ebb, and to give them from six weeks to three months in a setting similar in spirit to our summer camp. In these very informal schools, the young people studied Danish history to familiarize themselves with the soil of their own culture, and the Lutheran religious tradition together with the Bible, to discover the religious roots of their Danish life. The schools were co-educational, and folk-dancing and other recreation alternated with a set schedule of lecture periods to comprise the program. There were few rules in these schools, but one which was strictly enforced was that nobody could take notes at lectures. The endeavor was to secure virogous and moving lecturers in every case, because what was desired above all else for the students was the encounter of person-to-person communication by means of the spoken word. According to various accounts of these schools, they were not without a high degree of success in this endeavor.

THE STORY

Another most important teaching form especially suitable for younger children, although its possibilities in the teaching of adults should not be overlooked, is the story. While the story may have more frequent use with children, it should not however be regarded as a graded method especially geared to children.

257

Jesus' rather extensive use of parables was not prompted only or even chiefly by the recognition that people had to have truth illustrated for them. Unfortunately, it is often assumed in preaching that we have to illustrate general truths for people; so we state some supposedly true proposition, and then try to illustrate it, often with a story. This is a misconception almost without foundation in the Bible and in the art of communication. It is more likely that Jesus chose the medium of the parable because he could convey truths to people by narrative and metaphor that could not be conveyed by exposition or by explanatory signs. There is a direct connection between the assertion just made and what was said earlier concerning the function of the symbol in communication.[6] The specific contention here is that the story as a teaching form is not a graded method, but that it is valuable for youth and adults as well as for children.

Just what is the story? It is a form which is more moving than explanation or exposition, but which is not as spectacular as drama. A story is not a play in the sense in which the word is used in the legitimate theatre or in motion pictures or in television. The story itself may be symbolized by another figure; the telling of a story is like the relating of happenings which one viewer sees as he looks out the window and which he reports to other occupants of the room who cannot see out the window. In other words, a story is not as exciting or moving as drama, yet it is not lacking in movement, as is most often the case with exposition and explanation. There is constant movement in it developing toward a climax, and, for the most part, in the telling of the story speech becomes direct conversation rather than indirect report of what is said. This does not mean posturing and changing voice for the different characters as in drama.

A few suggestions for telling a story may be ventured, although the author finds himself in a position reminiscent of Rousseau's in relation to the teaching art; in his Emile he admits, "Since I am not fit to be a tutor, I will write a book to tell you how to be one, a second best but a safer venture!" Certainly, since the story is one of the most difficult teaching forms, we make a grave mistake with students when we start their practice with small children, assuming that they can get by with telling a story. Now directly to the sug-

[6] See pp. 139–149.

gestions, misgivings having been expressed, the chief proposal that the story should be told freely rather than read from a book. This is not to exclude the reading of stories to their children by parents in the intimacy of the family. But in a class, it is much better to tell the story than to read it. This means that it must be gotten well in mind in advance of the telling session; but getting it in mind does not mean trying to remember every detail precisely and in the exact words of the text. To be so bound to the text by memory is to read the story from memory, instead of reading it from the book; there is little difference, in fact the latter may be preferable. What is desired is freedom; and this means freedom from memoriter repetition as well as from the book. In telling the story then, not trying to remember everything precisely, let yourself go as unselfconsciously as possible while you are telling it. Don't act, don't dramatize, don't overdo it. You have to be yourself at the same time that you tell the story and letting yourself go means being yourself, it does not mean dramatizing. Remember also as you tell the story that it is part of a total teaching act and is not an end in itself.

THE UNIT OF STUDY

As with the story, it is difficult to deal with the unit or the project by written discourse or lecture; by comparison, it is easier to demonstrate or exemplify them. First of all, it will be well to make clear what the unit of study is and what the project is. The unit is a segment of study, assigned work, or class activity, which is carried forward both within and without the classroom and which is unified internally because it is built around a unity of subject-matter or a unity of interest. The unit commonly starts in present interests or problems of students, but it need not start there; it may begin at a point beyond felt problems, needs, or interests and still become a valuable unit of study. In contrast, the project is likely to be a particular piece of activity, operation, or job within a unit of study. For example, a class may have a unit of study on the customs of the Hebrew people in the times of Jesus. It would not be difficult to win the interest of a junior-age group, or even a junior-high group, for a program of study which would find out, as authentically and accurately as possible, what the customs of these people were. In such a unit one project, among others, might well be the making of clothes to reproduce, as authentically as possible, the way the Hebrew people dressed. There would no doubt be other comparable projects of serving a meal as they did, acting out a marriage ceremony as their customs dictated it, and so forth. But all of these specific projects would be parts of the unit and not the whole of it; when you narrow attention to a particular job such as the making of clothes, you are dealing with the project, whereas the unit is a more broad and inclusive whole.

The unit had its origin in progressive education and the influence of John Dewey.[7] We have discussed these in some measure heretofore and will not return now to the sources of the method involved; we are concerned here with the use of this method and its value. There are possibly some weaknesses in the unit and project which may be avoided if due precaution is followed. One mistake is to limit the scope more narrowly than is necessary by trying to start every unit in interest. Conceivably there may be units in which there is no solidity of content or no fundamental transaction educationally. This is not to say that formal class sessions are a prime necessity for a good and effective unit. One vacation-school class running for two weeks had only one formal class session; yet the members were working hard all of the time and their learnings were considerable. The chief danger, of course, is that activity, of which there may be an abundance, will be mistakenly identified with solid learning. The value, however, is that the unit can be put to very effective use in overcoming the artificiality and piecemeal character of our conventional Sunday-by-Sunday, lesson-by-lesson practice. There is something very artificially fragmented about this practice, time-honored though it may be, and it is well that many editors of curriculum materials have, for a number of years now, been doing much to correct it. Examine a number of Church-school curricula, and you will very frequently find that a general subject is the focus of study for four Sundays, or six, or even sometimes more. This is the result of the impact of the unit idea; it is a wise attempt to deal with subjects of study in larger blocks. It is wise because it gets away from segmentation and deals in large blocks of variously interrelated subjects, much more similar

[7] See Chapter 7.

260

to the widely related episodes of experience we have to deal with in real life.

It must already be evident that the unit requires very careful and, indeed, comprehensive preparation. This is one of its chief dissuading aspects; it takes more time, more work, and more resourcefulness on the part of the teacher than the more conventional modes of teaching. But there is imposing evidence that it elicits genuine learning and moves far beyond the academic ground rules which restrict much conventional school-keeping. The example of the study of symbolism, given earlier in the discussion of the Vacation Church School, may serve to make more concrete the technique and the values of the unit and the project method.[8]

[8] See pp. 185–186.

261

CHAPTER 16

Nurture in the Church and Curriculum

*T*he sequence of the preceding three chapters has been to proceed directly from consideration of the science of psychology to actual methods of teaching. The connection between psychology and methodology is quite evident and does not appear to need explication. There is a similar connection to be pointed out between psychology and curriculum. This is most evident, or at least most easily exemplified in the necessity that courses of study and study literature be adapted to the capacities of the respective age-levels, if learning is to take place.

DEFINITION OF CURRICULUM

Although it seems wise for this discussion of the curriculum of Christian education to deal for the most part with curriculum literature, we will first define curriculum. It is hoped that this will avoid the implication that all of curriculum is study liturature. It should also provide an appropriately broad context for a discussion which will otherwise be quite concrete and specific.

A Broad Definition

There are two valid ways of defining curriculum: the first of these may be termed the broader definition; the second the narrower. We will first propose the broad definition, approaching it in two ways.

For education generally, the curriculum is constituted by all of those influences and media of communication by which the less mature are nurtured in the culture of the community of which they are a part. Such a statement is of course bristling with problems, because it assumes, at least for the time being, that the secular culture nurtures individuals, possibly implies that it has the right to do so, and may even further suggest that the values implicit in the secular culture are valid and that the individual should be nurtured in them. Fortunately, we are not under the necessity of working through these ramified problems in order to offer the definitions needed for this chapter. We can proceed descriptively, merely observing that this is what goes on in secular culture and its institutions of education, without approving it. All that is being said is that when we try to define curriculum broadly in terms of education as a secular institution—with no disparagement intended because it is secular—we must refer to all media of communication and to all influences by which the individual is nurtured.

Narrowing the focus to the Church, not ideologically nor theologically, but in order to be concrete for the life of the Church and for the nurture that takes place within it, we again must define curriculum broadly. In this context curriculum is also constituted by all of those media of communication and all those influences by which the less mature are nurtured within the Christian community and, it is hoped, brought into effective relation to God and made partakers of the body of Christ. This returns our thought to our starting point at which a partial definition of nurture was derived from the nature of the Church. But the emphasis now is upon the meaning of curriculum in the relation of the Church to the individual it nurtures. And what we are saying is that curriculum is all of the media of communication and all of the influences by which the Church brings itself to bear upon the individual in nurture.

An observation is now in order concerning these broad definitions; it is that curriculum, viewed in this way, is much more than a study literature or a schedule of courses of study. But it is necessary to define curriculum in this broad way in order to avoid limiting it artificially and arbitrarily to specific curricular items to which major attention is soon to be given. There is a sense in which the Bible and the way in which it functions in the Church is curriculum. There is also a sense in which the theology, tacitly or officially accepted in any given church, is curriculum. Further, there is a sense in which the theologizing which may or may not go on in the Church is curriculum, either by its presence or absence. And finally, to mention one more important constituent, those who teach are curriculum. These and other comparable items are all a part of curriculum when broadly defined.

A Narrow Definition

Having acknowledged the necessarily inclusive context of curriculum concerns, we can now move on to the narrow definition of curriculum. The word "narrow" is not used disparagingly; the narrow definition is as justifiable as the broad, as long as it does not arbitrarily exclude the broad definition. According to it, curriculum, especially in Christian education, refers to courses of study and, even more specifically, to study literature. Curriculum commonly refers, therefore, to the study materials deliberately designed and prepared as a central agent, if not supposedly *the* central agent, in the Christian nurture of children, youths, and adults. While it is not as common in the church as in the school to think in such terms, curriculum more narrowly defined is also comprised of particular courses of study. In more recent years, when many churches have adopted systems of elective course for adults, curriculum has been conceived of as a program of study as well as a study literature.

With the context suggested by these two definitions at least stated, we can proceed to consideration of curriculum literature with some hope of avoiding the distortion that this is all there is to curriculum. At any rate, we must recognize partically that there is a growing body of curriculum literature which demands careful and critical study by the thoughtful student.

CURRICULUM LITERATURE

When we study curriculum literature, we will do well to come to it directly and concretely. We must not be satisfied to talk about curriculum, much less to talk around it; to do so is neither to conceive authentic theory nor to be sufficiently concrete to lead to effectiveness in practice. Our task is to go directly to specific literature, look at it, handle it, analyze it, try to understand its intended purpose, and finally criticize it. It is only in this way that we can develop sensible judgments about it and formulate criteria for judgment and selection of curriculum materials for particular situations. So still being somewhat general, but coming closer now to literature, we will take up some ways of classifying curriculum materials which may serve as a guide in getting acquainted with curriculum literature. There are different systems by which curricula may be classified, most of them disparate in relation to each other and representing different, but supplementary, approaches to analysis. Not infrequently, there are conflicting elements in these forms of analysis which present issues on which sides must be taken and critical judgments made.

Classification According to Age-Level Concerns

The first system of classification to be discussed is based on concern for the age- and grade-level of the child. This analysis system yields three types of materials: uniform lessons, closely graded lessons, and group- or cycle-graded lessons.

The Uniform Lessons. Historically, the uniform lessons constituted the first systematically ordered curriculum to be widely used in the Sunday School. They were first inaugurated, at least in the planning and writing stage, in 1872, about ninety-two years after the Sunday School first saw the light of day. The uniform-lesson plan was a seven-year sequence of study materials, covering the Bible, representatively as it were, and alternating between Old and New Testaments. Some minor changes came in later years, such as the reduction of the cycle to six years and the introduction of a "temperance" lesson once each quarter. But in essence the plan has remained the same from its inception to the present time. It is a program in which all members of the Sunday Church School, including adults, study the same lesson regardless of age- or grade-level. The assumption is that reasonably adequate adaptations of this one *uniform* lesson can be made so that it can be taught to the respective levels of maturity.

Closely Graded Lessons. A second type of study material, according to this same basis of classification, is the closely graded lesson. The idea of the closely graded curriculums was historically the first corrective which arose in reaction to the uniform lesson. While the uniform lessons were based on an overly simple idea, however easy to administer in practice, the conception of the closely graded curriculum was quite complex and difficult to operate, especially in a school which was made up largely of lay teachers with little training. In response to the idea of the uniform lessons, that everyone should be studying the same lesson at the same time, with some adaptation to different age-levels, the movement of reaction virtually said, "No, we must have a particular lesson particularly prepared for each age and each grade." This, of course, was the diametrical opposite to the principle of the uniform lessons. This new principle in the planning of a curriculum proposed that each age, from four on up to the high school ages, have a separate and unique course of study, peculiarly and particularly designed for that age. Theoretically at least, according to this plan, it is possible that no two ages will be studying the same lesson at the same time. Each age- or grade-level will be studying a lesson, of which both the content and form are tailor-made for it, not a lesson of which the form is adapted so as to make it fit reasonably well. One assumption implicit in this principle is that the uniform idea breaks down at the point of adaptation, and that neither all subjects nor all forms are adaptable to all grade levels. It is assumed that the subject has to be changed if a lesson is really going to be effective with a particular age or grade. This is the closely-graded idea.

Group-Graded Lessons. The third type of lesson, according to this method of classification, is a modification of the closely-graded idea, known as the group-graded, departmental-graded, or cycle-graded curriculum. This conception of curriculum materials does not assume, as in the uniform lesson, that everyone should be studying the same thing at the same time. It assumes that there must be adaptations, not only in material, but in method and approach. But in partial correction of the closely-graded idea, it is further assumed that it is not necessary for every age to have its separate material and that, within certain reasonably designated limits, there can be duplications both of subject and approach. The group-graded idea has emerged in the very familiar departmental organization common to most Sunday Church Schools. In this organization the four- and five-year-olds constitute the kindergarten department. These children, if group-graded lessons are used, study the same lesson at the same time throughout the two-age span, but on a two-year cycle. In year A all four- and five-year-olds study the lessons of the first year of the cycle. In year B they all study the lessons in the second year of the cycle. At the end of these two years, the children who have already studied the first year of the cycle will move into the primary department. The children remaining in the kindergarten department, together with the new crop of four-year-olds coming in, will study in year C the first year of the cycle. And so it will continue on year after year. In the primary department the same procedure is followed, but on a three-year-cycle for ages six, seven, and eight. The procedure in the junior department is the same for the preadolescent ages of nine, ten, and eleven; and essentially the sequence is the same for junior high school and senior high school departments. It certainly can be seen that this procedure offers economy, greater ease of administration, and yet quite adequate adaptability of lesson content and form to age-levels. The group-graded lessons are constantly being reissued, incidentally providing occasion for improvement and more complete revision; the closely graded lessons are not commonly reissued, at least until some complete or radical revision warrants it.

Classification According to Sponsorship

Another way of looking at curriculum materials is in terms of the sponsorship under which they are published. This may be more important than it first appears.

Denominational Curriculums. It is quite safe to say that the great majority of Sunday Church School curriculum materials are published denominationally. We may even go further and propose the value judgment (with which some may take issue) that this is as it should be. The principle of judgment involved here relates to what body, authority, or agency has, or should have, the prerogative of determining curriculum. Who should determine the curriculum that a given Christian community is going to study? Since the Christian faith is a very concrete faith, centered in concrete communities and specific literature, it is very normal that the respective

267

communions or confessional bodies should be the ones to determine what curriculum shall be studied within that particular communion. Accordingly, it is no accident that the great body of curriculum materials are published by the denominations.

There is also a financial aspect to this problem; it is most often the denomination that takes the risk of making the investment in the publication venture. The converse, however, is not necessarily true—that is that if anyone makes money on the material, it should be the denomination. After all, churches are not intended to be commercial institutions. The prior question is who makes the financial venture and hazards the very possible losses or sacrifices? One of the denominations, launching its new curriculum venture shortly after World War II, authorized the mortgaging of some of its holdings to underwrite the effort. The economic success of the publications, which could not be foreseen, nor by any means guaranteed, eventually made a mortgage unnecessary, but even so, large sums of money—as much as two or three million dollars—were involved, and the eventual return could in no way be made certain. This is the economic aspect of the principle of denominational sponsorship of the publication of curriculum. It is the confessional body or communion which has the responsibility of determining what the curriculum shall be, but this also means that it must make the venture of faith which publication costs assess upon the responsibility.

Cooperative Curricular Efforts. The counterpart of denominational curriculums is those materials which are planned and, less extensively, published by interdenominational cooperation. To be more precise, at their best, these materials are published as an ecumenical effort, of which cooperation among denominations is truly one motif—though only one among many and not the most important. In the most common of these cooperative efforts, the denomination does not delegate planning and writing to some interdenominational body. None of the national councils of churches in the various nations of the world is a superior body, higher in the polity-structure than the highest courts or authorities of the respective denominations. The various national councils of churches and the World Council of Churches function in other

268

more sensitive ways, which fully respect the uniqueness and self-determination of the different communions.

The way in which interdenominational cooperation in curriculum preparation has emerged has been quite sound and in harmony with the ecumenical spirit. It is this, that in the ecumenical or interdenominational body (which in this country used to be the International Council of Religious Education and is now the Division of Christian Education of the National Council of Churches) rather large committees representative of the member denominations project outlines for several years in advance. The different denominational bodies prepare their own materials as they wish, following the agreed-upon outlines in their own ways and making occasional modifications of the outlines. The extent of this interdenominational cooperation in curriculum preparation, it can be seen, is in planning, but not in the actual writing. This is true both for the uniform lessons and also for the graded series.

A less significant way in which the interdenominational principle has been followed is in the cooperative texts. These have been used most commonly in Vacation Church Schools and Weekday Schools. In the preparation of these texts, one denomination, by agreement, assumes the responsibility for preparation of the text for a particular age-level, another denomination assumes responsibility for another, and so on, so that texts will comprise a complete curriculum for a given year. In other words, the denominations farm out the work among themselves, and all who so choose use all of the materials when they are completed. The plan of preparation of the cooperative texts brings the actual writing of curriculum more into the interdenominational sphere than the lesson-outline committees do. At the same time, it does not adhere to the confessional principle quite as closely, in as much as texts written by several denominations may be used within a communication which has prepared only one of them, or maybe even none of them.

Nondenominational Materials. There are nondenominational publishers of curriculum materials, particularly for the Sunday Church School, which for the most part are commercial institutions. As a rule, they specialize in publishing uniform lessons, but there are some few which produce group-graded materials as well. It is not in order here to advertise these publishers, nor in any way to black-list them. The fair way to judge curriculum materials is on the merits of the literature itself. However, there is need to point out here that these nondenominational publishers are commercial, and not ecclesiastical institutions, and that they are not infrequently divisive influences in the congregations which buy their pub-lications.

Classification According to Focus

The third and last system of classification to be mentioned for analyzing curriculum materials has to do with the focus or inten-tion of the material. In this system of classification the concern is not adaptation to age and grade, nor the sponsoring body, but the center of gravity, as it were, of the material. This relates in part to earlier considerations of the place of theology and the Bible in nurture.[1]

Content-Centered Curriculums. One frequent characterization of curriculums within this classification system is that it is content-centered. If the conviction is that curriculum materials for the Sunday Church School, or for other teaching agencies of the Church, should be content-centered, then the further question must be asked as to what kind of content should be at a premium. The general concern that curriculum literature be content-centered corresponds directly to the learning theory that transmission is the primary, if not the entire, function of learning. Different kinds of content have been emphasized in content-centered materials. There have been Bible-centered materials, so-called, which have been both common and popular. Most of them are based on the assumption that the Bible is something to be known and that the important thing in the teaching of the Church is to give knowledge of the Bible to the students. Accordingly, the Bible is taken up in these materials, section by section, book by book, or in some similar way. The Uniform Lessons have been very clearly Bible-centered, with the slight exception of the quarterly "temperance" lesson that crept in some years ago when the temperance move-ment was strong. Another way of conceiving content-centered study in literature is to urge that it should be centered in doctrine, and

[1] See Chapters 9 and 10.

that materials should accordingly be comprised of theology or the confessional statements of the Church. Yet another way of conceiving content-centered materials is to argue that the study literature of the Church School should be Christocentric. Such a conception, implicitly or deliberately, assumes that christology is either prior to theology, or primary in it, or both, and that curriculum literature should give primary place to the life, ministry, and "work" of Christ.

Life-Centered Curriculums. Another type of material according to this system of classification is the life-centered curriculum. This policy regarding the focus or approach of curriculum is now more in the past than the present. Such curriculums were one of the consequences in the religious education movement of the influence of pragmatic educational philosophy and progressive educational practice.[2] It may be well to restate this connection concisely here. The pragmatic idea in learning is that learning always begins with a problem. Therefore, one of the very common concerns in the life-centered curriculum is to start a lesson or unit of study with a problem which, it is assumed, is present in the experience of the learner. It is also assumed that learning can move from this problem to the Bible or to the Christian Faith and find there the needed answer. It has the virtue of taking rather fully into account the experience of the learner; it may not, however, be successful in making the transition from a life-situation to the meaning of the Christian Faith.

The Unit of Study. A third and last type of curriculum to be mentioned within the system of classification primarily concerned with focus is the curriculum organized by units of study. This has already been taken up in connection with our examination of method in the preceding chapter, because the unit has both methodological and curricular aspects. One of the intentions of the unit of study is to get away from the artificiality and mechanical character of the Sunday-by-Sunday lesson. Put more affirmatively, to work by units is to recognize that the foci of solid teaching are bigger than this and cannot be broken down into neat little weekly packages. The unit is an attempt to catch these larger foci both in

[2] See Chapter 7.

271

experience and in subject-matter and to utilize them to the end of solid and meaningful learning. Put a bit more abstractly, the unit idea is an attempt to match the rhythm of life, which usually moves by larger and more complex fields than can be cut to fit a thirty-minute class session. In curriculum building, this is to organize a block of study in terms of its own nature, so that it can match more closely the almost intangible rhythms by which life moves. If the student examines one of the curriculums organized by the unit plan, he will find in the table of contents, for example, that four or five Sundays are clustered together under one topic and that there are subtopics for each particular Sunday. While more unity than this could certainly be desired, it is an attempt to adapt the unit idea and to deal with larger subjects in conceptions which approximate an adequate recognition of the magnitude and complexity both of Christian thought and of Christian life.

RECENT DEVELOPMENTS IN CURRICULUM LITERATURE

These three classification systems we have just discussed break down, at least in part, if not almost entirely, when we consider developments in curriculum since World War II. Some of the preliminary work on these new advances was begun before the war, but the yield in actual publications did not come until a few years after the war's close. The reference here is to the *Faith and Life Curriculum*, the *Seabury Series*, and other more recent departures, some of which are still in the preparatory stages.[3] Only the two of these, which have been in publication for several years, will be discussed here.

The *Faith and Life Curriculum* is a denominational curriculum, published by the United Presbyterian Church, U.S.A. It was not, however, ventured in opposition to ecumenical and interdenominational projects. It was initiated out of the conviction that curriculum improvement could be achieved more rapidly by the less

---

[3] United Presbyterian Church, U.S.A., *The Faith and Life Curriculum*, Philadelphia: Westminster, 1948 *et seq.*;

Protestant Episcopal Church, *The Seabury Series*, Greenwich, Conn.: Seabury Press, 1956 *et seq.*; see also

United Church of Christ, *United Church Curriculum*, Philadelphia: Board of Christian Education and Publications, 1960.

Presbyterian Church U.S., *Covenant Life Curriculum*, Richmond, Va.; Board of Christian Education, in preparation.

cumbersome striving of a single denomination. It also was accompanied by the continuing belief that religious faith is necessarily tied to concrete communities of faith. It departed therefore from any attempt to follow interdenominational outlines and was an attempt at a completely new beginning. *Faith and Life* follows in general a group-graded pattern, although its use for almost a decade and a half has accentuated the difficulties of adapting this pattern to the spread of abilities and interests embraced even by the two or three age-levels within a single department.[4] Accordingly, more recent adaptations in these study materials have been attempted which take into account more fully the differences between the more and less mature students in the same departments.

The curriculum strives to teach theology without arbitrarily transmitting doctrine. It is a serious attempt to be genuinely biblical in meaning and spirit, without naïvely assuming that this means large quantities of Bible content or a set sequence of study of books or chapters. *Faith and Life* is dynamic in approach, using the unit principle both in very broad scope and in the more limited range covering several weeks of study. The three successive years focus respectively on the Bible, Christ, and the history of the Church. Within each year there are several units of study dealing with some major aspects of the theme for the year. In general, the publication format of this new curriculum is comprised of the following items: parent-teacher magazines published quarterly for each departmental level; clothbound reading books for each age-group beyond the primary level; small paperbound booklets for the primary level and below. The parent-teacher magazines are a genuine attempt at a dignified and serious treatment which will elicit the best from teachers and engage the vital interest and participation of the home. It should be said, however, that, as might be expected, this attempt to engage the home in the religious nurture of the child has not met with notable success. For example, while the parent-teacher magazines may be regularly delivered to the homes, they are not commonly read nor taken very seriously by the parents. Possibly the actual achievement in this effort has been as good as could have been expected; nevertheless, new approaches to this primary institution of Christian nurture are urgently indicated and are also now under study by the denomination which publishes this curriculum. The clothbound reading

[4] See pp. 177–178.

books, the individual yearly readings for the student, are written by scholars in the various fields and are sold in the trade, as well as a part of the curriculum.

The *Seabury Curriculum* followed the *Faith and Life Curriculum* by a few years. In the preliminary stages of its development there was occasional conversation between the respective denominations sponsoring the two series, although each was forthrightly a denominational effort. Accordingly, *Seabury*, like *Faith and Life*, departed completely from the outlines of the interdenominational curriculum committees. Contrary to the plan of the *Faith and Life Curriculum*, *Seabury* follows the closely-graded plan and publishes separate items for each year or school grade. *Seabury* deals with major themes of the Church and of the Christian Faith, but seeks to do this by an approach which takes into account very fully the experience of the learner. In a less strict sense, the approach of the materials might be characterized as existential, as they try to deal with religious faith in the context of the actualities in which the child lives. The publication format includes a variety of elements. At lower age-levels there are good quality booklets for the child, which focus primarily in activities. There are clothbound books for most age-levels, all quite attractively designed. One of the most interesting of these, mentioned only by way of example, is a kind of theological word-book for age eleven, entitled *More Than Words*. Another completely new kind of literature, as far as the Christian education movement is concerned, is comprised of three volumes to be used in classes of parents and godparents of children in the Church School. A great deal of background thinking and writing was considered a necessary part of this curriculum effort of the Protestant Episcopal Church, and, as has already been noted, six major volumes on various aspects of the life of the Church were prepared by scholars and leaders in the Church in the hope that these volumes would become a part of the library of every home affiliated with the Episcopal Church.[5]

CURRICULUM AND PERSONNEL

We have now come to the point in our discussion of curriculum at which it will be well to introduce a note of caution about placing

[5] See p. 120.

too much trust in curriculum to fulfill the function of nurture in the Church. Curriculum problems and concerns are quite distinct from other aspects of the teaching ministry of the Church, and they should be recognized as such. The greatest danger is that we will depend too heavily upon curriculum, and too little on the persons who do the teaching. This is even more likely when we describe curriculum narrowly, as we have been doing for the greater part of this chapter. When this great confidence is placed in curriculum, there is also the danger of adopting a distorted content-centered emphasis and assuming that if we have the right curriculum, our problems will be solved. What is overlooked when this is done is that the best curriculum in the world will be of almost no avail, if it is not taught by teachers who are properly qualified.

We must remember that curriculum is only one factor in Christian nurture. It is of at least equal importance that there be qualified teachers who can effectively put curriculum literature to work and bring it to life. One of the discoveries that has come out of the recent and very serious efforts in curriculum development is that these new materials almost unavoidably place a heavy burden on the teacher. Consequently, there has been greater pressure toward a so-called leadership training, a very valuable accompaniment of curriculum development. Instead of the new and improved curriculum making the teacher less important, it has placed greater demands upon him.

COPING WITH CURRICULAR PROBLEMS IN THE CONGREGATION

We will conclude this chapter and bring this discussion of curriculum to a close by venturing some practical suggestions as to how the installed minister, or some other responsible leader of the congregation, may approach curricular problems in the local church. The proposals made here do not constitute an orthodoxy nor the only mode of procedure; there are a variety of procedures which may be followed, as long as we work in a manner which is in harmony with the spirit and character of the Church.

First of all, unless there is a dearth of plans and virtually no curriculum literature being used at all, a first step may very well be to continue the materials being used at least until the important preliminary steps can be taken which will lead to change. We can scarcely expect to make changes the first day we arrive on the scene, or the first month thereafter, or even possibly the first several months. The period before changes are begun should be long enough to enable the new leader to get acquainted with the situation, to perceive as many as possible of its nuances, and to begin to win the confidence of the people. This initial period of acceptance should be long enough for development of a plan of attack which makes sense and will not appear ill-considered.

A second consideration is that the authorized leader of the congregation will need to have some well-deliberated judgment concerning the curriculum materials of his own denomination. This must be an honest and forthright judgment, free from evasiveness and rationalization. If it is a critical judgment, it may be well for him to hold it privately, at least until it may be understood by others. Nevertheless, he must form such judgments clearly and with conviction. In this connection, it should be said that there is truth in the qualification that a local congregation cannot be an isolated entity and still be the Church; it is necessary for any congregation to be related to the larger life of the Church for it to be the Church. After all, the Church is a historical stream in which there is the backward look to the events of revelation and the forward look of expectation to the last things. The relevant question here is, "How does a congregation become in actuality a part of this stream, unless it is somehow related historically to an actual tradition?" A part of the answer is that, with rare exceptions, it is necessary for a congregation to be related to a denomination in order for it to be part of the Church. The point here is that the adoption and use of curriculum materials is involved in this relationship. This is not to justify denominational materials of poor quality nor a salesmanship approach in behalf of any materials, however excellent they may be. It is to say rather that it is normal for a congregation to use the curriculum materials prepared by the denomination of which it is a part. This is one way among others by which a congregation relates and identifies itself with its denomination and thereby may become a part of the historic Church.

Finally, it may be wise to suggest how to go about guiding a congregation facing a decision about curriculum adoption or change, or how to bring a congregation to face this decision, if it is necessary, or how to carry forward the consciousness in the congregation that some serious study should be given to curriculum. First of all, the minister, or possibly the minister of education in a larger church, faces an educational task at all levels in his church as to curriculum study. This is the task of guiding leaders in the kind of study of curriculum which will provide the basis for a valid program. Those engaged in this study should include elected officials of the church, the superintendent of the Sunday Church School, department heads and teachers, and the committee or board of Christian education. All levels of leadership should be involved, and they must study curriculum materials in such a way that, when the decision is made, it will be the congregation, through its officially designated authorities, which will knowingly make the decision. In fact the minister should be sufficiently objective, both about the careful study and the considered decision resulting from it, that it may be possible for a congregation to make a decision that he would not want made, were it left to his own preferences alone. There are certain hazards which have to be taken if we are going to be honest with people in seeking to lead them. Furthermore, just as we cannot make the decision ourselves, the decision cannot be made on only one level in the life of the Church, however high or low.

For example, here is a congregation, which in the course of the years made two mistaken decisions about curriculum and then, after a change in ministers, made a considered decision in a right way. The first mistaken decision was a multiple one, according to which each department in the Church School decided which curriculum it would use, without any review by a higher body. This, of course, lead to a chaotic condition satisfactory to no one; so after some months, the highest official body of the congregation took another action, without consulting teachers and department heads. This action discontinued the existing mixed curricula and adopted one of the more divisive nondenominational materials for all departments except the adult classes. Eventually, after a change in ministers (which had no connection with this problem) a committee on Christian education was formed in the highest official body governing the congregation. One of its first actions was to institute a very careful study of curriculum, in which most, if not all, of the teachers and other officers involved were consulted. The eventual decision was to adopt the curriculum of the denomination to which the congregation belonged, not out of a sense of denominational loyalty, but in the considered judgment that it was the best curriculum available.

As this example may suggest, it is not enough for the minister to make this decision; nor is it right for the governing body of the congregation to make this decision alone, although legally it may have the right to do so. This decision must be considered at all levels and then brought into the governing body by means of a recommendation on which that body may act. Other ways of approaching curriculum decisions will prove unsatisfactory, because they lead to fragmentation and to the assumption of misplaced prerogatives. The minister or minister of education must exercise throughout a kind of leadership, which is really a kind of teaching. While no disparagement is meant, it is very clear that this must be honest and pure teaching, and not selling. It is both dishonest and doomed to failure for the minister to manipulate a curriculum study in such a way as to bring his teachers, officers, and official bodies around to his views. Accordingly, since the chief basis of the decision is study, the important thing is to make available to all involved the widest possible range of curriculum literature. It may cost some money to buy curriculum sets from the various presses, denominational and otherwise, but this is the only way to provide the people with the breadth of acquaintance and thoroughness of understanding necessary for such an important decision. It will probably prove to be a practical necessity to choose one curriculum for the entire Church School in order to have the required sequence, integrity, and interrelatedness, but even so, this should not be considered an unalterable necessity. The basic necessity is that the Church School have a curriculum which hangs together and that individual departments and segments of the school do not go off in different directions without regard for, or knowledge of, the courses of study in all other parts of the school. This may mean in most cases the adoption of one single curriculum, but it does leave the door open to using the materials of different presses, as long as the responsible authorities in the congregation see to it that these are interrelated to constitute a valuable course of study for the individuals who follow it over the years.

278

CHAPTER *17*

The Church, Nurture, and Administration

*I*n approaching consideration of the administration of Christian education or nurture in the Church, we should speak first of all about its over-all motif or theme. It is so easy for us to make unexamined borrowings from our culture at this point, particularly because we Americans have a penchant for organization. Consequently, we may capitalize upon our apparent successes in business, for example, and take over forms and patterns into the Church with very little criticism or adaptation of them to the life of the Church. This is not to frown upon the Church learning or borrowing from so-called secular institutions; it is rather to complain about uncritical and blind borrowings.

To get the motif of administration in the Church, we must look back to the original figures or concepts that express the nature of the Church, some of which we explored in Chapter 1. If, for example, the Church is the body of Christ, then it should seek to order its affairs in a way which is in harmony with its nature as the body of Christ. To say this does not argue that we do not need organization and administration in the Church. It is to argue for order in the Church very firmly, but at the same time to insist that this order must be indigenous to the authentic nature of the Church. And this latter demand makes it impossible to transfer bodily administrative patterns, techniques, policies, tactics, and what have you, from so-called secular institutions to the Church. In speaking of the body of Christ here, we are taking one of the New Testament figures for the Church and exemplifying by it the way in which any or all of the comparable New Testament figures characterizing the Church may be normative in judging the policies and patterns borrowed from the secular order.

SOME ADMINISTRATIVE POLICIES

There are a few necessary policies of organization which may serve as guide lines in ordering the affairs of the Church pertaining to nurture in a way which derives from the nature of the Church. Some of these will now be discussed.

Authenticity

The first policy to be stated is that there should be a quality of authenticity in the organization of the life of the Church. Members should be able to discern in its organization that their church partakes of the authoritative Church. Conceivably, there can be effective, and even efficient, organization in the church which lacks authenticity. Such an organization is no more the Church than any other efficient organization. The ordering of the affairs of the church, to be authoritative, involves, among other things, a vital relation to the Church as the historic movement of Christianity in the world. Now, concretely, what does this mean? As history would seem to show,[1] the Sunday School movement and individual Sunday Schools often had very little or very tenuous connection with the Church. There is little wonder that the religion taught by the Sunday School frequently, if not commonly, lacked authenticity.

It is largely the burden of the installed minister, and his professionally trained associates if he has them, to bring authenticity into the organization and life of the congregation. One difficulty is that the minister too often misinterprets his authority as a line-of-command authority. The minister does have authority, but he has it by virtue of the fact that he is a *servant* of the historic Church, in his proclamation, in his relation with his people, and in his leadership of various groups and official bodies in the church. This does place a heavy burden on the minister, but, nevertheless, it is essential that he be in the councils where important decisions are made, not because he is an authority in the external sense which makes

[1] See Chapter 4.

his word law, but because he is the installed minister, who in his person and in his functions symbolizes and expresses the authentic Church. He is, as it were, at the center of the currents of the life of the congregation in a way in which no other person is, and there is a sense in which he can speak for the body of the church in a way no other person can. It is hoped that he will avoid exaggerations and distortions of his authority which can vitiate it just as much as his failure to exercise it. To negate one rather gross exaggeration, for example, the minister's function is not that of watchdog, smelling out and preventing heresy.

Representation

The second policy to be mentioned may be designated as representation, or representativeness. This may be made clear and possibly also authentic by referring to the body figure. If a body is going to act as a body, there is need for its different parts to be interrelated and in communication with each other. We should, of course, not be unmindful of the similarity of this policy to a central ideal in our American representative government. This ideal had at least two sources; one of them was the French enlightenment, and the other the Protestant Reformation, particularly as expressed in the government of Geneva in the time of John Calvin. It is submitted here that in order for a church to act as a body, there must be representative participation of the parts in the whole. Specifically, for nurture in the church, this means that the committee or board of Christian education must be a representative body. These representatives may be appointed by the governing body of the congregation, or the groups they represent may elect them. It is important for it to be clear however that they are not instructed representatives, bound to the will of the group they may represent, but that they should act according to their own convictions, when deliberating and making decisions.

Coordination

A third policy is coordination, which means that when organization is representative, its different parts are provided a means for talking to one another; the left hand can know what the right hand is doing. Many times in our churches, we simply lack knowledge of what other parts of the church are doing. Granted that this knowledge by itself does not go very far toward improvement, it is a step in the right direction for every part of the church to find out what every other part is doing. It is conceivable that when the parts get closer together, they may not like each other any better, or possibly not even as well as when they were further apart. While this may be the case, it is still important, if a body is going to be a body, that the parts have some perception, some appreciation, and some judgment of what the other parts are doing. In this context, when objectives are laid out, they are laid out as the whole body thinking together, rather than some one group launching out in an effort, without any reference to the remainder of the church. If tensions arise on occasion in a representative body such as a committee or board of Christian education, at least the tensions are out into the open. The group may have to approach and back away several times, before eventually—by the grace of God—it comes to see what is just and fair, what is really Christian love in the situation. It is doubtful that such co-ordinative functioning is possible for the life of the whole congregation, unless there is representativeness in official bodies. Of course, it is by no means all sweetness and light, nor can it be, if decisive actions are to be taken. Very often on the most critical matters there are hidden agendas and power struggles, which have to be brought out into the open, not crudely nor bluntly, but, nevertheless, sufficiently for people to see them for what they are and eventually to dispose of them with the constraint of Christian love.

Planning

The fourth policy to be mentioned is planning, which, at the least, is not out of harmony with an authentic understanding of the nature of the Church. Which is more in harmony with the Church understood as the servant of God in the world, *laissez faire* or deliberations prayerfully intended? Do we impede the intention and purpose of God any more by planning than by allowing things to happen as they will? There is a heavy weight of inertia in the institutional church, which virtually proclaims that if God wants something done he will see to it that it is done, and that we do not need to plan for it or exert effort to bring it about. On the other hand, there is also a dynamism in the Church—we trust, of the Spirit of God—which without human presumption insists upon struggling hard at serving God in the world. According to the spirit of this approach, people say, "We are going to sit down, think prayerfully, and try to determine what it is that God wants this church to do." Such an approach is not held rigidly by its plans, yet it is determined to have plans, however much they have to be changed in the course of events. This is the policy of planning and is submitted here as more of the nature of the Church than of *laissez faire*.

Distinction Between Planning and Operation

The fifth and last policy to be mentioned is that, for the sake of clarity, we need to distinguish between planning and operation. Strictly speaking, committees and other deliberative bodies are not action groups or functionaries. Professional staff, teachers, officers, and department heads, are functionaries, who are supposed to put into action the decisions made by deliberative bodies. While many individuals may legitimately "wear two hats"—now being a member of a deliberative body and later an acting functionary—it is very confusing when a single body both forms policy and carries it into action. It is much clearer, and lines of authority and responsibility are much more precise, when the deliberative and active functions are kept distinct. Deliberative bodies form policy, but, if confusion is to be avoided, they do not carry it out.

THE MINISTER IN ADMINISTRATION

One thing should be said concerning the minister in the administration of Christian education; because of its importance, it should be made a special point and not said incidentally to some other subject. It is hoped that this entire book converges upon the imperative that the minister must be the one responsible if the ministry of nurture in the congregation is to be both authentic and effective.

He cannot evade or delegate this responsibility. This is expedient in the small church, in which the one minister has to do everything that is done at the professional level as a kind of jack-of-all-trades. It is usually true, although not always and not necessarily, that nothing happens in the teaching ministry of the church, unless the minister makes it happen. This is as true in the larger churches of 1000, 2500, or even 6000 members. Such churches may have a very fine professional staff, a multiple ministry comprised of highly qualified and well-educated experts, among whom there may be very well-conceived and well-defined divisions of labor and delegations of duties and responsibilities, but still the senior minister cannot delegate all of the responsibility and authority for nurture in the church. He himself must have the vision of what should be done, and he himself must be able to convey this vision to his professional associates and to his people. He cannot excuse himself from at least this basic responsibility. He cannot, for example, say to the minister of education, "Education is your bailiwick, and I am going to stay out of it." One minister of education, when being inducted into a church, was taken by the minister to a particular door in the building, which happened to be the entryway between the educational unit and the remainder of the church building. As the two of them stood facing this door, the minister of education was told, "Everything beyond this door is your responsibility; everything on this side of the door is my responsibility." While this is a neat physical way of making a distinction in jobs, it simply isn't true and simply won't work. The installed minister of the church, who is regarded by the congregation as the leader of the church, must have more vision than this and must not evade his responsibility. He must know what he wants to see happen in Christian education; indeed, he must engage in a number of functions in relation to nurture (which we will soon mention), if anything significant is going to happen in this area of the life of his church.

This involves matters already implied, which may well be stated more specifically. It cannot be sufficiently emphasized that the minister needs to supply vision for the program of nurture in the church. This means that he will have to think things through carefully enough that he will know what he wants to see happen in his church and that he can convey this vision to other people. The minister should certainly be at least an ex officio member of the committee or board of Christian education, and not just in a token relationship. He must be vitally involved and an active force in this body, as the almost necessary means of authentic nurture taking place in his church. For one thing, if this committee or board performs its primary function, it will be making important policy decisions at virtually every meeting. If the minister is not involved or does not have adequate vision, this official body will probably not rise to its primary task. And if, by some stroke of genius on the part of its members, it makes policy recommendations without the participation of the minister, why should there be the wasted motion of his later review of the recommendations? He should participate instead in their initial formulation.

A PLAN OF ORGANIZATION

Our discussion must now become more concrete and propose a plan of organization. (See the chart on the following page.) Although it is forthrightly acknowledged that no plan of oraganization has finality, there are various ways of building relationships which are acceptable as long as the policies from which they stem are good. While the plan proposed is offered as an example of good organization, it is also presented out of conviction and as worthy of high recommendation. In line with the policy of authority already enunciated, the plan of organization should take fully into account the relation of the congregation to the officer or official body immediately above it in the organization of the denomination. The minister is the connecting link, of course, but if there are other ministers and if the higher authority is an official body, they also may be members of the organization.

The minister who has overall responsibility for the congregation and the minister or director of Christian education should both be at least ex officio members of the Christian education committee or board. As far as regularity is concerned, they should both sit in on the deliberations of this body as staff members whenever possible. Their function is not so much to determine the deliberations and decisions, as to enlighten and guide the committee without restricting the honest and free thought of the members of the group. The minister and, particularly, the minister of education are professionals who should be able to offer insights which the other members of the committee are not likely to have. In a real sense, they are servants of this policy-making body. They are present in it also, therefore, in order to see to the execution of the decisions of this body. And this relates to the policy, already mentioned, that planning and execution should be kept distinct as functions.

It is desirable that every official body of the church be represented in the committee or board of Christian education, as well

A Plan for the Administration of the Program of Nurture in the Congregation

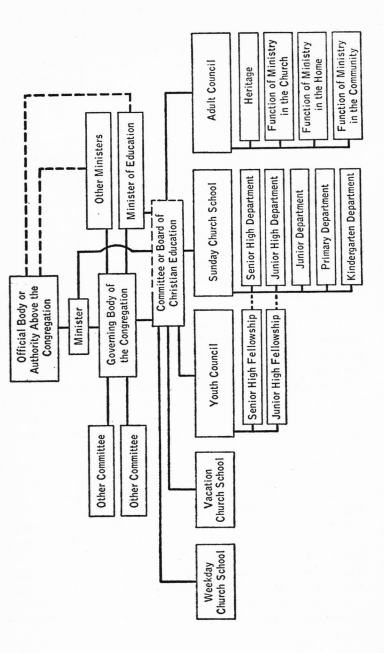

as all the different agencies or parts of the teaching program of the church. In addition, it is usually wise to have other kinds of representatives, such as different ethnic, social, and economic groups, if the congregation is that cosmopolitan. Some members may be chosen because their standing and acceptance enable them to speak for the church at large. In such ways as these, the committee or board is so composed that it can really think about the whole life of the church, as far as its teaching and nurture is concerned, in a way which will be accepted by the whole congregation. When its recommendations come to the governing board of the congregation, of which the committee is a subsidiary or under which it serves, they will come from a sufficiently broad base in the congregation that they will carry real weight. This exemplifies in organization the policies of representation, co-ordination, and planning.

The function of this committee or board is not actual teaching, it is not actual leadership education, and it is not actual assignment of teachers to different departments of the Church School. It is rather a plan for the entire teaching effort of the church, to see to it that there will be recruiting and training programs for teachers and officers adequate to make available to heads of departments, youth councils, adult councils, etc., a reservoir of qualified personnel.

As indicated on the chart of this plan of organization, it is proposed that all youth work be tied together in a unified program, as well as adult education, including leadership education and education for Christian family life. These relationships should be made somewhat more explicit.

It is proposed that there be a youth council which will be represented in the committee or board of Christian education. On the one hand, it will be related to and in communication with all other aspects of the effort toward nurture in the church. On the other, it will be in a position to plan for and administer specifically all youth activities. Embraced within its planning and administration will be all youth fellowships, all youth departments of the Sunday Church School, all youth choirs, and all scout organizations, if there are any housed by the congregation or under its sponsorship.

It is proposed that there be a similar council to embrace the overseeing and planning of all adult education in the congregation.

As indicated on the chart, this will include at least four aspects of the nurture of adults. First of all and, in a real sense, the basis for all the rest, there will be a program of study dealing with the Christian heritage. This will be comprised of serious courses in various aspects of the Bible, the history of the Church, and theology. With these genuinely adult courses as the context, there will also be three related programs of study in the functions of the ministry of the Church, in which laymen must be given their real part and for which they should be educated.

The first of these is commonly referred to as leadership education and officer training. We prefer to refer to these—we believe, more properly—as the functions of the ministry of the Church. It is in this part of the adult program that a reservoir of so-called leadership for the church will be developed.

The second of these areas in functions of the ministry will be a kind of ministry to the family in a program of study. It will be for parents and prospective parents and will be designed to help them build Christian families and fulfill their God-given ministry in the home.

The third and last of these functions of the ministry will be a program of study in community services. It will be the purpose of these courses to give a vision of the responsibilities of the Christian for social action. They will also help adults to see how they have a place of service to fill in the community, not only as citizens, but as those who are a part of the ministry of the Church to the world.

SUPERVISION

Administration may be conceived of as having at least three aspects. There is the structural aspect, which is organization. There is the functioning aspect, including both planning and operation, which is administration in action, and to that extent, a narrower definition of administration. And there is the supervisory aspect, which has to do with seeing that plans are carried out at the level of excellence which the Church deserves. We will look more closely at this supervisory part of administration as the final step in this chapter.

There are at least three purposes which may be fulfilled by

supervision. By it we may be able to check actual achievements in the program of teaching in the church against the functions and ends which are intended for it. By it we may also strengthen weaker and less mature teachers, if not actually teach them more about how they can do their jobs better. By supervision it may also be possible to coordinate more closely the work of the Church School as a whole, helping to make it the strong program of nurture it should be.

Good personal relationships are necessarily a prior condition to good supervision. Mutual acceptance between the supervisor and the supervised will go a long way in getting supervision done satisfactorily and to good ends. It is important for the supervisor to understand and be sympathetic toward the person he supervises and to fully appreciate his qualities and achievements. At the same time, of course, this willingness to understand should not blind the supervisor to the faults and failures of the supervised. As a part of the empathetic aspect of a good relationship between the two, there should be full cognizance, on the part of the supervisor, of the personal objectives toward which the supervised is moving. After all, each person in a Church School is in his own peculiar place in the life cycle, and in relation to it, his teaching may be a comparatively small consideration in his own subjective experience. This cannot be overlooked, whatever the quality of the teaching. When the time comes for discussion of what goes on in the classwork of the supervised, there should be both forthrightness and specificity in what is said. It probably will not be enough in most cases for criticisms to be implied; they must be direct, though at the same time kind. And since directness is necessary, it will be the part of wisdom to be specific in criticisms, so that that the supervised will clearly understand. Often a vague and general criticism is interpreted as meaning something much worse or more threatening than is intended. It is therefore the part of respect for the supervised, to be concrete and precise in meanings. There should always be willingness on the part of the supervisor to allow for freedom and variety in the ways and means by which agreed-upon ends may be accomplished. There are many legitimate ways of doing things, and the preferred schemes of the supervisor, while they may be better for him, can scarcely be proposed as norms by which the procedures of others are to be judged.

The question of who shall do the supervising is somewhat more difficult to answer for the Church School than for the day school. Should it be the minister? While in the smaller church his duties will be more than he can easily cover, he may, nevertheless, be the only person who is qualified to supervise. In larger and more adequately staffed churches, he will be relieved of this particular and often arduous task by staff-members who are especially assigned to the overseeing of the educational work of the church. Even so, in some of the administrative responsibilities—from which, we have held, the minister should not excuse himself regardless of the size of the church—he will also be incidentally fulfilling supervisory functions.

In larger churches in which there is a minister of education or director of Christian education, such specialists may very well find that a major part of their work is supervision, in a variety of forms. At the same time that he accepts the burden of supervision, the minister of education should by no means overlook the potential for supervisory responsibility in some of the so-called volunteer members of the Church-School staff. The superintendent of the Sunday Church School, the director of the Vacation Church School, or the director of the Weekday Church School are all qualified for supervision, if they are of sufficient caliber to be assigned the responsibilities which they have in their respective administrative positions. This may also very well be true of the superintendents or chairmen of the respective departments in the Sunday Church School. In fact, it is difficult to see how they can effectively guide their departments without fulfilling the supervisory function, at least in informal relationships and at department meetings.

Another nearly as important question has to do with the means by which supervision shall be accomplished. The person who supervises is of utmost importance, but how he goes about his supervision is scarcely a secondary consideration. In general, it can be said at the outset that by no means is all supervision carried on by means of the supervisory visit. The supervisor must first of all build relations of confidence and trust as the basis or context for acceptance of his supervision. There are many ways in which he may do this, some of which can be mentioned. He can build such trust by the general quality of his personal relationships, in informal associations, and in settings other than those in which assigned functions are carried out. He can also build this confidence in the line of duty, for example, in staff meetings at various levels. This may be more particularly true of the departmental meeting, where the work is more detailed and the focus of discussion narrows more closely toward classroom performance.

The supervisor must work in close proximity and rapport in the various formal meetings he may have with those under his supervision. He must do this, not only to establish relationships of trust and confidence, but in order to become genuinely involved with them in a common labor. As an accompaniment of this, he will learn much about the quality of classroom work prior to, and as a basis for, class visits. It will probably be wise for this kind of relationship to be cultivated over a sustained period before actual visits begin, if they prove to be necessary at all.

There will wisely be presupervision conferences and visits with teachers. There will, no doubt, be need, in the normal course of events, for personal conferences with teachers about their work. It will be preferable if these are initiated by the teachers rather than by the supervisor. And such conferences can be clearly invited both by one's action and general bearing, as well as by the spoken word. As far as teachers are concerned, it is possible for a supervisor, especially if he is the department head, to be in and out of classes frequently enough on other errands, and without hidden design, to pave the way for the visit which clearly focuses on supervision. He may become so much accepted both by pupils and teachers as a frequent and welcome visitor that a visit of any kind becomes the normal expectation.

As to the supervisory visit itself, there are some suggestions which may be made. First of all, it is assumed that the relationships have been established which make the visit a psychological possibility, as well as a physical one. The supervisor's presence is, or should be, already accepted before he appears on the scene. Secondly, the supervisory visit should be a sympathetic and cordial one. Both directly and indirectly, he should indicate his desire to be included as a part of the group, rather than just an observer, during the time he is in the class. Finally, he will want to make mental note of significant items in class procedure—the good, the bad, and the indifferent. But, like the good case worker, he will never be so formal as to use pencil and paper for this purpose, however precise he may be in his observations.

To complete the cycle, it will probably be wise to follow visits with supervisory conferences, in which the significant matters noted are discussed with the teacher. In these conferences, a special point should be made of giving commendation for achievements, as well as calling attention—helpfully, if at all possible—to failures and mistakes. Regarding the parts of the performance in class which were poor, they should be discussed emphatically, frankly, and specifically. As urged before, generalities, which can be so grossly misinterpreted, should be avoided. Adequate attention should also be paid for variant ways of getting things done—even if they are unfamiliar to the supervisor—if they seem to be possible means of good teaching. This leaves the door open to creativity on the part of the supervised, and this door should never be closed. In the case of more mature teachers, both visits and the conferences following them may possibly be more peremptory. We should, nevertheless, be on our guard against allowing familiarity and long tenure to become an illusion of excellence.

A final question, which all of this discussion of supervision may raise in the minds of some, is, "Should the supervisor have a schedule of standards which constitute a pattern for his supervision and consequent evaluation?" Admittedly, much can be said in favor of such a schedule; it will give purpose and direction, and it may keep the supervisor alert to things he should be watching.[2] However, the suggestion is submitted here that it is wise not to have any such pre-arranged schedule. It can easily become too rigid and constitute a kind of stereotype for the supervisor, thus giving him false confidence and possibly inhibiting his interest in the new and unprecedented. In any event, if some such schedule is used, it should be revised frequently, if not before each visit. Like most sermons, it is not worth preaching twice without being rewritten, or at least reworked.

---

[2] See, for example, Nevin C. Harner, *The Educational Work of the Church*, New York: Abingdon-Cokesbury, 1939, pp. 206–207.

CHAPTER 18

The Ministry of the Church and Nurture

*T*he subject of this final chapter is the ministry of the Church. As will be observed as the chapter proceeds, we are speaking of the ministry in its broadest sense. It is the ministry of the Church which is our concern and not just the ministry of the ministers, as it were, as a profession. In fact, the latter more narrow focus is a mistaken one and lacking in authenticity; the ministry belongs to the Church as a whole and not to some special group or profession.[1]

We make this our concluding subject for two reasons. As the book began with the nature of the Church, it is both normal and cogent for it to conclude with the ministry of the Church to the world. But there is also a more specific reason which relates to the emphasis this book has placed upon the nurturing aspect of the life of the Church. It is in nurture, or Christian education as it has been more commonly, but not so wisely, known in recent times, that a great many so-called lay or volunteer leaders are needed for the Church to do its work. In recent times this concern has been expressed under the captions of leadership and leadership education. Our preference is to deal with this important subject in the context of the *ministry of the Church*. We believe this is its proper and authentic designation.

It will be necessary, as will become clear later, for us to take at

[1] See H. Richard Niebuhr, *The Purpose of The Church and Its Ministry*, New York: Harper, 1956.

least a brief look at the ordained ministry of the Church, as well as
to consider what part the laity has in the ministry of the Church.

TOWARD AN AUTHENTIC CONCEPTION
OF THE ORDAINED MINISTRY

At the present time, in the United States at least, we think of
the ordained minister first of all as the preacher. His main task, according to our folkways, is to prepare and to deliver sermons. The
word "proclamation" has been deliberately avoided in this statement, because proclamation should be understood as more generic
and, therefore, more inclusive than the act of preaching. In somewhat more precise terms, we often speak in church groups of "the
ministry of the Word and Sacrament." Accordingly, we assume
that the reason a man is ordained is to preach the Word of God
and to administer the sacraments. Although this reference to the
ordained ministry may be more exact than the word "preacher," it
is still more a folkway than an authentic conception. Somehow it
has become established in our minds, even in more radically
Protestant churches, that the ordained minister is set apart to a
sacerdotal function, and, possibly without knowing it, we have as
often as not made the minister a priest. For all practical purposes,
in emphasizing the functions of preaching and administering the
sacraments, we have set ordained ministers apart as a different class,
if not a different kind of Christian, from laymen in the Church.

The second function which we assign to the ordained minister
is that of being pastor to the people, by which we chiefly mean two
things. We mean that he should call on the members of the church
in their homes with some degree of regularity and that he should
call on those "outside" the Church who might be evangelized and
brought into the Church. In some measure, we have also come to
think of the pastoral function as including counseling, but, in
spite of all the emphasis it has received in recent years, this is
probably still minor in our conception. According to this second
aspect of the pastor's function, he is one who wins the confidence
of people, so that they disclose to him their inner life and their
problems, possibly make confession of sin, and seek his help.

We should now try to achieve a better perspective by looking
at the ministry, as it apparently was in the primitive Church. This

is not to imply that the primitive Church is the norm by which all succeeding generations of the Church are to be judged; however, it was in the primitive church that the functions of the ministry first emerged.[2] We know that the original Apostles were an exalted group, having a special status because of the historically original position in which they stood. Saint Paul achieved the status of Apostle in the mind of the Church by the peculiar and radically courageous position of leadership to which he arose and by his unrelenting service in establishing and nurturing churches.

In the early Church, prophecy had a priority of importance, at least in Saint Paul's estimation. Saint Paul suggested that the work of the prophet and the function of proclamation are unique, because they deal with the noumenal, as opposed to the phenomenal—the internal essence or reality of things in distinction from appearances. The prophet had to do with visions, with revelations, with a kind of initiation into divine secrets. In the *Didache*,[3] the prophet is once referred to as a high priest.

The teacher's function in the primitive Church apparently was instruction in the more pedestrian sense. His job was to inform concerning doctrinal content, as distinct from giving utterance to inspired revelation. As compared to teaching the prophetic function was proclamation, which was itself a kind of revelation of truth. Prophecy and teaching were not separately designated functions, identified with distinct persons having their peculiar status-levels in the church. Sometimes, it is true, prophecy and teaching were exercised by different persons; but it was also common for these functions to be exercised by the same person. In other words, the functions could be distinguished, but people could not be separated into groups or classes because they exclusively performed one of these functions. Specifically, it appears that there were no separate offices for the prophet and for the teacher.

Apparently sex distinction had no connection with differentiation of functions in the early Church; women shared both in the gifts and the labors of the ministry. Several examples can be cited

---

[2] See John Knox, "The Ministry in the Primitive Church," chap. 1 in H. Richard Niebuhr and Daniel D. Williams, eds., *The Ministry in Historical Perspectives*, New York: Harper, 1956.

[3] *Ibid.*, p. 14.

from the letters in the New Testament to verify this. As can be readily indicated by reference to the New Testament, women had their share, as well as their prominence, in the administrative and pastoral work of the churches. It would seem likely that they also exercised comparable leadership in the early love-feast, the antecedent of the later and more formalized sacrament of communion.

A very interesting and striking fact is that in the local churches, it was "administrators" and "helpers" who first received official status in the Church, comparable to ordination.[4] The system of government by councils of elders understandably made this necessary. It was people who did not fulfill the prophetic function, or even the teaching function, but whose responsibilities were the administering and ordering of the day-by-day affairs of the various churches, who were apparently first given official status in the Church. By the end of the first century, these people, who became known as bishops and deacons, were beginning to take over the instructive and liturgical functions of the prophets and the teachers. But in the first instances, there seem to have been pragmatic rather than charismatic reasons for the emergence of those who first had official status. Their reason for being rose out of the necessity for local congregational organization and for church councils at higher levels, so that there should be order and management, not chaos, in the affairs of faith.

The whole point in introducing this reference to the practice of the primitive Church is to set it in contrast to our present folkways, which, dictate to us what the ordained ministry is supposed to be. In the early Church, there were a number of specialized functions in the ministry, but there was no special status of separateness, until the need for administering and ordering affairs became urgent. Our present folkways governing the ordained ministry do not square very well with the facts. Yet even these folkways constitute a kind of romanticized ideal, which has been carried over from former generations and which the pressures of today prevent us from practicing, however much we verbalize them. There are some indications that today the ordained minister, whether he wishes it or realizes it, actually spends far more time in administrative functions than in those tasks assumed to be his by our folkways. In part, it is the complexity of modern society

4 *Ibid.*, p. 19.

which has caused this. In the United States at least our churches are bigger; it is not at all uncommon for individual congregations to have more than a thousand members. In a few instances, the membership runs to several thousand, unwise as this may be. The complexity is not only a matter of size, however; it is also the quality of complex involvement of our civilization, much of which tries our best efforts to understand it and cope with it. Accordingly, the conviction is often voiced that things other than the familiar and time-honored activities need to take place in the life of the church. Whether there is one minister or a staff of six, there is a great deal of organization that has to be done somehow, and above the level of the congregation we have been forced to develop large organizations and bureaus, employing great numbers of people, many of them ordained ministers.

A close parallel to this pressure of complexity can be seen in the curriculums of theological seminaries. For the most part the curriculum of theological education today lacks integrity—not ethical integrity, but intellectual integrity. It does not hang togeher and it is not internally interrelated. In an earlier time, theological schools could and did have integrity, but it was an easy and overly simple integrity. Education of ministers could be conceived of simply as being derived from the heritage; this made it comparatively simple. But the pressures that have emerged, particularly in the late nineteenth and the twentieth centuries, have forced theological education to spread out and to include several disciplines resulting from the impact of the various sciences. As yet, theological education has not been able so to interrelate these new disciplines with the heritage as to have intellectual and curricular integrity. This transitional situation is not all bad, even though it is painful and disconcerting to the student. The old integrity may have been adequate for its time, but it was far too easy for this and coming generations. It is hoped that in the remaining decades of the twentieth century, if the hands of human destruction are stayed, that the theological schools will be able to establish a new and more difficult integrity, not just wrought out of the heritage, but also in relation to the complex world to which the Church now ministers. It is submitted here that hard work at the critical labors of theology will have more to do with bringing this about than a rigidly dogmatic theology.

There are two main elements in the conception of the ministry which is coming and which will be more adequate and more authentic. The first is that the ordained ministry of the Church is one ministry and not many ministries. Sometimes suggestions are made in the councils of the Protestant churches that we should have different orders in the Church and that some people should be ordained as preachers, some as teachers, others as pastors, and so on throughout a long list, supposedly providing for all the different functions of ministering. Fortunately, such proposals are resisted as a rule with a strength of conviction equal to, and commonly stronger than, that of the proposal. The ordained ministry of the Church is one ministry, at least within Protestantism, and it cannot be divided into several or many orders, only one of which is authorized to administer the sacraments. When a person is ordained to the ministry, he is ordained not just to one function, but to all functions of the ministry. And this is as it should be; the ministry is one ministry.

Within this unity, however, there is a plurality of functions for which specialization of training and service is legitimate. This means that all who qualify before the proper authorities should be ordained to the one ministry and be authorized thereby to fulfill any and all of the functions of ministering in the Church. But it also means that, within this one ministry, they may specialize and devote themselves to particular functions; in situations and circumstances calling for it, such specialization may be exclusive. Some may be pulpit ministers; some pastors; some teachers in parish, college, or divinity school; some may be administrators; and so on. But all have full standing in the one ordained ministry of the Church.

Such a conception should eventually have its effect upon education for the ministry in our schools of theology. If it does, it will mean that theological education will give a common education to all candidates for the ministry to the extent that it is necessary for all to be grounded in the knowledge and disciplines essential to the ordained ministry. It will also mean that opportunities will be offered for the various specializations needed to equip persons for various specialized functions of the ministry. These opportunities should be in scholarly pursuits in the respective areas of knowledge and theological disciplines, as well as in so-called vocational functions. It might also mean a common academic symbol for the qualified minister, such as the B.D. degree, paralleling the common ecclesiastical symbol of ordination.

TOWARD A CORRECTION OF THE CONCEPTION OF THE LAITY

Our discussion now moves on to what appears to be the necessary correction of the conception of the laity which has been current in the Church for centuries. The correction is that the layman in the Church is only a layman in the sense that he has received neither professional training for the ministry nor a formal call to be minister of a congregation, on both of which ordination is commonly based. This is the only authentic distinction between the layman and the ordained minister. Both have received the call to be a Christian, in comparison to which all other distinctions are minor. This is to say that the only authentic difference between the ordained minister and the layman is a functional one, providing for divisions of labor in the Church. There are some who, of necessity, have to give full time and commitment to the ministry and the service of the Church in the world. But this makes them no more ministers in terms of quality or kind, than the so-called laymen in the Church, who also are ministers by virtue of the fact that they are Christians. Actually the Greek term, from which our word "layman" comes, referred, without distinction, to all the people within the context of the Church as the "people of God." Conceivably, in our present-day churches there is sometimes no basis in fact for the distinction we accept between laymen and minister. While it may not happen frequently, there are ministers who have to preach Sunday by Sunday to so-called laymen who know more about the Bible, theology, or church history than the minister does. But does this make them any less ministers to these laymen, or does it vitiate in any way the responsibility laid upon them to proclaim the Word of God to these laymen? This very mixture of heterogeneity and homogeneity existed in the primitive Church and apparently was not regarded as having any bearing upon distinctions between classes among the members of the body of Christ.

It would appear, therefore, that the norm for the nurture of so-called laymen in the Church should be that they have both the opportunity and the encouragement to go as far as their abilities and their time permit. This is what adult Christian education should be—the opening of the way and the providing of the means by which laymen can progress as far in the understanding of the faith as possible. Although this is coming, and is actually happening in churches here and there, it is far beyond what most churches are now doing. In the majority of cases, we are still settling for Sunday morning adult classes, that are often weak and insipid and struggling to stay alive. Very often there is little awareness in them of the crisis of our day, of what the Christian faith has to say in the face of it, and of the responsibility of adult Christians to be genuinely adult in their faith.

Nevertheless, the layman is no less a part of the ministry of the Church than his minister, and he must study seriously the faith and the ministry of the Church to the world, in order that he may fulfill his responsible part in that ministry. The layman has no less responsibility than the minister for understanding and thinking his faith, to the degree his life circumstances make possible. It is also his responsibility to minister to men and to the world as a part of the ministry of the Church, to whatever extent his native gifts, his preparation in serious study, and his stewardship of his time make possible—this is his calling as a Christian and as a member of the body of Christ.

IMPLICATIONS FOR ADULT EDUCATION AND LEADERSHIP IN THE CHURCH

What does this proposed correction have to say concerning adult education and leadership in the Church? For one thing, we now have to deal with these two as one. There must be sufficient and serious adult nurture in the Church to enable the so-called layman to participate to the full extent of his responsibility in the ministry of the Church. This adult education will be of at least two kinds: nurture in the Faith, and education in the functions of the ministry.

Nurture in the Heritage

The foundation of adult nurture is the kind of serious study which will lead to understanding the Faith and thinking the Faith.

And this means understanding it biblically, understanding it historically, and understanding it theologically. Such an educational effort would constitute a program of study for adults in the Church which refuses to settle for a Sunday-School religion. Instead, it makes each congregation a kind of theological seminary, to the extent that people are taking the Faith seriously, and studying it biblically, historically, theologically as though their lives depended upon it—which, in all reality, they do. In such a program there is room for all kinds of courses, for a well-stocked library, for book lists to guide the reading of members, with all kinds of gradations to accommodate different levels of achievement. There is room for many other similar provisions and innovations which will challenge people to serious study and assist them in it. Is there any reason why many laymen in the Church should not be reading the theological books used in schools of theology? We undersestimate most of them; they are ready for more than the innocuous diet we commonly feed them.

Proficiency in the Functions of the Ministry

It is in this setting that so-called leadership education can find its proper and authentic place in the Church. With nurture in the Faith as foundation and context, there should be study by adults of the functions of the ministry of the Church. It is hoped this will eventually take the place of so-called leadership education and officer training, so that these will have their proper setting as parts of the ministry. As adults are studying the Faith in terms of its heritage, they should also, in conscious relation to it, be studying the ministries that are specific and concrete functions in the life of the Church. It is in this way that leadership education and officer training should be conceived.

Finally, there are important derivatives which may follow from such a program of adult education. One of the derivatives is the parent's place, as a parent, in the ministry of the Church in the home. It is here that education for family life finds its proper context. In this setting it is not just family education as such, but home life and parenthood as a part of the ministry of the Church. Also derivative from this conception of adult nurture is broadening the church's ministry to families to include more than preparation for marriage and Christian family life. In other words the

301

church assumes partnership with the home in nurturing children. Still another derivative is qualification of volunteer leaders, not only for teaching and administrative responsibilities within the church, but also for ministry outside the church—possibly in social organizations and agencies, for example, or in official positions in government. Equipping and helping volunteer leaders to know how to be Christians and to render a Christian ministry in a recreational agency, in a character-building agency, or possibly as a board member of one of the community organizations, is a phase of its ministry to the world that no congregation can afford to overlook. In this conception of adult nurture, the Church is virtually saying to its so-called laymen, what is said poetically in one of the liturgies of ordination to the ministry: "We give you the right hand of fellowship, to take part of this Ministry with us."

Bibliography

CHAPTER 1

Bonhoeffer, Dietrich. *Life Together*. Translated by John W. Dober-
stein. New York: Harper & Brothers. 1954. Chapter 1.

Brunner, Emil. *The Misunderstanding of the Church*. Translated by
Harold Knight. Philadelphia: Westminster Press. 1953.

Grimes, Howard. *The Church Redemptive*. New York: Abingdon
Press. 1958.

Newbigin, Leslie. *The Household of God*. New York: Friendship
Press. 1953.

Niebuhr, H. Richard. *The Purpose of the Church and Its Ministry*.
New York: Harper & Brothers. 1956.

Sherill, Lewis Joseph. *The Gift of Power*. New York: The Macmillan
Co. 1955. Chapter 3.

Webber, George W. *God's Colony in Man's World*. New York:
Abingdon Press. 1960.

Welch, Claude. *The Reality of the Church*. New York: Charles Scribner's Sons. 1958.

CHAPTER 2

Clement of Alexandria. *The Instructor*. Volume IV. *Ante-Nicene
Christian Library*. Edited by Alexander Roberts and James Donaldson. Edinburgh: T. & T. Clark. 1867.

Didache. Volume I. *The Apostolic Fathers*. Translated by Kersopp
Lake. Cambridge, Mass.: Harvard University Press. 1952.

Eby, Frederick, and Arrowood, Charles Flinn. *The History and Philosophy of Education Ancient and Medieval*. New York: Prentice-
Hall, Inc. 1940. Chapter 13.

Hodgson, Geraldine. *Primitive Christian Education*. Edinburgh: T. &
T. Clark. 1906.

Jaeger, Werner, *Early Christianity and Greek Paideia*. Cambridge,
Mass.: Harvard University Press. 1961.

Marrou, H. I. *A History of Education in Antiquity*. Translated by
George Lamb. New York: Sheed & Ward. 1956.

Sherrill, Lewis Joseph. *The Rise of Christian Education*. New York:
The Macmillan Co. 1954. Chapters 6 and 7.

CHAPTER 3

Calvin, John. *Institutes of the Christian Religion*. Seventh American
Edition. Translated by John Allen. Philadelphia: Presbyterian Board

303

of Christian Education. 1936. Book I, Chapters 3, 4, and 15; Book II, Chapters 1 and 2.

Comenius, John Amos. *The Great Didactic.* Translated and Edited with Biographical, Historical and Critical Introductions by M. W. Keatinge. London. A. and C. Black Ltd. 1921. Two Volumes.

Cubberly, Ellwood P. *Readings in the History of Education.* Boston: Houghton Mifflin Co. 1920. Reading 190: "The Massachusetts Law of 1642": Reading 191: "The Massachusetts Law of 1647."

Eby, Frederick. *The Development of Modern Education.* Second Edition. New York: Prentice-Hall, Inc. 1952. Chapters 3, 6, and 7.

Keatinge, M. W. *Comenius.* New York: McGraw-Hill. 1931.

Luther, Martin. "Letters to the Mayors and Aldermen of All the Cities of Germany in Behalf of Christian Schools." Robert Ulich. *Three Thousand Years of Educational Wisdom.* Cambridge, Mass.: Harvard University Press. 1947. Pp. 218–238.

Luther, Martin. "Sermon on the Duty of Sending Children to School." Robert Ulich. *Three Thousand Years of Educational Wisdom.* Cambridge, Mass.: Harvard University Press. 1947. Pp. 238–249.

Smith, J. W. Ashley. *The Birth of Modern Education.* London: Independent Press Ltd. 1954.

CHAPTER 4

Beard, Augusta Field. *The Story of Jean Frederic Oberlin.* Boston: The Pilgrim Press. 1909.

Browning, Webster E. *Joseph Lancaster, James Thomson, and the Lancasterian System of Mutual Instruction.* Privately printed. 1936.

Butler, J. Donald. "Sunday School." *Twentieth Century Encyclopedia of Religious Knowledge.* Grand Rapids, Mich.: Baker Book House. 1955.

Dawson, Marshall. *Oberlin, A Protestant Saint.* Chicago: Willett, Clark and Co. 1934.

Graves, Frank Pierrepont. *A History of Education in Modern Times.* New York: The Macmillan Co. 1937. Chapter 3.

Gregory, Alfred. *Robert Raikes: Journalist and Philanthropist.* New York: Anson D. F. Randolph and Co. 1879.

Jones, Mary Gladys. *The Charity School Movement.* Cambridge: The University Press. 1938.

Kendall, Guy. *Robert Raikes: A Critical Study.* London: Nicholson and Watson. n. d.

Lancaster, Joseph. *Improvements in Education as It Respects the Industrious Classes.* New York: Collins and Perkins. 1807.

Leopold, Richard William. *Robert Dale Owen.* Cambridge, Mass.: Harvard University Press. 1940.

Sherrill, Lewis Joseph. *Presbyterian Parochial Schools 1776–1870.* New Haven: Yale University Press. 1932.

Society for Promotion of Christian Instruction, *The Principles and the Plan of the Society.* London: The Society. 1828.

CHAPTER 5

Eby, Frederick. *The Development of Modern Education.* Revised Edition. New York: Prentice-Hall, Inc. 1952. Chapters 13, 17, 18, and 19.

Froebel, Friedrich William August. *The Education of Man.* Translated and Annotated by W. N. Hailman. New York: D. Appleton and Co. 1887.

Graves, Frank Pierrepont. *A History of Education in Modern Times.* New York: The Macmillan Co. 1937. Chapters 2, 5, and 7.

Herbart, Johann Friedrich. *Textbook in Psychology.* Translated by Margaret K. Smith. New York: D. Appleton and Co. 1897.

Herbart, Johann Friedrich. *The Science of Education.* Translated by Henry M. and Emmie Felkin. Boston: D. C. Heath. 1893.

Krusi, Hermann. *Pestalozzi: His Life, Work, and Influence.* New York: Wilson, Hinkle and Co. 1875.

Marenholtz-Bullo, Bertha Maria. *Reminiscences of Friedrich Froebel.* Translated by Mrs. Horace Mann. Boston: Lee and Shepard. 1894.

Pestalozzi, Johann Heinrich. *Leonard and Gertrude.* Translated and Abridged by Eva Channing. Boston: D. C. Heath. 1891.

Pestalozzi, Johann Heinrich. *How Gertrude Teaches Her Children.* Translated by Lucy E. Holland and Francis C. Turner. Syracuse: C. W. Bardeen, 1915.

Rousseau, Jean Jacques. *Emile.* Everyman's Library. London: J. M. Dent and Sons, Ltd. 1943.

Ulich, Robert, Editor. *Three Thousand Years of Educational Wisdom.* Cambridge, Mass.: Harvard University Press. 1947. Pp. 383–425, 480–507, 508–522, and 523–576.

CHAPTER 6

Bushnell, Horace. *Christian Nurture.* With an Introduction by Luther A Weigle. New Haven: Yale University Press. 1947.

Fallaw, Wesner. "The Role of the Home in Religious Nurture." Chapter 13 in Marvin J. Taylor, Editor. *Religious Education.* New York: Abingdon Press. 1960.

Munro, Henry C. *Protestant Nurture.* Englewood Cliffs, N.J.: Prentice-Hall, Inc., 1956. Chapter 3.

Sherrill, Lewis Joseph. "A Historical Study of the Religious Education Movement." Chapter 1 in Philip Henry Lotz, Editor. *Orientation in Religious Education.* New York: Abingdon-Cokesbury Press. 1950.

CHAPTER 7

Aikin, Wilford M. *The Story of the Eight-Year Study.* New York: Harper & Brothers. 1942.

Dewey, John. *A Common Faith.* New Haven: Yale University Press. 1934.

Dewey, John. *Democracy and Education*. New York: The Macmillan Co. 1916.

Dewey, John. *Experience and Education*. New York: The Macmillan Co. 1938.

Dewey, John. *Logic, the Theory of Inquiry*. New York: Henry Holt and Co. 1938.

Meyer, Adolph E. *The Development of Education in the Twentieth Century*. Second Edition. New York: Prentice-Hall, Inc., 1949. Pp. 1–162.

Progressive Education Association. *Thirty Schools Tell Their Story*. New York: Harper & Brothers. 1943.

White, Morton G. *The Origins of Dewey's Instrumentalism*. New York: Columbia University Press. 1943.

CHAPTER 8

Bower, William Clayton, and Hayward, Percy Roy. *Protestantism Faces Its Educational Task Together*. Appleton, Wis.: C. C. Nelson Publishing Co. 1949.

Butler, J. Donald. "Religious Education." In Chester W. Harris, Editor. *Encyclopedia of Educational Research*. Third Edition. New York: The Macmillan Co. 1960. Pp. 1147–1155.

Cully, Iris V. *The Dynamics of Christian Education*. Philadelphia: Westminster Press. 1958.

Miller, Allen O. *Invitation to Theology*. Philadelphia: The Christian Education Press. 1958.

Miller, Randolph Crump. *The Clue to Christian Education*. New York: Charles Scribner's Sons. 1950.

Miller, Randolph Crump. *Biblical Theology and Christian Education*. New York: Charles Scribner's Sons. 1956.

Sherrill, Lewis Joseph. "A Historical Study of the Religious Education Movement." Chapter 1 in Philip Henry Lotz, Editor. *Orientation in Religious Education*. New York: Abingdon-Cokesbury Press. 1950.

Smart, James. *The Teaching Ministry of the Church*. Philadelphia: Westminster Press. 1954.

Smith, H. Shelton. *Faith and Nurture*. New York: Charles Scribner's Sons. 1946.

Stolz, Karl R. "Historical Development of Religious Education in America." Chapter 1 in Philip Henry Lotz and L. W. Crawford. *Studies in Religious Education*. Nashville, Tenn.: Cokesbury Press. 1931.

Taylor, Marvin D. "A Historical Introduction to Religious Education." Chapter 1 in Marvin J. Taylor, Editor. *Religious Education*. New York: Abingdon Press. 1960.

Vieth, Paul H., Editor. *The Church and Christian Education*. St. Louis: The Bethany Press. 1947. Chapter 2.

CHAPTER 9

Bailey, Albert E. "Philosophies of Education and Religious Education." Chapter 2 in Marvin J. Taylor, Editor. *Religious Education*. New York: Abingdon Press. 1960.

Barrett, Clifford. *Philosophy*. New York: The Macmillan Co. 1935.

Barth, Karl. *Dogmatics in Outline*. Translated by G. T. Thomson. New York: Philosophical Library. 1949.

Broudy, Harry S. *Building a Philosophy of Education*. New York: Prentice-Hall, Inc. 1954.

Brunner, Emil. *The Christian Doctrine of God*. Volume I of *Dogmatics*. Translated by Olive Wyon, Philadelphia: Westminster Press. 1950.

Brunner, Emil. *The Christian Doctrine of Creation and Redemption*. Volume II of *Dogmatics*. Translated by Olive Wyon. Philadelphia: Westminster Press. 1952.

Butler, J. Donald. *Four Philosophies and Their Practice in Education and Religion*. Revised Edition. New York: Harper & Brothers. 1957 (Particularly Chapters 23 and 24).

Casserly, J. V. Langmead. *The Christian in Philosophy*. New York: Charles Scribner's Sons. 1951.

Cully, Iris V. *The Dynamics of Christian Education*. Philadelphia: Westminster Press. 1958. Chapter 3.

Dillenberger, John, and Welch, Claude. *Protestant Christianity*. New York: Charles Scribner's Sons. 1954.

Ferm, Vergilius, Editor. *Classics of Protestantism*. New York: Philosophical Library. 1959.

Haroutunian, Joseph. "A Protestant Theory of Education." Chapter 2 in John Paul von Grueningen. *Toward a Christian Philosophy of Higher Education*. Philadelphia: Westminster Press. 1957.

Kimmel, William, and Clive, Geoffrey, Editors. *Dimensions of Faith*. New York: Twayne Publishers. 1960.

Miller, Allen O. *Invitation to Theology*. Philadelphia: The Christian Education Press. 1958.

Miller, Randolph Crump. *The Clue to Christian Education*. New York: Charles Scribner's Sons. 1950.

Niebuhr, Reinhold. *The Nature and Destiny of Man: A Christian Interpretation*. Volume I, *Human Nature*. New York: Charles Scribner's Sons. 1941.

Niebuhr, Reinhold. *The Nature and Destiny of Man: A Christian Interpretation*. Volume II, *Human Destiny*. New York: Charles Scribner's Sons. 1949.

Niebuhr, H. Richard. *Christ and Culture*. New York: Harper & Bros. 1951.

Niebuhr, H. Richard. *Radical Monotheism and Western Culture*. New York: Harper & Brothers. 1960.

Park, Joe, Editor. *Selected Readings in the Philosophy of Education.* New York: The Macmillan Co. 1959. Parts 5 and 6, pp. 299–429.

Smart, James D. *The Teaching Ministry of the Church.* Philadelphia: Westminster Press. 1954. Chapter 2.

Tillich, Paul. *Systematic Theology.* Chicago: University of Chicago Press. Volume I. 1951 and Volume II. 1957.

Williams, Daniel D. *What Present-Day Theologians Are Thinking.* Revised Edition. New York: Harper & Brothers. 1959.

Williams, Daniel D. "Current Theological Developments and Religious Education." Chapter 4 in Marvin J. Taylor, Editor. *Religious Education.* New York: Abingdon Press. 1960.

CHAPTER 10

Anderson, Bernard W. *Understanding the Old Testament.* Englewood Cliffs, N.J.: Prentice-Hall, Inc. 1957.

Butler, J. Donald. *Four Philosophies and Their Practice in Education and Religion.* Revised Edition. New York: Harper & Bros. 1957. Pp. 543–549.

Foss, Martin. *Symbol and Metaphor in Human Experience.* Princeton, New Jersey: Princeton University Press. 1949.

Kee, Howard Clark, and Young, Franklin W. *Understanding the New Testament.* Englewood Cliffs, N.J.: Prentice-Hall, Inc. 1957.

Langer, Susanne K. *Philosophy in a New Key.* Cambridge, Mass.: Harvard University Press. 1942.

Miller, Randolph Crump. *Biblical Theology and Christian Education.* New York: Charles Scribner's Sons. 1956.

Smart, James D. *The Teaching Ministry of the Church,* Philadelphia: Westminster Press. 1954. Chapter 7.

Tillich, Paul, *Dynamics of Faith.* New York: Harper & Brothers. 1957. Chapter 3.

CHAPTER 11

Bachmann, E. Theodore. *The Activating Concern.* New York: National Council of the Churches of Christ in the U.S.A. 1955.

Cayton, Horace R., and Nishi, Setsuko Matsunaga. *The Changing Scene.* New York: National Council of the Churches of Christ in the U.S.A. 1955.

Johns, Ray, and DeMarche, D. F. *Community Organization and Agency Responsibility.* New York: Association Press. 1951.

Stroup, Herbert Hewitt. *Community Welfare Organization.* New York: Harper & Brothers. 1952.

CHAPTER 12

Blair, W. Dyer. *The New Vacation Church School.* New York: Harper & Brothers. 1939.

Bone, Maurice D. "Camps and Conferences." Chapter 20 in Marvin J. Taylor, Editor. *Religious Education.* New York: Abingdon Press. 1960.

Bower, William Clayton, and Hayward, Percy Roy. *Protestantism Faces Its Educational Task Together.* Appleton, Wis.: C. C. Nelson Publishing Company. 1949. Chapters 6–9.

Butt, Elsie Miller. *The Vacation Church School in Christian Education.* Nashville, Tenn.: Abingdon Press. 1957.

Dirks, J. Edward. "Religious Education in Church-Related College and University." Chapter 27 in Marvin J. Taylor, Editor. *Religious Education.* New York: Abingdon Press. 1960.

Fallaw, Wesner, *The Modern Parent and the Teaching Church.* New York: The Macmillan Co. 1957.

Fallaw, Wesner. "The Role of the Home in Religious Nurture." Chapter 13 in Marvin J. Taylor, Editor. *Religious Education.* New York: Abingdon Press. 1960.

Goddard, Alice L. "Weekday and Vacation Church Schools." Chapter 21 in Marvin J. Taylor, Editor. *Religious Education.* New York: Abingdon Press. 1960.

Heim, Ralph D. *Leading a Sunday Church School.* Philadelphia: Muhlenberg Press. 1950.

Johnson, F. Ernest, Editor. *American Education and Religion.* New York: Harper & Bros. 1952.

LeFevre, Perry. *The Christian Teacher.* New York: Abingdon Press. 1958.

Maves, Paul B. "The Christian Education of Adults." Chapter 12 in Marvin J. Taylor, Editor. *Religious Education.* New York: Abingdon Press. 1960.

Michaelsen, Robert. "Religious Education in Public Higher Education Institutions." Chapter 28 in Marvin J. Taylor, Editor. *Religious Education.* New York: Abingdon Press. 1960.

Miller, Alexander. *Faith and Learning.* New York: Association Press. 1960.

Miller, Randolph Crump. *Education for Christian Living.* Englewood Cliffs, N.J.: Prentice-Hall, Inc. 1956. Chapters 6–9.

Moore, Raymond S. "Protestant Full-Time Weekday Schools." Chapter 22 in Marvin J. Taylor, Editor. *Religious Education.* New York: Abingdon Press. 1960.

Newby, Donald O. "The Churches' Ministry to Youth." Chapter 11 in Marvin J. Taylor, Editor. *Religious Education.* New York: Abingdon Press. 1960.

Niebuhr, H. Richard, *et al. The Advancement of Theological Education.* New York: Harper & Brothers. 1957.

O'Neill, James M. *Religion and Education Under the Constitution.* New York: Harper & Brothers. 1949.

Presbyterian Church, U.S.A. "The Church and the Public Schools." Philadelphia: Board of Christian Education. 1957.

Shaver, Irwin L. "Remember the Weekday, to Teach Religion Thereon." Chicago: National Council of Churches, Department of Weekday Religious Education. n. d.

Snavely, Guy E. *The Church and the Four-Year College*. New York: Harper & Brothers. 1955.

Smith, Huston. *The Purposes of Higher Education*. New York: Harper & Brothers. 1955.

Vieth, Paul H. *The Church School*. Philadelphia: Christian Education Press. 1957.

Westcott, Regina. *The Family Lives Its Religion*. Revised Edition. New York: Harper & Brothers. 1954.

Wynn, John Charles. *Pastoral Ministry to Families*. Philadelphia: Westminster Press. 1957.

CHAPTERS 13 and 14

Allport, G. W. *Personality*. New York: Henry Holt. 1937.

Blair, A. W., and Burton, W. H. *Growth and Development of the Preadolescent*. New York: Appleton-Century-Crofts. 1951.

Broudy, Harry S. *Building a Philosophy of Education*. New York: Prentice-Hall, Inc. 1954. Chapters 3, 6, and 9.

Butler, J. Donald. "Theology and Psychology: Some Points of Convergence." *Encounter*. Volume XIX, Number 4. Autumn 1958. Pp. 391–406.

Cantor, Nathaniel. *The Teaching-Learning Process*. New York: Dryden Press. 1953.

Conklin, E. S. and Freeman, F. S. *Introductory Psychology for Students of Education*. New York: Henry Holt and Co., Inc. 1939. Chapters 9 and 10.

Cully, Iris V. *The Dynamics of Christian Education*. Philadelphia: Westminster Press. 1958. Chapter 4.

Dewey, John. *Logic, The Theory of Inquiry*. New York: Henry Holt and Co. 1938.

Gesell, Arnold, and Ilg, F. L. *Infant and Child in the Culture of Today*. New York: Harper & Brothers. 1943.

Gesell, Arnold, and Ilg, F. L. *The Child from Five to Ten*. New York: Harper & Brothers. 1946.

Gesell, Arnold, Ilg, F. L., and Ames, L. B. *Youth: The Years from Ten to Sixteen*. New York: Harper & Brothers. 1956.

Hall, C. S., and Lindzey, Gardner. *Theories of Personality*. New York: John Wiley. 1957.

Havighurst, Robert J. *Human Development and Education*. New York: Longmans, Green and Co. 1953.

Henry, N. B., Editor. *The Psychology of Learning*. The Forty-first Yearbook of the National Society for the Study of Education. Bloomington, Ill.: Public School Publishing Co. 1942.

Herbart, Johann Friedrich. *Science of Education*. Translated by Henry M. and Emmie Felkin. Boston: D. C. Heath. 1893.

Linton, Ralph, *The Cultural Background of Personality.* New York: Appleton-Century. 1945.

May, Rollo, et al. *Existence.* New York: Basic Books. 1958.

Mead, Margaret, and Wolfenstein, Martha, Editors. *Childhood in Contemporary Cultures.* Chicago: The University of Chicago Press. 1955.

Mowrer, O. Hobart. *Learning Theory and Personality Dynamics.* New York: The Ronald Press. 1950.

Murphy, L. B., and Ladd, Henry. *Emotional Factors in Learning.* New York: Columbia University Press. 1944.

Pfuetz, P. E. *The Social Self.* New York: Bookman Associates. 1954.

Sherrill, L. J. *The Struggle of the Soul.* New York: The Macmillan Co. 1951.

Yeaxlee, Basil. *Religion and the Growing Mind.* Greenwich, Conn.: Seabury Press. 1952.

CHAPTER 15

Cantor, Nathaniel. *The Teaching-Learning Process.* New York: Dryden Press. 1954.

Chaplin, Dora. *Children and Religion.* New York: Charles Scribner's Sons. 1948.

Clemmons, Robert S. *Dynamics of Christian Adult Education.* New York: Abingdon Press. 1958. Chapters 3, 4, 5, and 7.

Cully, Iris V. *The Dynamics of Christian Education.* Philadelphia: Westminster Press. 1958. Chapters 5–7.

Cully, Iris V. "Children's Work in the Church." Chapter 10 in Marvin J. Taylor, Editor. *Religious Education.* New York: Abingdon Press. 1960.

Gable, Lee J., Editor. *Encyclopedia for Church Group Leaders.* New York: Association Press. 1959.

Grimes, Howard. *The Church Redemptive.* New York: Abingdon Press. 1958. Chapters 7 and 8.

Haiman, Franklin S. *Group Leadership and Democratic Action.* Boston. Houghton Mifflin Co. 1951.

Ham, Harold M. "The Church School and Techniques of Teaching." Chapter 17 in Marvin J. Taylor, Editor. *Religious Education.* New York: Abingdon Press. 1960.

Horne, Herman Harrell. *Story-Telling, Questioning and Studying.* New York: The Macmillan Co. 1916.

Little, Sara. *Learning Together in the Christian Fellowship.* Richmond, Va.: John Knox Press. 1956.

Maves, Paul B. "The Christian Education of Adults." Chapter 12 in Marvin J. Taylor, Editor. *Religious Education.* New York: Abingdon Press. 1960.

Miller, Randolph Crump. *Education for Christian Living.* Englewood Cliffs, N.J.: Prentice-Hall, Inc. 1956. Chapters 10–15.

Newby, Donald O. "The Churches' Ministry to Youth." Chapter 11 in Marvin J. Taylor, Editor. *Religious Education.* New York: Abingdon Press. 1960.
Weigle, Luther A. *The Pupil and the Teacher.* Philadelphia: The United Lutheran Publishing House. 1929. Chapters 13, 14, 18, and 19.

CHAPTER 16

Broudy, Harry S. *Building a Philosophy of Education.* New York: Prentice-Hall, Inc. 1954. Chapters 6 and 7.
Butler, J. Donald. *Four Philosophies and Their Practice in Education and Religion.* Revised Edition. New York: Harper & Brothers. 1957. Pp. 254–258; 367–370.
Denominational Boards: A selected list of some to which inquiries may be directed for curriculum literature.
Disciples of Christ, Division of Christian Education, 222 South Downey Avenue, Indianapolis 7, Indiana; also Christian Board of Publication, 2700 Pine Boulevard, St. Louis 3, Mo.
The Methodist Church, Board of Education, 119 Seventeenth Avenue South, Nashville 2, Tenn.
Northern Baptist Convention, American Baptist Publication Society, 1701–3 Chestnut Street, Philadelphia 3, Pa.
Presbyterian Church in the United States, Board of Education, 8 North Sixth Street, Richmond 9, Va.
Protestant Episcopal Church, Department of Christian Education, Greenwich, Conn.
United Church of Canada, Board of Christian Education, 299 Queen Street West, Toronto, Ontario, Canada.
United Church of Christ, Board of Christian Education and Publication, 1505 Race Street, Philadelphia 2, Pa.
United Lutheran Church in America, The Parish and Church School Board, 1228 Spruce Street, Philadelphia 7, Pa.
United Presbyterian Church in the United States of America, Board of Christian Education, Witherspoon Building, Philadelphia 7, Pa.
Division of Christian Education. *A Guide for Curriculum in Christian Education.* New York: National Council of Churches of Christ in the U.S.A. 1955.
Kearney, Nolan C., and Cook, Walter W. "Curriculum." In Chester W. Harris, Editor. *Encyclopedia of Educational Research.* Third Edition. New York: The Macmillan Co. 1960. Pp. 358–365.
Miller, Allen O. *Invitation to Theology.* Philadelphia: The Christian Education Press. 1958. Part 3, Pp. 153–184.
Miller, Randolph Crump. *The Clue to Christian Education.* New York: Charles Scribner's Sons. 1950.

Miller, Randolph Crump. *Biblical Theology and Christian Education.* New York: Charles Scribner's Sons. 1956.
Smart, James D. *The Teaching Ministry of the Church.* Philadelphia: Westminster Press. 1954. Chapters 6 and 7.

CHAPTER 17

Denominational Boards: A selected list of some to which inquiries may be directed for manuals on administration. (See the list included above in the Bibliography for Chapter 16.)
Gable, Lee J. *Christian Nurture Through the Church.* New York: National Council of the Churches of Christ in the U.S.A. 1955.
Gable, Lee J., Editor. *Encyclopedia for Church Group Leaders.* New York: Association Press. 1959. Chapters 19–22.
Miller, Randolph Crump, *Education for Christian Living.* Englewood Cliffs, N.J.: Prentice-Hall, Inc. 1956. Chapters 17 and 18.
Vieth, Paul H. *The Church School.* Philadelphia: Christian Education Press. 1957.
Vieth, Paul H. "The Local Church Organized for Christian Education." Chapter 23 in Marvin J. Taylor, Editor. *Religious Education.* New York: Abingdon Press. 1960.

CHAPTER 18

Clemens, Robert S. *Dynamics of Christian Adult Education.* New York: Abingdon Press. 1958.
Ernsberger, David J. *A Philosophy of Adult Christian Education.* Philadelphia: Westminster Press. 1959.
Grimes, Howard. *The Church Redemptive.* New York: Abingdon Press. 1958. Chapter 10.
Gwynn, Price H., Jr. *Leadership Education in the Local Church.* Philadelphia: Westminster Press. 1952.
Kraemer, Hendrik, *A Theology of the Laity.* Philadelphia: Westminster Press. 1958.
Niebuhr, H. Richard. *The Purpose of the Church and Its Ministry.* New York: Harper & Brothers. 1956.
Niebuhr, H. Richard, and Williams, Daniel D., Editors. *The Ministry in Historical Perspectives.* New York: Harper & Brothers. 1956.

Index

Abbotsholme, 105
Administration, 279-292
  and the Church as the body of Christ, 279, 280
  the minister and, 283-285
  policies of, 280-283
Adolescence, 214-220, 241-243
Adult council, 286, 287, 288
Adult classes, 178, 242
Adult Education Program, 286, 287, 288, 299, 300
  and leadership in the Church, 299-302
  and thinking the Faith, 300, 301
Age levels, 73, 89, 128, 129, 213-214
  curriculum classified according to, 265-267
American Sunday School Union, 66
Apperception, 81, 82
Aquinas, 25, 131, 198
Aristotle, 101
Art and symbolism, 142-145
Asbury, Francis, 59
Associative groups, 170, 171
Atonement, the, 124
Augustine, 25, 131

Bacon, Francis, 232, 244
Badley, J. H., 105
Baptism, 26-27, 91
Barnard, Henry, 90
Barth, Karl, 103, 117
Bedales, 105
Being, 110
Belief, 1, 2, 131, 132
Bell, Andrew, 57, 58
Bernreuter Personality Inventory, 205
Bible, the, 50-52, 116, 117, 118, 120, 125, 128, 132, 136-154, 200, 221, 223, 224, 235, 237, 258, 263, 265, 270, 271, 288
  content in teaching and, 150-154
  forms of literature and, 148
  functions of, 137-138, 151-154
  symbols of communication and, 139-145

  symbols in, 139-149, 218
  as revelation, 139, 150, 151, 154
Board of Christian Education, see Committee of Christian Education
Bonhoeffer, Dietrich, 247
Boville, Robert G., 184
Broudy, Harry, 233
Brunner, Emil, 16, 103, 117
Bushnell, Horace, 36, 91-104

Calvin, John, 40-43, 98, 131, 132, 281
Calvinism, 93, 94, 97, 98
Carlyle, Thomas, 94
Catechetical instruction, 29-30
Catechumenal instruction, 26-29, 130
Champaign decision, 188, 189
Channing, William Ellery, 94
Chappell, Nelson, 64
Character education, 226
Character building agencies, 168-171, 174
Character Research Project, 115, 116, 138
Charity School Movement in England, 54-58
Childhood, see Growth and development in childhood
Children's stories, biblical, 153, 154
  method of using, 258, 259
  See also Story
Christ, 7, 8, 9, 10, 12, 13, 14, 17, 20, 21, 145-148
  the Church and, 10, 11, 19, 20, 21
  in Church School curriculum, 129, 149, 150, 263, 273
  and the king figure, 147, 148
  and the parables, 285
  and the religious education movement, 116
  and the servant figure, 18, 19, 147
  in theology, 117, 118, 124
Christian Community, biblical record of, 149, 150
  curriculum and, 263

315

316

INDEX

Primary department of the Sunday Church School, 177, 286
Problem solving, learning as, 230–233
Proclamation, 295
Progressive education, 105–112, 255, 260, 271
Prophecy, 295
Protestantism, 39–40, 117, 130, 134–135, 198, 208
Protestant Reformation, 281
Psychology, 197–221, 222–237
  and Christian education, 216–217
  and the Church School, 129, 213
  depth psychology, 207
  influence of the Church on, 197–198
  influence on the Church, 198
  learning theories, 222–237
  and method, 239–241
Pubescence, 214–215

Question, the, 249–257
Qumran Community, 28

Raikes, Robert, 59–64
Rauschenbusch, Walter, 99
Recreation, 174
Reddie, Cecil, 105
Redefinition, 229–230, 232–233
Redemption, 124
Reformation, Protestant, 281
Religious education, 78–79, 87–88, 89, 90, 99, 102, 111
  and psychology, 197–198, 216–217, 230–233
Religious Education Association, 113–116
  journal of, 114
Religious education movement, 113–121
Retreat, the, 208
Revelation, 1, 2, 123–125, 127, 128, 132, 149–150, 153–154
  the Bible as, 125, 137–139, 149–151, 153–154
  the Church and, 1–2
  and communication, 132–133
  and nurture, 236–237
Revivalism, 94–95
Roman Catholic Church, the, 114–115, 134, 197–198, 207–208
Rorschach Test, the, 211

Rousseau, Jean Jacques, 68–73, 74, 78, 89, 258–259

School, day or public, 173, 187–190, 195
Science, 150, 199
Seabury Curriculum, 120–121, 139, 274
Selfhood, 206–210, 217
Synagogue, the, and weekday instruction, 190
Sense-perception, 86–87
Senior High Department of the Sunday Church School, 178, 182, 286
Senior-high fellowship, 181, 286
  See also Youth fellowship
Servant figure, 147
Sign vs. symbol, 141–143, 145, 146
Sin, 124, 387
Smart, James, 121
Smith, H. Shelton, 118–119
Social action and the Church, 158–161, 288
Social agencies, 166–174
Social science, 203–204
Social Security Act, 166
Social theory, 153
Society for the Promotion of Christian Knowledge, 56–57
Socrates, 255
Spencer, Herbert, 225
Stock, Thomas, 60, 62
Story, the, 153–154, 257–259
Summer camp program, 174
Sunday Church School, 176–180, 193, 213, 279–292
  and congregational worship, 179
  and curriculum materials, 265–278
  departments of, 177–178
  and the minister of education, 176
  and the responsibility to integrate thought, 173, 179
  and the Superintendent, 176, 290
  and the Youth Council, 182
Sunday Church School curriculum, 128, 129, 130, 153–154, 213, 233, 264–278
  the adoption of, 275–278
  and the Bible, 128, 139, 150–154, 263

320